MICHAEL W. BALFE

Statue of Michael William Balfe, erected in 1874, Theatre Royal, Drury Lane, London.

Michael W. Balfe

A Unique Victorian Composer

BASIL WALSH

Foreword by
RICHARD BONYNGE

IRISH ACADEMIC PRESS
DUBLIN • PORTLAND, OR

First published in 2008 by Irish Academic Press

44 Northumberland Road,
Ballsbridge,
Dublin 4, Ireland

920 NE 58th Avenue, Suite 300
Portland, Oregon,
97213-3786

www.iap.ie

Copyright © 2008 Basil Walsh

British Library Cataloguing in Publication Data
An entry can be found on request

ISBN 978 0 7165 2947 7 (cloth)

Library of Congress Cataloging-in-Publication Data
An entry can be found on request

Printed by Biddles Ltd., King's Lynn, Norfolk

Such a career as that of Balfe is rare – unprecedented in this country [Britain], where so little account is ordinarily taken of the labours of our own musicians, however conscientious and hard-toiling. It may justly be likened to the career of Rossini in Italy and of Auber in France. Balfe, indeed was our Rossini, and also, in a measure, our Auber; for his eclectic genius led him to amalgamate the styles of those two distinguished men, while giving a colouring to the amalgamation which was his own and no one else's ... he had the gift of melody [and] upon his stores of melody he could draw on at will. His melodious invention never failed him.

The Times (London)
12 June 1874

Contents

APPENDICES

List of Illustrations

(AUTHOR'S COLLECTION)

Cover: Balfe at age forty-two in London.
Frontispiece: Statue of Michael William Balfe, erected in 1874, Theatre Royal, Drury Lane, London.

1. Advertisement by Balfe's father in Wexford, June 1813.
2. The house at 10 Pitt Street, Dublin, where Michael W. Balfe was born in 1808.
3. Balfe's first published song, Dublin, *circa* December 1822, when he was fourteen years old.
4. Rotunda Concert Rooms, Dublin, where Balfe performed during the early nineteenth century.
5. Renowned singer Maria Malibran, a friend of Balfe's.
6. Portrait of Balfe as a young man.
7. Libretto for *I rivali di se stessi*, Balfe's first opera, as performed in Italy in 1829.
8. Libretto for *Un avvertimento di gelosi*, Balfe's second opera, performed in 1831.
9. Libretto for Balfe's third work, *Enrico IV, al passo della Marna*, which had its premiere at the Teatro Carcano, Milan, 1833.
10. The soprano, Giulia Grisi, whom Balfe first met in Bologna in 1829.
11. Malibran and Balfe in *La sonnambula* in Venice, 1835.
12. The Teatro Malibran in Venice, 2006.
13. Playbill of *The Siege of Rochelle*, Balfe's first London opera, 1835.
14. Malibran in Balfe's *The Maid of Artois* in 1836, London.
15. Balfe's *Falstaff* with Luigi Lablache in the title role, premiered in 1838.
16. Portrait of Balfe's young wife, Lina Balfe.
17. Portrait of the thirty-eight year-old Michael W. Balfe in Vienna.
18. Louisa 'Gigia' Balfe, the composer's first-born child.
19. Balfe's youngest daughter, Victoire Balfe.

Foreword

I welcome this important new study, which brings to light much of the little-known life of Michael William Balfe and which deals in great detail with his lesser-known works.

That the majority of his works are so little heard is a shame. He was of supreme importance during the great bel canto epoque of the nineteenth century, and it is certainly time that his works be rediscovered and re-evaluated. His melodic genius, allied with the innate simplicity of his compositions, give his work a freshness which will never die.

A protégé of Rossini, he was a singer of international renown who in his early years sang with Maria Malibran and Giulia Grisi. He composed operas for the great singers of the day including Rubini, Tamburini and Lablache, as well as the above-mentioned ladies.

A recent recording of the *Maid of Artois*, which was written for Malibran, is certainly a step in the right direction, but there is a great deal more of real worth to be considered. Basil Walsh's passion for the music of Michael William Balfe has urged him to extensive research and in this book he brings forth so many details of Balfe's personal life and corrects a great deal of misinformation which has appeared in previous publications.

Balfe, along with his compatriot William Wallace, must be considered as the greatest composers of operatic music in nineteenth century Britain, and their neglect is woeful and shameful. This book will hopefully encourage many musicians and especially many young musicians to look at this treasure trove of opera and song.

I thank Basil Walsh for his dedication to the music of Balfe and for his inspiring writing, which can only help to revive the work of Ireland's great composer.

Richard Bonynge, AO,CBE
Les Avants, Switzerland
8th January 2007

Preface

Balfe has always been a fascinating character for me. His time was at the start of the Romantic period in the arts in Europe. His name is intrinsically linked with so many legendary musicians, singers, statesmen, business people and even royalty.

Most of us have been familiar with selected pieces from his very popular opera *The Bohemian Girl*, but not too many people know very much about the other operas he wrote for London. Or for that matter the ones he wrote for Paris and Milan or the reworked German or Italian versions which were so successful in Vienna, Berlin, Frankfurt, Milan, Trieste, Bologna and other places.

It has always been the 'unknown' Balfe that has intrigued me, more than the familiar Balfe. As a result, I decided to research the composer, his family and the extent and scope of his work and influence. This is not a musicologist's view of Balfe, but more a study of the man: the scope of his work, his lifetime achievements and his family. Among other things, it documents his works, his multi-language operatic premieres and the singers who performed in them.

Strangely, Balfe never wrote an autobiography; if he had, it would have been a fascinating document. He did keep diaries, we know that. However, apparently he regularly destroyed his diaries at the end of each year. Some short extracts have survived and they give us a very brief glimpse of how he recorded selected events.

Balfe somehow has eluded his biographers, as no real satisfactory biography of the composer is extant, which is surprising given the great resurgence and interest in Victorian culture and studies over the past several decades, particularly in Britain and Ireland. Balfe was certainly an important Victorian. Musical activity in Britain in the Victorian years is extremely well documented and Balfe, as the leading composer of vocal music, was at the centre of it during the decades that spanned the mid-century.

During his time, Balfe was to music what Charles Dickens was

Michael W. Balfe

to literature. As with the novels of Dickens, Balfe's music was immediately accepted by the masses and had equal acceptance throughout the English-speaking world and beyond. Balfe and Dickens knew each other well, and were good friends. They had a lot of things in common. Basically they were of the same age. Dickens was a frequent visitor to Balfe's home, even presenting the composer with a special *Pickwick Papers* initialled snuffbox gift on one occasion.

Balfe's restless nature and his pursuit of new challenges frequently caused him to travel extensively throughout continental Europe, even as far as Russia, for long periods of time. Perhaps that was the root cause of the problem for most of his biographers. Most research takes a long time to complete; foreign research takes much longer and is more expensive to accomplish. Musical performances are well documented for continental Europe – however, these periodicals have not been easily accessible to writers and researchers, not to mention the language problems.

Balfe was fluent in French and Italian and had some German, and as a result there were times when he appeared to have been more comfortable working in continental cities. Perhaps that was a matter of how music as a profession was accepted in continental Europe, versus Britain. Yet Victorian Britain was the place where his reputation was made and where most of his income came from.

The two early anecdotal Balfe biographies, one by Charles Lamb Kenney (1875), the other by William Alexander Barrett (1882), which can be found in most libraries today, have created considerable confusion. Each has numerous inaccuracies and misstatements. Neither provides documentary support for many of the statements. Regrettably, much of what they said has been pickedup and perpetuated in many current reference works, primarily because the proper research work has not been done. Another early short anecdotal biography by Henry St Leger (1870), in which the author claimed a strong personal relationship with the composer, also offers some conflicting information.

In any event, this study endeavours to correct the situation as much as possible, and in the process, to help provide significant new information and facts about the composer, his works and his family. It covers the scope of his work and his contribution to Victorian society as one of its leading musical figures. It also offers a perspective of the composer and his success as he worked in London, Paris, Dublin, Berlin, St Petersburg, Vienna, Milan, Palermo and other places.

Additionally, another objective of this book is to bring together, in one central work, detailed information about Balfe's most significant musical compositions, a chronology of their premieres, the singers who performed them and, most importantly, the location of the associated music and scores today.

The libraries and other places where most of Balfe's music resides today are identified along with their reference numbers for those interested in further study. This includes information on early Italian operatic material that previously has been deemed "lost" by most major reference sources, including *Grove*. It also includes other works and music by the composer, not previously known to exist.

Some years after the composer's death his widow, Lina Balfe, donated her large collection of his original manuscript operatic scores and other items to the British Library, in the hope that his music would be available for future generations. That collection still exists, and represents the most significant part of Balfe's lifetime achievement and his legacy.

However, numerous other manuscript scores, operatic sketches, sheet music from some of his very early Italian operas, French operas and German-language versions, in addition to cantatas and songs, are scattered around libraries in Britain, France, Italy, Austria and America. Possibly some also exist in Ireland, since at the time of writing much of his material in the National Library in Dublin has not yet been fully catalogued.

His personal correspondence and the many letters written by his wife have suffered the same fate. The majority are in private collections and libraries on at least two continents, undocumented in any central source. This is a task in itself, and is not covered by this work.

Balfe's operas continued to be performed long after the composer's death. In the early twentieth century touring companies in Britain, Ireland and America continued to mount his operas up to the 1930s. A hundredth anniversary performance of *The Bohemian Girl* was given in Dublin in 1943. Sir Thomas Beecham funded a lavish production of *The Bohemian Girl* in Liverpool in 1951 for the Festival of Britain. In August of the same year the production was taken to London with the same casts, and given nineteen consecutive performances at the Royal Opera House, Covent Garden. There were two casts for these performances. The opera had a reworked libretto by the writer Dennis Arundell. The Wexford Festival in Ireland opened its inaugural season in November 1951, with a performance of *The Rose of Castille*. The late Dr Tom Walsh, a delightful person who was the founder of the Wexford Festival, was a great Balfe aficionado. Later Wexford also did another Balfe opera. In June 1958 at a gala concert at the Royal Opera House, Covent Garden, Australian singers Joan Sutherland (on the brink of her brilliant international career) and tenor John Lanigan sang excerpts from *The Bohemian Girl*. Beyond this activity not much else happened in Britain in the succeeding years up to 1980.

In 1981, the book *The Romantic Age* was published in London by Blackwell Ltd, as part of its *Music in Britain* series. This excellent work was edited by Nicholas Temperley, with the section relating to Balfe and his contemporaries contributed by Michael Hurd. Two years later, in 1983, Eric Walter White published his ground -breaking, *History of English Opera*, which provided much new information on Balfe and other composers of his generation.

Several years elapsed before George Biddlecombe published his *English Opera from 1834 to 1864 with Particular Reference to the Works of Michael Balfe*, in 1994, which was the first book to provide an analysis of Balfe's music and a fresh approach to the scope of Balfe's work. While each of these modern writers does an excellent job in dealing with Balfe, and his contribution to the Victorian musical landscape, their basic focus is significantly broader by reason of their overall subject matter.

As far as recordings of Balfe's music are concerned, the distinguished conductor and musicologist Richard Bonynge took the lead with the first complete CD recording of *The Bohemian Girl* in 1991. Subsequently Mr Bonynge has had various other CD releases that included many relatively unknown Balfe tenor and soprano arias. These CDs and others are listed in the discography section of this book.

Early in 2000, as I finalized my book *Catherine Hayes: The Hibernian Prima Donna*, I decided to look at Balfe the man, the composer and his achievements, as his path had crossed that of

Catherine Hayes in London of the 1850s. Given the fact that Balfe's bicentenary was on the near horizon the timing also seemed logical. I initially launched a Balfe website in June 2000, which became the platform for my subject. I also contributed articles on the composer to various magazines and to the Donizetti Society newsletters and the Oxford University Press journal *The Opera Quarterly*.

Concurrent with my efforts, I discovered other people who were at different stages of writing about Balfe. Most important of these was the late William Tyldesley of Liverpool, a retired academic and musicologist. Bill Tyldesley and I inevitably became good friends, and since he was further along with his task than I was, he filled me in on what he was doing so that there was no duplication of effort. Subsequently, his excellent book *Michael William Balfe, His Life and His English Operas* was published in England in 2003. It provides the most comprehensive study to date of Balfe's English operas, i.e. operas that were written for the London stage with an English-language libretto. It primarily deals with the musical structure of Balfe's English operas and their success; it also contains a short biography with some new information on the composer.

However, ultimately, I felt that a new more comprehensive book about the composer would be beneficial for a variety of reasons, particularly to redefine the scope, breath and impact of his work in the field of opera in the nineteenth century. Regrettably, because of time constraints I was not able to include detailed information on the 250 songs or more that Balfe wrote over a period of forty years. However, a reasonably comprehensive listing of most of his songs currently does appears in *Grove*.

In the various biographies available, references to Balfe's family, particularly his father, mother and sisters and his own family life, were vague, inconsistent and undocumented. The larger scope of Balfe's work in Britain and Ireland has not been fully explored in detail or documented. His work in continental Europe has had very limited coverage, yet it was very significant and very important for a British composer to be recognized in this way. His musical influence on Victorian middle-class society has never really been touched on.

Some of the greatest Italian, British, French and American

vocalists in the nineteenth century sang in Balfe's operas, yet no current Balfe reference provides any details of who sang in which opera or which role. This information obviously would help provide a perspective on how well the composer's music was accepted during his lifetime by some of the most renowned singers of the period. This is corrected in this work.

Balfe never visited America, yet no one has ever delved into his rationale for not crossing the Atlantic when so many of his associates were so successful there. New documentation on his feelings and desire about going to America has come to light that fully explains his reason for not making the journey which might have changed his life, or certainly his financial situation in his later years.

Virtually all reference books and biographies today state that the music for the three operas he composed in Italy in the early 1830s has been lost. This is not correct. A considerable amount of this music is available today for those interested in studying Balfe's early compositional style. Details are provided. This study is meant to supplement the earlier books mentioned above. In general, it covers a different aspect of Balfe, his life and his family and origins. It also provides much information about the composers that has not appeared anywhere previously.

The period Balfe spent in Italy learning his craft was the subject of an article, 'Balfe in Italy', which I wrote for *The Opera Quarterly*, (volume 18, number 4, Autumn 2002); a journal of the Oxford University Press. I wish to thank the publishers for their permission to use some of the text from that article. The research I've done since will also correct and update some of the references in my article.

Throughout my references and end notes mostly use the reviews from the London periodical *The Musical World* (editor J. W. Davison and Sub-editor Desmond Ryan), and sometime the *Times*, which in my judgement were significantly less biased than the *Athenaeum* (musical editor H.F. Chorley). Chorley was a very eccentric and strange character. He obviously did not care for Balfe and so his reviews were almost always negative. He wrote one song for Balfe but never got the opportunity of a libretto for an opera, which may have been the problem. He did write a libretto for one of Wallace's operas. Chorley's obituary of Balfe was so negative that the Drury Lane orchestra members wrote to the *Press* about it. The following is an extract.

> One of the most unfriendly biographies we have seen is the mortuary notice of Balfe by Mr. Chorley. Even if it were possible to agree with Mr. Chorley's estimate of the dead composer, the proprietory of publishing such sentiments at the present time would remain open to strong objections. But as it is, the bias in the writer's judgment is equally cruel and unjust. Mr. Chorley doubtless congratulates himself that Balfe never set [a] libretto of his ...

Any reference to Britain or the British throughout the text generally means England, Ireland, Scotland and Wales, unless Ireland is specifically separated out for discussion purposes. During the period under study and beyond, Ireland was completely under British rule for all of the nineteenth century.

Abbreviations shown below in parentheses are used to define a singer's type of voice throughout this work.

Soprano (s); mezzo-soprano (ms); contralto: (ct) tenor (t); baritone (br); bass (bs); buffo-bass (bfb).

Whenever possible, I have endeavoured to provide the date of birth and death when a person's name appears for the first time in the text, which I feel is always useful in terms of the context and time period. If this information does not appear after a name, then generally it means that I did not have access to the details or dates at the time of writing.

It is my hope that an organization, academic or otherwise, will consider establishing a central Balfe repository where information on this important Victorian composer and his musical compositions can be accessed for study. While the British Library does an excellent job with the material it holds, the daily pressures on its staff because of the demand for their large holdings does not make it an ideal environment for study of Balfe's works. To have a central repository where copies of all known Balfe music is made readily available, either electronically, or on microfilm at one central source, would be extremely valuable.

In conclusion, in an age when Verdi's *Nabucco* and other Italian operas are being recorded with *English librettos*, surely it is also time for recordings of Balfe's *Falstaff*, *Les quatre fils Aymon*, and some of his English operas for which the full orchestral scores are available in the British Library?

If this occurs, it will certainly help realize Lina Balfe's desire that her husband's musical works would be easily accessible to all future generations, for study or performance.

Basil Walsh
Delray Beach, Florida
January 2007

Acknowledgements

It takes about seven years to research a work of this nature. Without a lot of help from many people around the world, and a significant amount of personal travel and research it would never have been possible to complete the task. Of course, the internet also played an important part.

How wonderful it is to be able to go online to the British Library in London and search their incredible holdings and order copies of most documents over the internet. Since the library has the largest Balfe collection in the world, thanks to Balfe's wife, it is an important source for a study of Balfe and his music. As always I wish to thank the curator, Nicholas Bell, and his staff for all of their help.

On a more personal note, I also wish to thank my family, in particular my wife, Eileen, and my son, Jay Walsh, who lives in Cambridge, MA, and my brother, Derek Walsh of Dublin, for their encouragement, enthusiasm and help with my work relating to this unique nineteenth-century composer.

My thanks also go to Lisa Hyde and editor Sian Mills of the Irish Academic Press, London, for all their help and suggestions, and to Rachel Milotte of the Irish Academic Press, Dublin. Appreciation is also expressed for the help and assistance in the form of a grant provided by the Arts Council, Merrion Square, Dublin.

I wish to express my appreciation to the following, each of whom has contributed in various ways: Richard Bonynge, Switzerland, Roberta Peters of the Metropolitan Opera and her husband, Bert Fields, New York/Florida, Dr Philip Gossett, Chicago, Alexander Weatherson and Pip Clayton, of the Donizetti Society, London, Tom Kaufman, Maryland, Angela Hubert and her late husband, Tom, Sussex, England, Mary Quinton, Hertfordshire, England, Dr Una Hunt, Dublin and Dr David Rhodes, Waterford, Ireland.

I also want to thank the following for their help: and encouragement, Dr Giorgio Appolonia, Varese, Italy, Harold Bruder, New

York, Dr Peter Clive, Ottawa, Canada, David Collopy, *Opera Ireland*, Dublin, Karin Coper, Berlin, Stan Cory, Arizona, Barbara Davies, Jersey, CI, Bill Ecker, Harmonie Autographs and Music, New York, Fiona Fitzsimons, Eneclann, Dublin, Kurt Gänzl, Rangiora, New Zealand, Mario Genesi, Piacenza, Italy, the late Dr Tom Glasow of *Opera Quarterly*, Tommy Graham, *History Ireland*, Dublin, David Grant, Waterford, Ireland, Roger Gross, New York, Friederike Hammer, London, Dr Geerd Heinsen, Berlin, George Jellinek, New York, Dieter Kaegi, *Opera Ireland*, Dublin, Dr Axel Klein, Bonn, Germany, Clarissa Lablache, Florida, Andrew Lamb, Croydon, England, Dr. Valerie Langfield, Cheshire, England, Dumont Laurent, Paris, Dr Joe Law, Ohio, Denis Leonard, Limerick, Ireland, Dr Roberta Marvin, Iowa, Dave Moran, Tasmania, Australia, Theo Mortimer, The Old Dublin Society, Dublin, Colman Morrissey, Dublin, Dr Michael Murphy, Limerick, Ireland, Mike Quinn, Brisbane, Australia, Helen Rappaport, Oxford, England, Thomas Schulz, Vienna, Caroline Shaw, Rothschild Archives, London, Barry Smith, London, Dr Bradley Strauchen, London, the late, William Tyldesley, Cheshire, England, John Ward, Lancashire, England, Granville Walker, Germany and Raymond Walker, Cheshire, England.

My appreciation is also extended to the following for helping me obtain copies of selected Balfe-related documents: Dr Paola Chiapperino, and Anna Bogo, Biblioteca della Casa di Goldoni, Venice, Dr Anna Claut, Biblioteca Nazionale Marciana, Venice, Biblioteca della Fondazione Giorgio Cini, Venice, Dr Marcello Eynard, Biblioteca Civica Angelo Mai, Bergamo, Dr Agostina Zecca Laterza, Biblioteca del Conservatorio di musica Giuseppe Verdi, Milan, Dr Francesco Melisi, Biblioteca del Conservatorio di Musica S. Pietro a Maiella, Naples, John Eeckloo, Koninklijk Conservatorium, Brussels, Dr Barbara Lesák, Österreichisches Theatre Museum, Vienna, Brigitta Pamperl, Österreichische Nationalbibliothek, Vienna, Don McCormick, curator, and Sara Velez, Rogers & Hammerstein Archives of Recorded Sound, New York, Julia Creed, Royal Opera House Collection, Covent Garden, London, Catherine Fahy, Collette O'Flaherty and Jennifer Doyle of the National Library of Ireland, Dublin, Leah Benson and Marie McFeely, the National Gallery of Ireland, Dublin, Tom McCanna, University of Sheffield Music Library, England, Ian Graham, Bowdoin College Library, Maine, the staff at the Richter Library, Microfilm Department, University of Miami, Florida, the University of Indiana, Music Library and the Ontario University Library, Hamilton, Canada.

CHAPTER ONE

Dublin and London –
Background and Beginnings
1808–1825

Balfe's remarkable musical talents secured a unique position for him in Britain during the middle of the nineteenth century. Having spent a number years in France and Italy learning his craft and performing the operas of Rossini, Donizetti and Bellini, he arrived back in London in May 1835, aged tenty-seven, married and with a three-year-old daughter.[1]

His first operatic work for the London stage was the *Siege of Rochelle* (1835), which ran for more than seventy nights at the Theatre Royal, Drury Lane. It augmented a new format that had been introduced the previous year by John Barnett (1802–1890), in his opera *The Mountain Sylph*. Balfe with his Italian training and gift for melody added a completely new continental style and flavor to English language opera which had great appeal and which immediately gained great popularity. The opera represented a major advance in which music became the dominant factor as opposed to the drama. The format eventually changed tastes by making the play with music format which had been London's basic entertainment for generations, obsolete.

Balfe quickly followed it with *The Maid of Artois* (1836). This one he composed especially for his friend, the renowned mezzo-soprano Maria Malibran (1808–1836). He had become friends with Malibran when he sang with her in Paris and Italy. She sang the title role with great virtuosity and sensational results, both musically and financially. Malibran, though born in Paris, was fluent in several languages including English. She had been educated at an English school, so an English libretto presented no problems for her.

Malibran's celebrity and importance had encouraged some leading composers to write or adapt an opera for her, during her short life. Balfe was one; the other of importance was Gaetano Donizetti (*Maria Stuarda*) in 1835. Vincenzo Bellini had adapted one of his scores (*I Puritani*) for her particular vocal range, but she never actually sang it.

The new composer was the talk of the town, so much so that when the young Queen Victoria made her first visit to the theatre shortly after her accession to the throne it was to see a Balfe opera. This publicity greatly enhanced the new composer's position and his pocketbook.

For the next thirty-five years Michael Balfe was to be the dominant British operatic composer of the Victorian era. Outside Britain, he received great personal recognition in the major cities of continental Europe and elsewhere, where several of his operas continued to be performed through the end of the century. The scope and breath of this multi-talented man's activity were spectacular and far-reaching.

While Balfe died in October 1870 his music lived on for a time, particularly in continental Europe, Britain and Ireland and to a lesser extent in other parts of the English-speaking world. Eventually, as with many other composers, including Rossini, public taste changed and music from the earlier part of the century was overtaken by Verdi, Wagner and later Puccini.

Balfe's ever popular opera *The Bohemian Girl*, which premiered in 1843, and which had such great success in the nineteenth century, managed to have a life of its own. It achieved a new and very different audience in the early twentieth century. In an amazing turn of events, in 1922 a silent film version of *The Bohemian Girl* was released in London, starring the young Ivor Novello and Gladys Cooper, with the composer's melodies as background music. How well it did is not known.

However, London wasn't the only place to see new adaptations of this unique work. In 1930 the wonderful film, *Song o' My Heart* was produced in Hollywood featuring the great Irish tenor John McCormack, and quite naturally some of Balfe's music was heard in it. In 1934, Balfe's music was also heard on Broadway, New York at the Lyric Theatre in a show called *Gypsy Blonde*, using Balfe's *Bohemian Girl* score and produced by Dmitri Ostrov.[2] There were twenty-four performances, and by all accounts it was somewhat of a success during those difficult bleak Depression years.

The opera itself had first been heard in New York at the Park theatre in 1844, and there were many subsequent productions throughout the nineteenth century in the United States. In 1911 the opera ran for twenty-four performances at the Majestic Theatre on Broadway and the Majestic saw it again in 1934, when it ran for eleven performances, perhaps playing off the success of the Broadway *Gypsy Blonde* musical version shown a little earlier the same year.

In 1936, a further adaptation of this resilient Balfe work was launched by no less a distinguished person than the legendary Hollywood film immortal, Hal Roach. The film produced by Roach was called *A Comic Version of The Bohemian Girl, An Opera by Balfe*, and it starred Stan Laurel and Oliver Hardy. A number of Balfe's famous musical pieces from the opera were featured throughout. The movie is now available on VHS/DVD from internet video retailers. And even later than that, some of Balfe's music from the opera was also used in *Lassie Come Home* the 1943 Hollywood movie.[3] The famous Irish writer James Joyce also immortalized Balfe's name and works in his *Ulysses* and *Dubliners*. Quite amazing when one thinks about it.

Indeed, there is little doubt, that if Michael William Balfe had been born in the twentieth century instead of the early nineteenth century chances are he would have been just as great a success in London and elsewhere given his musical style and abundance of melody. In fact, if one of today's ambitious producers or arrangers wanted to find a source for new music for a show they would only have to look to the past and Balfe's marvellous scores, and there are lots of them available (see the appendices section), and adapt the music for the Broadway or Drury Lane stage.

Michael William Balfe was born in Dublin on 15 May 1808 at 10 Pitt Street, which was renamed Balfe Street in 1917 by the Dublin Corporation. The home he was born in was demolished in the 1960s to make room for a hotel which stands on the site today. A plaque in Balfe's honour is attached to a wall at the rear of the hotel complex.

Documentary proof of the composer's birth date is not forthcoming, since official registration of births, marriages and deaths in Ireland did not start until January 1864. However, the date has normally been accepted as 15 May 1808. His death certificate and gravesite confirm the year of his birth. Documentation relating to Balfe's baptism, which according to his early biographers occurred some weeks after his birth at St Ann's Anglican Church in Dawson Street, Dublin (a short distance from where he was born in Pitt Street), is not available either. Baptismal records of St Ann's prior to 1873 have unfortunately been destroyed.

In 1922 during the civil war in Ireland, major fires at the Four Courts Building complex in Dublin which housed the Public Records Office tragically destroyed most Irish public records, including many church parochial records relating to baptisms and a wide range of other documents.[4] This event left a huge void for historians and biographers.

Balfe's father was also named Michael William Balfe (he is generally referred to as 'William' Balfe in most biographies).[5] The father died 6 January 1823, according to the composer's early biographers. However, while nothing could be found in the Dublin newspapers about this event, it does seem almost certain that his death did occur in Dublin around this time given the subsequent action of his young son Michael during that period. Where the father might have been buried is not known. Two of Dublin's oldest cemeteries, Mt Jerome and Glasnevin, were not officially opened until some years after 1823. Balfe's mother Catherine (née Ryan) was born in 1782 in Dublin and died in London in 1839, age 57, where she lived with her son, his wife and family at 61 Conduit Street.[6] The Balfe Dublin family eventually consisted of Michael (the future composer) and two daughters. One of the daughters was named Amelia; the first name of the other daughter is unknown.[7]

One of his two sisters apparently was a singer and there is a record of her performing at a concert in Dublin in 1845, however her first name was not given and she was simply referred to as 'Miss Balfe, the sister of the composer'.[8] The other sister appears to have married and, as a result, her name changed to Mrs Dodd. A lady (formerly named Balfe) with this name offered vocal instruction from an address on Ormond Quay in Dublin in 1854.[9] While Amelia did show up as living at the Balfe's home at 61 Conduit Street in London in the 1841 census, it is still quite possible that she may have been one and the same person as Mrs Dodd given the time gap between the two events. Amelia Balfe does not show up in later London census data. In any event, clearly music was part of the Balfe family life from an early period.

William Balfe (the father) married Catherine Ryan in Dublin in 1807. It was a mixed marriage, the mother being Catholic, the father Anglican. The practice then was for a son to be baptized in the father's religion and a daughter in the mother's.

The family initially lived at 10 Pitt Street. It appears that Pitt Street was fashionable for people in the musical profession. Balfe's mother and father went to live there shortly after their marriage in June 1807. It was a short street (as Balfe Street still is today) so there were probably about ten or twelve houses there. At least two if not three were homes occupied by prominent musicians. The musician Sir Robert Stewart and his family lived there for several years. He was a Balfe contemporary. At an earlier time, the important Giordani musical family also lived on this street.

Balfe's father was a musician and dancing master. Balfe senior offered dancing classes in Dublin and Wexford from around 1810 to 1817, or later. He usually spent about six months at each location. While some of the composer's early biographers have questioned the father's occupation and the fact that he was even a musician, there is now evidence to show that he was in fact a dancing master.[10] He plied his trade between Dublin and Wexford on Ireland's southeast coast, a distance of about one hundred miles, at different times of the year.

In 1818 the Balfes moved to 2 Hamilton Row, Dublin (now known as Fenian Street), a socially less desirable neighborhood at the time of their move. However, it was a short walk from their former residence, so patrons did not have to travel too much farther. The father continued to offer dancing lessons on Mondays and Thursdays at this address. It was also at this location that the father most probably died in January 1823. Their move to Hamilton Row may have been an indication of deterioration in the father's health and a declining financial situation, since the father was only forty years old when he died, possibly from tuberculosis or typhus which had an outbreak in Dublin around that period.

Annually from about 1810 in late June or July, and again in December, William Balfe advertised his arrival or departure in local Wexford newspapers saying that he was offering lessons in 'waltzes, minuets, hornpipes, reels and the most fashionable dances'.[11] He didn't appear to advertise too much in Dublin, which might suggest that he had a reasonably good base of patrons in the city who knew him. The dancing master profession was a well-established business in Ireland during those years, particularly in the southeast area of the country.[12]

Logically, young Balfe would have received his initial musical training from his father, who was a violinist. The father had recognized his son's musical talents early on and had later placed him with various music teachers in Wexford and Dublin. He spent time under the tutelage of a Wexford-based music teacher, T. P. Meadows, and later in Dublin, initially with William O'Rourke (afterwards in London known as Rooke) and then with James Barton, both of whom worked as violinists. O'Rourke and Barton were with the Crow Street theatre orchestra. Later Barton was associated with the Theatre Royal orchestra for many years.

Where Balfe junior might have received his basic education and for how long is unknown. Formal schooling was not introduced into Ireland until the 1830s. Even as a youth he appeared to be quite literate. His mother and father possibly came from good backgrounds and perhaps he was home educated, which was not uncommon in Dublin in the early nineteenth century.

There is also an undocumented reference to the fact by one of the composer's early biographers that Balfe's mother was related to the notorious Leonard McNally, of Harcourt Street, Dublin. McNally was a prominent lawyer, songwriter, and later a spy for the ruling administration. If there was in fact a relationship, then it possibly meant that she could have been from a well-educated family and as a result could have been young Balfe's teacher of basic subjects.

During these early years Balfe, a child prodigy, participated in concert life in Dublin at such places as the Rotunda Concert Rooms and the Crow Street Theatre. Dublin's theatre life was remarkably busy during the early decades of the nineteenth century. Generally, there was an ongoing stream of actors, singers and musicians who regularly visited the Irish city when the London season drew to a close each year.

The musical works being performed in Dublin around the second decade of the nineteenth century were more like plays with music than operas, particularly those of the English composer

Henry Bishop (1786–1855) or, a little later, Bilbao-born Michael Rophino Lacy, (1795–1867), a musician and arranger with an Irish wine merchant father and a Spanish mother who studied music in Paris and who was particularly successful with his arrangements of other composer's dramatic musical works in London.

Operas which Michael Balfe would later become very familiar with such as Rossini's *L'Italiana in Algeri*, *Il barbiere di Siviglia* and *La Cenerentola* were just receiving their premieres in Italy at this time. Donizetti's most famous operas, *L'elisir d'Amore* and *Lucia di Lammermoor* and Bellini's *Norma*, and *La Sonnambula* would have premieres some years later, while Verdi's first operatic success was almost twenty years on the horizon.

At nine years old Balfe performed at his first professional concert at the Rotunda Concert Rooms on 30 May 1817. He next performed on 20 June at the Crow Street Theatre with excellent reviews, having played a work on the violin by one of his teachers, James Barton, who was then leader of the orchestra. He appeared again, five nights later, in a benefit concert for Barton. These activities were followed in quick succession by additional concerts either at the Rotunda or the Crow Street Theatre over the next several months.

He continued to perform at concerts in Dublin and other places with considerable success. His first composition, a song called 'The Lover's Mistake', with words by Thomas Haynes Bayly (1795–1839), was published by Isaac Willis in Dublin in December 1822. The British Library and the National Library of Ireland both hold copies of this original early Balfe composition. These early years of learning his craft by performing as a soloist would prove to be extremely valuable as Balfe's career developed.

A great deal of change was occurring in Ireland during the early years of the new century. The Act of Union, which was enacted on 1 January 1801 eliminated the Irish Parliament and moved the government to London, creating a great deal of uncertainty for the Anglo-Irish ascendancy. The ascendancy had been the primary supporters of the arts and music in Dublin for decades.

However, despite these economic concerns the early years of the century also saw great expansion in the city. Because of its large population, which was around 200,000, and its strong military base and affluence the city had always been the musical focal point

in Ireland. Handel's *Messiah* had it premiere there at the Great
Musick Hall, also referred to as Neale's Musick Hall, in Fishamble
Street in April 1742 with the composer directing. Handel came
for a short visit but stayed several months before returning to
England. He was quite complimentary about the quality of the
musicians. The Philharmonic Society of Dublin was involved with
the production.

In 1819 Dublin saw its first Mozart opera, *Don Giovanni*, with
one of the great baritones of the day, Giuseppe Ambrogetti, in the
title role. Two years earlier the opera had its first London performance. As time progressed Dublin became an important venue
for visiting Italian and English opera troupes.

The population supported several theatres, music rooms and
concert halls, most of which had been in operation for decades.
The beautiful Rotunda Concert Rooms was built in the 1760s (the
building still exists as of this writing, though sadly it is virtually
derelict) as part of a fundraising venue for the adjacent hospital. It
could accommodate 2,000 people due to the fact that the remarkable ceiling with its chandeliers, beautiful curvature and recesses,
had no central support columns, which left the entire floor space
open for seating and standing room. As a result, it was reported to
have perfect acoustics.[13] During Balfe's early years the Rotunda
Concert Rooms were particularly active. He performed there on
the violin many times as a child prodigy, from around 1817 to
1822.

Virtually from its inception, the unique Rotunda 'round room'
developed a long history of hosting balls, masquerades, political
and religious meetings, choral performances, and classical musical
concerts, both instrumental and vocal. Legendary artists, such as
the Dublin born child prodigy, pianist John Field (1782–1837),
violinist Nicolo Paganini (1782–1840), pianist Ignaz Moscheles
(1794–1870), violinist, Ole Bull (1810–1880) and the renowned
Franz Liszt (1811–1886), and others performed in the Rotunda
round room. Composers whose music was featured at some of
these concerts included Handel, Vivaldi, Corelli, Geminiani, and
later Rossini, Donizetti, Bellini and others. Vocal concerts usually
featured visiting artists from London and the continent and local
Irish artists including the very young Irish soprano Catherine
Hayes (1818–1861), who participated in one of Liszt's concerts in

1841.[14] Vocal concerts usually featured music by Handel, Dibdin and Arne along with a mixture of Italian arias and Irish and Scottish songs.[15]

In January 1821 the 3,000-seat Theatre Royal opened its doors in Hawkins Street on the south side of the River Liffey, which divides the city's north and south sides. The experienced Henry Harris of London's Covent Garden theatre was the manager of the Theatre Royal. The Royal in Dublin was reported to be one of the largest theatres in Britain. It cost £50,000 to build; an enormous sum in those days. As a demonstration of its affluence, innovation and elegance the theatre added gas lighting in 1823. For almost sixty years the theatre was the centre for opera in Dublin. Michael Balfe was destined to sing there in opera and have a number of his operas performed there in the years ahead.

During the same year the Theatre Royal opened its doors, King George IV visited Dublin. He attended the theatre for a performance of Sheridan's *Duenna*. King George was the first reigning British monarch to visit Ireland.

Within a short period of time the Royal became the venue for a wide variety of performances including English composer Henry Bishop's (of 'Home Sweet Home' fame) bowdlerized adaptation of Mozart's *The Marriage of Figaro*, with an English libretto. The fourteen-year-old Balfe most probably saw this performance in 1821, because he was obviously very impressed by Mrs Ann Humby, who sang the role of Cherubino. In fact, Master Balfe was so impressed with Mrs Humby that he dedicated his first published song, 'The Lover's Mistake', to Mrs Humby when it was produced in 1822 in Dublin. Ann Humby was considered to be a fascinating actress and singer who was immensely popular at the Theatre Royal and in Britain. Obviously, young Balfe was one of her ardent admirers.

Early in 1822 Charles Horn, a vocalist, musician and composer with an excellent London reputation, arrived in Dublin to perform in English opera. Horn returned again to Dublin a year later in early January 1823 for twelve nights of English opera with the soprano Cathy Stephens. Horn's visit this time would have a significant influence on Balfe's future career.

In August 1823 the renowned Italian soprano Angelica Catalani revisited Ireland and gave a concert at the theatre, to a sold-out house. She had first appeared at the Rotunda Concert Rooms in 1807.

The Theatre Royal eventually became one of the primary places of choice for internationally established artists who visited Dublin for concerts and opera during the nineteenth century. Singers such as, Giovanni Battista Rubini (1794–1854), Fanny Persiani (1812–1867), Luigi Lablache (1794–1858), Giulia Grisi (1811–1869) Giovanni Mario (1810–1883), and others arrived, some broadening their visits to include Belfast, Cork, Limerick and sometimes Kilkenny as places beyond the "Pale" became more sophisticated and interested in classical music. A number of years later Balfe himself would return a number of times to perform in opera at the Theatre Royal. On one occasion his wife Lina Roser Balfe (1808–1888), and the pianist Sigismond Thalberg (1812–1871), accompanied him.

Dublin was also gradually developing a significantly new skyline as the early century progressed along with greatly widened streets. Most of the buildings which still exist were constructed during the 1780s and later. These included the dominant Custom House, the impressive Four Courts complex; Henry Grattan's Parliament, which had been built at an earlier time, took on a new look as it became the Bank of Ireland building with the transition of the Irish parliament to London. The Royal Exchange and the General Post Office were opened during the early part of the century. Also Nelson's pillar in the city centre was constructed early in the new century. Outside the city, the work on the spectacular new harbour at Kingstown (now Dun Laoghaire) also commenced around this period.[16]

It was paradoxical, as Dublin was also struggling with the recession that came about with the end of the Napoleonic Wars in 1815, when thousands of Irish-born British soldiers were demobilized and returning to Ireland without any work. The British economy at the same time was faltering on bankruptcy.

Throughout all of this, music continued to be an important part of life in Dublin. It wasn't too long before visiting Italian operatic troupes were singing operas by Rossini and others at the Theatre Royal. However, despite all that was happening around Balfe, the musical scene in Dublin was just not robust enough for the aspiring young Dublin composer. Whatever motivated him generally appeared to come from within, driven by a restless need to move on. His lifetime pattern would demonstrate this time and again.

From the outset Michael William Balfe never lacked confidence. His actions as a boy and later as a teenager showed a remarkable level of intelligence and self-assurance combined with a decisiveness that worked for him most of the time. If he had any failings, they were not always obvious during these early years. People seemed to like him and to want to help him. He appeared to have a very positive attitude. In later life this was particularly apparent when it came to his family and close associates.

There is little doubt that given the young musician's driving ambitions and restless personality that his life in Dublin during these early years was becoming too routine. One way or another he would ultimately have been drawn to London, where the opportunities were so much greater. Visiting musicians would also have encouraged this given his personality and talent. However, it was actually the death of his father at the beginning of January in 1823 that precipitated the first major change in his life, either because of the need for change, or because the family's economic situation was drastically impacted by the death of the father, or possibly a combination of both.

Balfe set off for London towards the end of January 1823. While he didn't know it then, London would really only be a stepping-stone for him during this initial period before he went on to a greater learning experience in France and Italy for several years. He crossed the Irish Sea in the company of the musical performer and song writer, Charles Horn, as an articled apprentice.[17] Horn had just completed a successful season of English opera at the Theatre Royal, when Balfe apparently approached him about going to London. The two had first met in June 1818, when Balfe performed at a benefit concert for Horn and Mrs Isaac Willis at the Rotunda Concert Rooms. Again, Balfe's persuasive personality and sincerity of purpose probably played a role is getting Horn to agree to take him to London. This, it seems, was done with the consent of the young musician's mother.

Horn was a highly competent musician who was born in London in 1786 His father was Charles (Carl) Frederick Horn (1762–1830) a musician from Nordhausen in Germany who became organist and music teacher at St George's Chapel Royale at Windsor.[18] Horn senior also had several members of the Royal family as pupils. During these early days in London, Balfe also received instruction from Horn's father; presumably it was arranged by the son.

As Charles Horn grew up in London he assisted his father in the instruction of some of the junior pupils. Possibly this early learning experience made him compassionate in terms of helping the young Dublin musician improve his skills. In any event, Charles Horn also continued to perform in musical dramas and English opera for many years in Britain, before going to New York, where he became the manager of the Park Theatre in October 1827. He returned to London occasionally. He was married twice, once in England in 1810 and again in America in 1838. There were children from both marriages. He eventually died in Boston in 1849.[19]

Almost immediately on arriving in London, Balfe started working with the orchestra at Drury Lane theatre as a violinist. It's very possible that Horn arranged this, as he was also scheduled to commence a series of performances at Drury Lane in February 1823. The music director there was the highly talented Dublin born musician and composer Thomas Simpson Cooke (1782–1848). The young Dubliner's skills as a violinist were immediately obvious, with the result that he gave his first solo, a new violin concerto, on the stage of the Drury Lane theatre on 19 March 1823, under the direction of the important musician, Sir George Smart.[20] It was a remarkably fast London debut. Again, it was indicative of Balfe's decisiveness, confidence and persuasive personality, even at an early age.

The concert, which was announced in the *Times* as part of an 'Oratorio' series involved a number of distinguished musicians such as, the French harpist and composer, Nicholas Bochsa (1789–1856), soprano Mary Ann Paton (1802–1864) and others. It made reference to Balfe's appearance as follows; 'A new concerto on the violin, [by] Master Balfe (his first appearance)'.

While some of the critics praised him for his efforts, others were more cautious, saying that he had youth on his side and that no doubt his talents would fully develop with time.

For the next two years Balfe continued to work in the orchestra, with Cooke as its director and Nicholas Mori (1792–1839) as the leader. Balfe maintained his position as a violinist, even on some occasions substituting as the leader. His readiness to take on new duties resulted in opportunities to work on copying orchestral parts and related activity for James Mapleson[21] (the grandfather of Lionel Mapleson, librarian at the Metropolitan Opera and famous for his early cylinder recordings), the librarian and copyist at Drury Lane.   Balfe was now also maturing; he turned seventeen years old in May 1825, and found himself with a reasonably good-quality baritone voice.

His exploits led him to take on new sets of challenges some of which he was ill prepared for.   He became part of an operatic venture in Norwich, where it appears that he took on the role of Kaspar in an English version of *Der Freischütz*. While the documentary newspaper evidence recording the evening's activities was apparently lost at this point in time, due to a fire, it does seem that some of his early biographers had access to the information as they recorded the event. However, there is new evidence available that places Balfe in Norwich at this time, which tends to support his first venture into opera.[22]

As it turned out, the young baritone was not able to handle the role or performance due to stage fright. The role of Kaspar was also written for a bass voice not a light baritone. The evening eventually ended in a disaster for him and the entire cast with a fire, which may well have been caused by Balfe's ineptness.   However, this Norwich experience did not seem to have any lasting affect on our young musician. He returned to London unabashed, ready to continue his activities at Drury Lane.

Frequently over the years critics would refer to Balfe as the 'indefatigable Balfe' as he dealt with difficult challenges and adversity, particularly in the opera house.   Perhaps his quick recovery after the Norwich fiasco was indicative of this characteristic.

Many years later, at the peak of his success, he was to visit Norwich again. This time he went as the accompanist for the famous soprano Jenny Lind (1820–1887), who was giving a concert there. No doubt Balfe, in his own unique humorous style, would have recounted his youthful operatic indiscretions to the famed prima donna, given their close relationship.

London in the early nineteenth century was an important musical centre. It had its Italian opera seasons and it was frequently visited by many of the leading continental performing artists. However, it was not normally a city that saw world premiere performances of

large-scale lasting musical works or major operas, with a few
notable exceptions. It didn't yet have the status of Paris or Vienna,
where operas and orchestral works by leading composers were
premiered on a regular basis. It would be a few years before the
city on the Thames fully achieved that distinction.

The Royal Philharmonic Society had inaugurated its first concert in 1813. Sir George Smart became its leader. The German
composer Carl Maria von Weber arrived in the city in 1825, to
premiere his opera *Oberon.*

Balfe's time in London during these years exposed him to a very
different level of musical performance particularly the *Italian Opera*
at the King's Theatre and the other musical works being performed
at Drury Lane. It was around this time that he is reported by his early
biographers to have met a wealthy Count Mazzara from Rome who
was visiting London. It was further stated that Mazzara, who had a
wife and home in Rome, was immediately struck by the young
Balfe's resemblance to his recently deceased son. As a result, he
invited Balfe to Rome to meet his wife and to study music there.
Without all of the facts on Mazzara, and what his interests may
have been, particularly in London, it is difficult to dispute the early
biographers' version of the facts. Patrons for young aspiring musicians were not uncommon during the nineteenth century.

Research shows that there was in fact a Louis Phillippe
Baldersar Mazzara who visited London and who lived in Rome.
The French forenames possibly relate to the fact that Mazzara
appears to be a family name from Sicily, which was governed by
the Bourbons of Naples in the early nineteenth century. What his
occupation or interests in London may have been is unknown.
Louis Mazzara was widowed by 1839. In September of that year
he married Felicia, the young daughter of the famous violinist and
Beethoven friend George Polgreen Bridgetower (1778–1860), in
the fashionable St George's Church, Hanover Square, London.[23]
These events might suggest that Mazzara's interests had something
to do with music, given his bride and the Hanover Square setting,
which was a central area for music-related businesses and residences. However, since his specifics are unknown it is difficult to
verify the information. Additionally, it is also not possible to know
if this was the actual individual that Balfe might have met in
London in 1825.

Regardless of Mazzara, we do know that Balfe did make his way to continental Europe towards the end of 1825 and in the process he first visited Paris, where he met, among others, the composer Luigi Cherubini (1760–1842). He spent some time studying with Cherubini before departing for Italy, presumably with his patron, Mazzara.

It would be many years before Balfe would eventually return to make London his home. When he did arrive in London, he came as an experienced musician and with many years as a singer in Italy behind him. He also brought with him a young and beautiful continental wife and his firstborn child, Louisa Catherine Maria. By then he was also fluent in French and Italian.

It was the beginning of a brilliant career that would stretch out across Europe and beyond, and it was remarkable by any standard.

NOTES

1. Balfe returned to London in May 1835, not 1834, as stated in the *New Grove Dictionary of Opera,* in Tyldesley's biography section of his Balfe book and in the early Balfe biography by Barrett. Balfe was performing in Venice with Malibran as late as 8 April 1835. Also see reference in the *Times,* 25 May 1835, to a proposed 'Mr. Begrez Annual Morning Concert', at the King's Theatre, London of 29 May 1835 announcing 'Signor Puzzi, who will play a new fantasia, composed for him by Signor Balfi, who has just arrived in London'.
2. See www.ibdb.com – Michael Balfe – Internet Broadway Database.
3. See www.Imdb.com – The *Earth's Biggest Movie Database.* An Amazon.com company.
4. *A Table of Church of Ireland Parochial Records and copies*: Irish Family History Society, Nass, Co. Kildare, Ireland. May 2005, editor, Noel Reid.
5. Death Certificate of Catherine Balfe showing she was the 'Widow of Michael William Balfe, a Professor of Music'.
6. Death Certificate of Catherine Balfe showing her death as 24 January 1839, age of fifty-seven.
7. While Balfe was visiting Dublin in the early 1840s he composed a song, 'Keep one kind thought for me' with words by Hugh O'Reilly, which states on the front page, 'Composed expressly for and dedicated to his sister, Amelia Balfe'. The piece was published by Robinson & Bussell, Dublin. The National Library of Ireland, Dublin, has a copy of it.
8. *The Musical World,* London, March 1845, page 162. 'Mr McIntosh completed a season at the Dublin Music Hall having had Giulio Regondi, Henry Russell and the Misses Morgan and Balfe (sister of the composer) as vocalists.'
9. This reference is from p. 53 of the book *To Talent Alone* (see bibliography) in which the author refers to Mrs Dodd as being Balfe's 'daughter.' This is an error; it was probably was one of Balfe's sisters as neither of Balfe's daughters were married to anyone called Dodd and neither ever lived in Ireland. The author's reference comes from *The Freeman's Journal* of 23 November 1854.
10. See *Opera in Dublin 1798–1820, Frederick Jones and the Crow Street Theatre* by T. J. Walsh, page 191, in which the author details various references to the father's activities
11. Advertisement, front page of the *Wexford Herald,* 3 June 1813. Also see *Wexford Herald,* 5 December 1815, 21 December 1815, 13 May 1816 and 16 June 1817.

12. Friel, Mary. *Dancing as a social pastime in the South-east of Ireland 1800–1897.* Four Courts Press, Dublin, 2004.
13. Paper "The Rotunda Gardens and Buildings" read by Seamus Scully, Old Dublin Society, 1 March 1971.
14. See *Catherine Hayes: The Hibernian Prima Donna* by Basil Walsh, page 23.
15. *Rotunda Music in Eighteen-century Dublin*, pp. 152–153, by Brian Boydell
16. *Dublin Historical Record*, Vol. LIX, No. 2 Autumn 2006, pp. 182–200.
17. *Charles Edward Horn's Memoirs*, Charles Horn and Michael Kassler. There is no mention of taking Balfe to London as his apprentice in Horn's memoirs.
18. See, *Charles Edward Horn's Memoirs of his Father and Himself*, ed. Michael Kassler.
19. Ibid.
20. *The Times*, Wednesday 19 March 1823. Advertisement for an evening concert in which between the second and third parts 'a new concerto on the violin, Master Balfe (his first appearance) ... [will be performed]'.
21. James Mapleson was the father of the singer and impresario Col. James Henry Mapleson. Mapleson senior's other son was Alfred John Mapleson, who was the father of Lionel Mapleson, librarian at the Metropolitan New York and famous for his cylinder recordings from the "flies" of the Metropolitan Opera in the early 1900s.
22. The *Norwich Mercury* of 18 September, 1824 contained an advertisement that showed that 'Master Balfe, the Musical Prodigy' was going to be in Norwich with a group (Mr Ellar, Mr Beral, Signor Paulo, Miss Mason, Mrs Pindar, Mr G. Bennett, Mr Edw. Crook) from the Theatre Royal Drury Lane to present a 'Series of Novelty' for the Grand Festival, etc. My thanks to Pip Clayton of the Donizetti Society of London, for supplying this information and the copy of the Norwich advertisement.
23. The information about Mazzara was kindly provided by Helen Rappaport of Oxford, UK, who is working on a book on the nineteenth-century violinist George August Polgreen Bridgetower (Bridgtower)

CHAPTER TWO

France and Italy –
Singer and Composer
1825–1831

When Balfe arrived in Paris in 1825, Rossini's music was all the rage. The Italian composer was very active. Rossini had just signed an agreement in London at the French Embassy that his future compositions would be for the Académie Royale de Musique and the Théâtre-Italiens in Paris. His most important work for Paris, the monumental masterpiece *Guillaume Tell* (1829), was still in the future.

However, Balfe did not meet Rossini on this occasion, possibly because the Italian was too busy with his next compositions, or with his new role as director of the Théâtre-Italiens, which he offered to share with the incumbent director Ferdinando Paer (1771–1839). Paer, upset and dissatisfied with the appointment of Rossini, offered his resignation, but later withdrew it because he would have forfeited his other post as the King's *maître de chapelle* if he had resigned.[1]

Paer's contribution was later recognized in Paris when he received the cross of the Légion d'Honneur in 1828, and when he became a member of the Académie des Beaux-Arts. He later also taught at the Conservatoire until his death. Paer stayed in Paris, never returning to Italy. As a result, the references by one of Balfe's early biographers to the fact that the young musician studied with Paer while in Rome during 1826 could not be correct.[2]

During this period Balfe met with Luigi Cherubini in Paris; presumably it was arranged by Balfe's patron.[3] It was a fortuitous contact, however short, that would lead to important events for Balfe in the years ahead. The elderly Italian composer was then the director of the Paris Conservatoire, a position he had held from 1821 and would continue to hold until 1841. He took an immediate liking to the young student and was impressed by his musical talents. He talked to the youth about study and the opportunities in Paris for a musician, offering Balfe "gratuitous instruction" if he remained in Paris.[4] However, Balfe was not diverted from his desire to go to Italy, advising Cherubini that he would return to Paris if things did not work out in Italy.

Sometime later in 1825, probably in the spring, the young musician and his patron reached Milan where they spent some time. Balfe was invited to participate in a private concert in the home of Giovanni Ricordi (1785–1853), the music publisher who frequently arranged such events. Other singers included the noted French tenor, Gilbert Duprez (1806–1896), and another French tenor, Alexis Dupont (1796–1874), both on their way back to Paris.[5] There is no record of what was sung at the Milan concert. Dupont had performed leading roles in a number of Rossini operas at La Scala during the 1824–25 season, which ended in May 1825. Duprez was at the beginning of what would be an illustrious career.

Both of these singers later created numerous leading roles in Paris. Duprez, who became the more famous of the two, also created the role of Edgardo in Donizetti's *Lucia di Lammermoor* in 1835 in Naples. Some years later, Balfe was destined to compose a remarkable cantata for these two singers and others, while in Paris. Most important perhaps is the fact that Balfe's entry into Italy started in esteemed company, which says something for his talents and personal style.

While in Milan Balfe and his patron also visited the opera. Rossini's *Semiramide, Mosè in Egitto, La Cenerentola* and *Tancredi* were being performed at La Scala. These were operas that Balfe would become very familiar with in the future. Afterwards they departed for Rome. The year 1825 was a Holy Year in Rome; as a result all of the theatres were closed, which would have been a disappointment for Balfe.[6]

How much time Balfe spent during 1825 languishing in Rome is not really known. Whether he took music lessons or singing lessons or participated in any concerts is also not really known as no direct documentation has been found that might provide an insight into his activities during this period.

However, by early 1826 his patron deemed it desirable that his young guest should consider moving to Milan for study, where

there were experienced instructors and more opportunities to participate in concerts. Milan also had several opera houses.   The
patron also had the need to travel to England on business and on
the way he offered to take Balfe with him to Milan and to make
arrangements for him to study there. It seems he also provided the
young musician with an initial stipend to enable him to get established in the northern Italian city.

In Milan, Balfe worked with Vincenzo Federici (1764–1826)
through the summer of 1826. While Federici was associated with
the Milan Conservatory, Balfe actually took lessons with him
privately, probably because Balfe would have been over age for the
institution. It was this same Conservatory that refused to admit the
young Giuseppe Verdi a few years later because they considered
him too old, at the age of eighteen. In any event, Balfe continued
his tuition in counterpoint and harmony with the aging Federici.
The music teacher later died in Milan in August 1826 so Balfe was
left to continuing his studies with his singing teacher, Filippo Galli
(1783–1853), as his sole instructor.

It was also around this time that Balfe decided to branch out. He
made contact with various theatre managers in the area to see if
there were opportunities for him as a composer or singer or possibly as a copyist for orchestral scores. During the early nineteenth
century, orchestral scores were not printed. Most theatres had
copyists on staff or access to outside copyists for the purpose of creating the orchestral parts from a composer's autograph score.

There were several theatres functioning in Milan at the time,
including the Teatro Carcano, Teatro Cannobiana, Teatro Re,
Teatro San Radegonda and several other smaller places, all of which
presented opera in addition to the city's principal venue, La Scala.

During this time period Balfe also made contact with the
London-born Joseph Glossop (1793–1850), the son of a wealthy
London merchant and property owner. Glossop in his youth had
established the Royal Coburg Theatre in London, which went into
bankruptcy around 1822, forcing Glossop to depart London. To
avoid his creditors Glossop took off for the continent to try his
success there.   When Balfe arrived in Milan, Glossop in fact was
in charge of the Royal Theatres of Milan with an appointment
from August 1824 to May 1826. He also had the lease on the San
Carlo Theatre in Naples.

Through a somewhat audacious application to the ruling Austrian authority (Austria ruled Lombardy and Venetia at the time), Glossop gained control of La Scala, and the Teatro Cannobiana and other Milan theatres in August 1824, having already being appointed lessee at the San Carlo in Naples earlier that same year.

Glossop was a man of the theatre, as were his sons. He was first married in 1812 to the English soprano Elizabeth Férron (1797–1853). She established herself as an important singer and she was in fact singing at La Scala during this period also. In turn one of their sons, Augustus Harris Glossop (1825–1873), who was born in Naples, became a London impresario, and his son Sir Augustus Harris (1852–1896) became, perhaps, the most famous family member as the lessee of Drury Lane and Covent Garden Theatres in London, where he managed some of the greatest singers of the late nineteenth century. Glossop senior married a second time in 1827, this time to Josephine de Méric, another singer, who would also get to know Balfe at a later date through members of her family. Joseph Glossop died in Italy in 1853 and is buried in Florence. Balfe was destined to come in contact with various Harris Glossop family members again later in his life in London, in a different capacity.[7]

In 1826, Balfe was finally successful in gaining an assignment to compose a ballet, titled *Il naufragio di La Perouse*. This was gained through his relationship with Glossop. However, Glossop had concerns with a composer who was British and whose name is unknown. As a result, he assigned the work to one of his secondary theatres, the Teatro Cannobiana, not to La Scala. The sets and scenery were designed by an Englishman by the name of Barrymore. It was reported that the work was quite successful.[8] How many performances it may have had, is not known. The music has not survived and there does not appear to be any documentary information or reviews available. The Cannobiana being a secondary theatre in Milan, it would not always have had musical critics in attendance.

With Glossop gone from Milan and no real opportunities, Balfe became somewhat despondent with his limited progress and the fact that he was most probably short on money. Additionally, he continued to struggle with his thoughts of becoming a singer versus

a composer, trying to work both side of the street created a conflict. Balfe made up his mind to return to London, where he had
contacts and the opportunity to gain an income. Remembering
Cherubini's kind words he decided to visit Paris on the return trip.
It is also possible that he may have first actually returned to
London for a short time during this period because there is a reference to him in the *Harmonicon* (London) as having performed
at a private concert in London around this time.[9]

In any event, early in 1827, he returned to Paris. Once there he
immediately contacted the aging Italian composer Cherubini to seek
his advice and help. Cherubini was sympathetic to the young musician. He invited Balfe to dinner where his guests were Gioachino
Rossini (1792–1868) and his wife of five years, the successful singer
Isabella Colbran (1785–1845) and some other people.

As the evening progressed, Rossini in his inimitable style suggested some music and singing. Balfe was invited to display his talents.
The young Irishman, with great flair, accompanied himself on the
piano in a recital of Figaro's aria "Largo al factotum" from Rossini's
Il barbiere di Siviglia, to the amazement of all present, most of all the
composer himself. Rossini's response was quite complimentary.[10]
Balfe was about to turn nineteen years old at the time.

Rossini was so impressed with the erudite Balfe's performance
that he committed to helping him, at the same time promising him
that he would eventually perform at the Théâtre-Italiens, the premier Italian opera house in France. Another guest at Cherubini's
dinner party, a banker, agreed to underwrite the cost of Balfe's
vocal lessons with the singing teacher, Bordogni. For the next year
Balfe studied with Cherubini and took vocal lessons with the well
established singer and coach, Giulio Bordogni (1789–1856),
applying himself with great zeal according to reports.

Balfe's baritone voice had matured by now with his initial training
from Galli. He had a two-octave range, with significant flexibility,
that was suited to Rossini's music style. He was also an excellent
sight-reader of music, a talent rare among singers of that period.

Balfe's operatic debut occurred at the Théâtre-Italiens in January
1828 in the role of Figaro in nine performances of *Il barbiere di
Siviglia*. The Rosina of the cast was none other than the celebrated
Henriette Sontag (1806–1854), Giulio Bordogni (Balfe's teacher),
was the Almaviva, with Nicholas Levasseur (1791–1871) as Don

Basilio. By all accounts, it was a very successful debut. Following the fourth performance, Rossini advised Balfe that he would be receiving a three year-commitment from the opera's management, which was welcomed by the somewhat amazed Balfe.[11]

Over the next several months Balfe added the part of Dandini in *La Cenerentola* by Rossini, with the renowned Maria Malibran (1808–1836) in the title role. Domenico Donzelli (1790–1873) sang the tenor role of the Prince. Balfe's next portrayal was that of Don Giovanni in Mozart's opera of the same name. He later sang in Rossini's *La gazza ladra* in the part of the Podesta with Malibran and the short comic role of Batone in *L'inganno felice*, which finished up a very successful season for him. This relationship with Malibran would be extremely valuable to Balfe in the future. The two would become close friends.

Towards the end of the season in Paris the theatre management decided to mount a production of Nicolo Zingarelli's (1752–1837) opera *Romeo e Giulietta* with Malibran in the part of Romeo. Malibran in her capricious style was not completely happy with some of Zingarelli's music. She requested Rossini to make some adjustments so that the music was more suitable for her vocal style. Rossini declined but recommended that Balfe be considered.[12]

Balfe jumped at the opportunity to compose music for Malibran and interpolate it into Zingarelli's score. And so his first musical effort included composing an overture, two choruses and a special scene for Malibran and an aria for the secondary role of the soprano. This was virtually a restructuring of the opera. However, Malibran was more than satisfied as was the theatre management, to the extent that they offered Balfe a libretto for him to compose a new opera, with the title of *Atala*.

As it turned out, Balfe only composed selective pieces for the opera, electing instead to return to Italy to gain more experience as a singer and possibly a composer. Before his departure there was a concert performed in which some of his musical pieces were performed. His friend Malibran participated, as did tenor Alexis Dupont, whom he had met earlier in Milan. The great tenor Adolph Nourrit (1802–1839), who would go on to create the role of Arnold in Rossini's crowning achievement, *Guillaume Tell*, in Paris a year later, was also on the programme.[13]

On 16 August 1828, apparently Rossini and his wife were

scheduled to participate in a concert at the Hôtel de Ville in Dieppe. Rossini brought Balfe along. The concert was for the Duchess du Berry. What they performed in not known. Obviously the relationship between the young Irishman and the famous Italian composer was excellent. On his return to Paris Balfe prepared himself for his journey to Italy and for what would be the start of the next stage of his career.

How Balfe got to Italy this time has been the subject of much speculation that will be touched on later. After leaving Paris he did not have much money after paying his debts, even though he had good earnings as a singer for several months. However, ever optimistic and with his mind made-up, he decided to return to Milan as quickly as possible given his new credentials from the Théâtre-Italiens. Rossini had also provided a letter of introduction for him to various people in Italy.

Balfe arrived in Milan in December 1828, where he most probably contacted Giovanni Ricordi, whose business was now flourishing, or possibly an ex-Ricordi employee, Francesco Lucca (1802–1872), who had started his own music publishing business in Milan in 1825. Lucca would publish some of Balfe's works in the years ahead.

Possibly because of his prior contact with Ricordi or maybe through his letter from Rossini he managed to gain a position in a concert being sponsored by the Garden Society of Milan on 7 December 1828 in which the featured singer was the great soprano, Giuditta Pasta (1797–1865), who was then only thirty-one years old and about to create major new roles in Milan for Bellini and Donizetti within a few years. Also sharing the concert platform was the tenor Berardo Winter and a mezzo-soprano, Marietta Tonelli, along with Balfe.[14]

The concerts consisted of excerpts from Giacomo Meyerbeer's (1791–1864), *Il Crociato in Egitto*, Rossini's *Tancredi*, Giovanni Paisiello's (1740–1816) *Nini* and Francesco Morlacchi's (1784–1841) *Tebaldo e Isolina* were performed by the singers. Balfe had not sung any of this music previously. However, given his ability to sight-read and being a quick learner no doubt he performed well. He would meet with Pasta again many years in the future in London when they would perform together with Balfe in a very different role.

During this time the composer Vincenzo Bellini (1802–1835), was also in Milan finalizing his new opera, *La Straniera*, which had originally been scheduled to premiere at La Scala for the opening of Carnivale on 26 December, but because of illness on the part of his librettist it was delayed until 14 February 1829. Balfe met Bellini during his stay in Milan as Bellini was later to convey his good wishes to Balfe through a friend (Andrea Monteleone in Palermo) when the baritone was about to sing in the local premier of Bellini's new opera, *La Straniera* in Palermo.[15] Balfe more than likely was introduced to Bellini by Pasta. While in Milan he presented the Rossini letter to the Conte San Antonio (later Duke of Canizzaro) and as a result an assignment was secured for him in Palermo at the Teatro Carolino for the spring/summer period 1829.[16]

After leaving Milan, Balfe made his way to Bologna to visit one of Rossini's wealthy musician friends, the Marchese Francesco Giovanni Sampieri, whom he had met in Paris. During his stay in Bologna Balfe was introduced to the future great soprano, Giulia Grisi (1811–1869). The two were initially attracted to each other. She and Balfe were destined to become lifelong friends.

The Marchese as a patron of the arts hosted various evenings and events for his friends. During the early months of 1829 Balfe and Giulia Grisi sang together at concerts. During the Lenten season, the Societa del Casino sponsored Rossini's *Mosè*, which was performed on 17 March with the eighteen-year-old Giulia Grisi in the roles of Sinaide and Balfe as Farone.[17] Balfe also sang one of his favorite arias, Figaro's 'Largo al factotum', at one of the concerts, much to the delight of Grisi. Shortly afterwards Balfe composed a cantata quartette (32 pages) for Grisi the tenor Francesco Pedrazzi (1802–1850?), and the composer and bass Giuseppe Tadolini (1789–1872) and one other voice. Pedrazzi was later to create leading roles in several operas at La Scala and elsewhere. Tadolini was a composer, vocal teacher, the husband of the soprano of the same name and a friend of Rossini's.

In Bologna Balfe also composed his first and only Sinfonia (88 pages), which was completed on 31 March, 1829, in honour of his host's birthday. It was probably performed by what would have been a small orchestra in the service of the Marchese. The complete autograph score of the cantata and the Sinfonia autograph score are both held by the library of the Accademia di Filarmonica in Bologna, under the name Guglielmo Balfe.[18]

The Marchese was so impressed by his young guest that he arranged for Balfe to be offered a lifetime honorary membership in the Società Filarmonica di Bologna. It was interesting to see that Balfe is described as being 'from Dublin', not London, and aged twenty in the official document dated 20 March 1829 that was submitted for his appointment.

The long formal document making his appointment official also included some other recommended applicants was dated 14 April 1829 in the signature section. At the top it was dated 27 March 1829. Apparently the document had to wait until the next meeting of the members before it became official. In the document Balfe is described as "Michele Guglielmo Balf, di Dublino" with the 'e" missing from his name. The document was signed by nine members of the Academy.

Shortly afterwards Balfe left for Palermo, where he was engaged to make his Italian operatic debut. Giulia Grisi left for Florence, where she would sign a contract with the impresario, Alessandro Lanari, as a prima donna assoluta. She and Balfe were destined to meet each other and perform together many times in the years ahead. Grisi had a remarkable career in London, Dublin, Paris and St Petersburg. She became one of the most important singers of the nineteenth century.

There seems to be some confusion among his biographer as to when Balfe actually arrived in Palermo. However, new evidence suggests that Balfe probably left Bologna in April and arrived in Palermo by the second week in May 1829.[19] Most probably he made his way first to Genoa or possibly to Naples and from either one then took a boat to Palermo.

On arrival in Palermo he joined the season at the Teatro Carolino. His debut there took place on 30 May 1829 in Bellini's opera *Bianca e Gernando*. This was followed by Donizetti's *L'ai nell imbarazzo*. It was during this time that the chorus threatened to go on strike either for increased pay or more likely for back pay. The administrator, Count di Sommatino, decided to mount an opera that didn't need a chorus; however, he didn't have the scores for a Cimarosa or a Rossini opera that did not require a chorus. It was then that the ever-resourceful Balfe stepped into the breach, suggesting that he could write an opera in the time allotted and probably flaunting his newly acquired credentials from Bologna.

Sommatino was able to provide a libretto based on a French vaudeville play by Antonio Alcozer, a librettist who was to later revise one of Donizetti's opera and so Balfe got to work immediately on creating an opera minus a chorus. The libretto for *I rivale di se stessi* (44 pages), states that it is a 'Melo-Dramma Comico per Musica'. It is a two-act opera with eight scenes. For details of the cast who premiered the work and other information see Appendix II-1 of this work.

By the time Balfe had composed the opera the newly published libretto mentioned that the music was specially written by Signor Maestro Guglielmo Balfe, of the Accademia di Filarmonica di Bologna; and honorary member of the Accademia di Palermo. So Balfe must have established his credentials almost immediately to have been appointed as a member of the Academy in Palermo on such short notice. Possibly his letter from Rossini created the opportunity.

His new work which premiered on 29 June 1829 at the Teatro Carolino was a success since it was repeated a number of times.[20] Balfe did not sing in it immediately, however it appears that he may have taken over the baritone part of Durmont in one or more of the later performances. It had a strong cast; some of the singers had previously created leading roles in Rossini and Donizetti operas.

The London *Harmonicon* newspaper, which had representatives throughout Europe reporting on local musical events, now featured a report on Balfe's exploits in far-off Palermo. The *Harmonicon* representative said:

> *Teatro Carolino;* At this theatre an opera, by the bass [the baritone voice during that period was generally known as a bass voice in Italy] singer Guglielmo Balfe, was given some months ago, of which the Bolognese Journal says that 'The opera by Signor Balfe is now beginning to please; and a new production by this professor may be shortly expected.' Other journals speak differently of this work, not even dignifying it with the title of opera. Be the merits of Balfe as a composer great or small, his vocal talent is unquestioned, and gave great delight in a piece composed by Maestro e Direttore La Manna, [Director and orchestra leader] which was introduced among many other pieces in Rossini's *Bianca e Falliero*.

Unfortunately the music for this first Balfe opera is lost. However, clearly this was an opera, not a musical play. The singers who performed it all had good operatic careers in major opera houses afterwards.

It seems that after this effort the chorus acquiesced and meekly went back to work as the season continued. Balfe sang in several more operas (see Appendix I for details) and his new opera was performed again in September and early in the New Year.

On New Year's Day 1830 he took on the principal baritone roles in the local premiere of Bellini's new opera *La Straniera*. The evening included a state visit by the Viceroy. Balfe's performance was loudly applauded, once the Viceroy indicated approval, particularly the second act aria, 'Meco tu vieni, o misera'. The native Sicilian composer's opera was of course a great success, with the opera being performed for seventy nights.[21]

As the season at Palermo wound down Balfe returned to the mainland, feeling confident and with some money in his pocket. He continued to build his career; however, he was still not sure of his overall direction. He was having some success at singing and new opportunities were beginning to open up for him. His first experience with composing an opera had been exciting and it too provided new scope and opportunities.

Meanwhile, continuing to use the name 'Guglielmo' Balfe, he had made contact with the Teatro Comunale in Piacenza and had reached an agreement with the management to perform there, during the latter part of the summer season in 1830. He agreed to sing in five operas, as follows: *Matilde di Shabran*, *La gazza ladra*, *Semiramide* and *Demetrio e Polibio*, all by Rossini, and the spectacular *Gli Arabi nelle Gallie* by Giovanni Pacini.

The *Harmonicon* (London) reported on his progress in Piacenza, saying:

> Two foreign artists, Madlle. Josephine Noël-Fabre, and an Englishman of the name of William Balfe, are great favourites here at present. The applause which they obtained, was of a very flattering kind.[22]

However, the report did not end there. There was an asterisk after Balfe's name to an extensive footnote that expanded considerably on Balfe's background, his talents and how he got to Italy, as follows:

This young man (an Irishman by the by), if all we have heard
of him be true, is a real musical genius. After making a kind
of *debut* some years ago, as a juvenile violin- player,   at   a
theatrical benefit [London], we have heard that, led by his
enthusiastic love of his art, he made his way to Italy *on foot*.
In that country he met with patronage which enabled him to
enter on a course of study; and his inclination, and a fine bass
voice, led him to cultivate, especially, composition and
singing... his voice was a bass voice of two octaves compass
from F to F; and he possessed much energy of manner, and
great flexibility of execution.[23]

This contemporary report on Balfe is one of the earliest reports
that provide information on his vocal capabilities and skills while
in Italy during these years. The reference to Balfe getting to Italy
"on foot" is also intriguing. A later report in the *Harmonicon*
refers to his history as being somewhat romantic, reinforcing the
fact that he had actually "walked [hitch-hiked?] to Italy" so that he
might have an opportunity of hearing and imitating the great
singers there. In any event, the *Harmonicon* was sufficiently interested in the young artist's career to continue to provide feedback
on Balfe's progress in Italy during the next few years.

We next find him in at the Teatro Sociale in the town of Varese,
north of Milan.[24] Here he opened the newly decorated theatre in
Filippo Celli's *La seccia la rapita* which had moderate success.
This opera and Bellini's *I Capuleti e I Montecchi* continue to performed over several weeks, after which Giovanni Pacini's
(1796–1867) *Il barone di Dolsheim* was introduced. In general he
received good reviews except for the Bellini opera, in which he
sang the tenor part of Tebaldo with disastrous results. This was a
mistake he never repeated. With the season over Balfe moved on
to Milan where there was exciting new operatic activity.

The Carnival season that year at Teatro Carcano in Milan had
been organized by a group of *dilettanti* who were upset at the way
La Scala was being run. In the process they offered leading composers such as Donizetti and Bellini special terms to write new
operas for their theatre, as a counter to La Scala's management.[25]
Donizetti came to Milan early in October to finalize arrangements
with his librettist and the Teatro Carcano for what would be one

of his masterpieces, his new opera *Anna Bolena*.[26] He also visited Bergamo to see his parents for the first time in nine years. His new opera was scheduled to premiere on the prestigious opening night of the Carnival season on 26 December 1830. The cast included Giuditta Pasta, tenor Giovanni Battista Rubini (1794–1854), Filippo Galli (1783–1853), and the mezzo Elisa Orlandi (1811–1834).

The score of *Anna Bolena* was completed by Donizetti at Pasta's villa at Blevio on Lake Como by 10 December, after which he returned to Milan. Balfe, who was in Milan during this period, had more than a passing interest in Donizetti's new opera. He was on personal terms with Pasta, and Galli, who had been his vocal coach in Milan for almost a year. There is no doubt that given Balfe's precocious nature he would have somehow arranged to obtain a seat for one of the performances of the new opera, which was anxiously awaited by the elite of Milan.

The Carnival season at Teatro Carcano that year also included someone that would have a major influence on Balfe's life, the young attractive soprano Lina Roser (1810–1888). Lina Roser had been born in Pest (Budapest). The correct year for her birth would appear to be 1810, based on biographical data received from Vienna. Her father, Franz de Paula Roser (1780–1830) was a well-established Austrian composer who was working in Pest (Budapest) as a composer and musician in the service of, Ignaz von Vegh from 1806 to 1811, when she was born. Despite the location of her birth her native language was German.

She was scheduled to make her debut at the Teatro Carcano on 30 December 1830 singing opposite Giuditta Pasta in the opera, *Malek Adel* by Giuseppe Nicolini (1762–1842). There were five performances of the opera and she was singled out for her fine soprano voice and excellent singing style.[27]

As soon as Donizetti left Milan after the *Anna Bolena* premiere the focus became the new opera by Bellini, *La sonnambula*, which was to premiere at the Teatro Carcano on 6 March 1831.

One of Balfe's early biographers (Barrett) states that Bellini was interested in giving the part of Amina to Lina Roser. However, the composer decided against it because Roser's knowledge of Italian was too limited. Instead, Pasta created the part. There is no evidence provided by Barrett to support his claim. It's possible that Pasta might have originally recommended Lina Roser to Bellini for the part. Barrett also claims that Pasta and Roser both had the same vocal coach, Alexandre Micheroux. Micheroux was certainly associated with Pasta, but there's nothing that documents that he was Roser's coach. In fact there is some evidence which would suggest the contrary.[28]

Roser's experience at the time of her Carcano debut was very limited. She was twenty years old, a fine musician, but she had no direct operatic experience so it seems very unlikely that Bellini would have risked assigning her the leading role in his new opera. With someone as experienced as Pasta on the roster he most certainly would have had her in mind for the part. No documentary support has been found to validate the claim that Lina Roser might have been considered for the part. Later on as Lina's career advanced she never in fact sang the role of Amina in Bellini's opera.

As we know Pasta, the tenor Rubini and bass Luciano Mariani (1801–1859) created a sensation in the premiere of *La sonnambula* in March 1831 at the Teatro Carcano no doubt Lina Roser was in the audience, possibly also Michael Balfe.[29] It was also during this period that Balfe first met his future wife. It's possible that they met through Pasta, who may have invited them to her villa at Blevio on Lake Como, where she frequently had guests. It was also a place that the two of them would visit together many years in the future, perhaps in reflection of their early days in the Milan area and on the beautiful lake. During 1831 they were destined to meet again in Bergamo within a few months, which would be a decisive moment for both of them.

In February Lina Roser sang the leading soprano role in Luigi Majocchi's opera *Rosamonda* with tenor Giovanni Battista Rubini and baritone Paul Barroilhet (1810–1871) who was then at the beginning of what would become a distinguished career. Lina and Michael Balfe would meet both of these singers in the future under very different circumstances; both would create operas for Balfe.

Balfe had a commitment to be in Pavia by April for the opera season. As part of his contract he also had to compose a new opera for the Teatro Condomini. During April he also sang in Rossini's *Il barbiere di Siviglia* and *Mosè*. April was also spent finalizing his new opera, his second composition, *Un avvertimento di gelosi*, a

one-act comedy with sixteen scenes which was scheduled to premiere on 11 May 1831 with an experienced cast. Possibly Balfe
may also have been the musical director of the orchestra. See
Appendix I–2 for details.

The opera was an immediate success. The librettist Giuseppe
Foppa (1760–1845) had provided librettos for Rossini, Paer,
Zingarelli and others. Balfe, ever vigilant and restless, spent the
next few months in the area, singing, working on some new compositions and looking for new opportunities that would give him
income. Clearly Balfe was making good progress as a composer.
His new opera was later performed in Milan with a distinguished
cast.

Early in June he was contracted to perform at the Teatro
Riccardi in Bergamo, Donizetti's home town. The Bergamasc composer was in Naples at the time. Balfe was scheduled to sing in
Pacini's remarkable opera, *Gli arabi nelle Gallie*. His partners were
the young attractive soprano Lina Roser, the renowned tenor
Giovanni David (1790–1864) and the bass, Carlo Cambiaggio
(1798–1880) who was also a librettist, a composer and eventually
an impresario at the Teatro Carcano. There was also a concert on
29 September at the Accademia in Bergamo in which Balfe participated with Roser and David.

Carlo Cambiaggio was well connected in operatic circles and he
became a good friend of Balfe's. They sang together in various performances over the next several years. Cambiaggio would also be
helpful to Balfe in premiering the Irishman's next opera in Milan.

Balfe was awarded an honorary membership in the Accademia
Filarmonica di Bergamo for his participation, giving him additional
accreditation for his work and adding to the recognition he
achieved in Bologna and Palermo.

Sometime between June and September 1831, Lina Roser and
Michael Balfe were married. Lina came from a Catholic family, so
it must be assumed that the marriage occurred in a Catholic
church, probably in Bergamo, as they were both singing at the
Teatro Riccardo during this period. Official records of marriages
from that time were controlled by Vienna and the Habsburg
Empire and most of those records are not available from Italian
sources today. Possibly they are retained somewhere in Vienna,
which requires further study. In any event, by October, when Lina

and Michael Balfe were singing together in Varese and other places she was using her new name, Lina Roser-Balfe, a name she continued to use while singing in Italy during the next few years.

Meanwhile Balfe's new opera composed in Pavia was now being performed in Milan at the Teatro Re, with an excellent cast that included the future great Verdi baritone, Giorgio Ronconi (1810–1890), who would create Verdi's first great operatic success, *Nabucco* in March 1842, at La Scala, Milan.

The tenor in the cast for Balfe's opera at Teatro Re was Timoleone Alexander (1798–1856?), a singer who was born in Parma. He had a successful career, with four operas being composed for him. Indirectly Timoleone became associated with the Glossop family through his marriage with Josephine de Méric, the former wife of Joseph Glossop.

Immediately after the Bergamo season was over, Michael and Lina Balfe set off for Varese, where they both had a contract to sing in several operas. This was the start of what would be a thirty-nine year marriage and a strong partnership that would bring both of them to several of the most important capitals of Europe and beyond in pursuit of music. Balfe would achieve great fame as a composer and Lina would support him along the way and become the mother of his four children.

NOTES

1. See Herbert Weinstock's biography, *Rossini*, pp. 142–143.
2. Barrett makes the statement that ... [Balfe] 'worked at composition under Ferdinando Paer' while in Rome and staying at his patron's home. This error also appears in Tyldesley's book and in the *New Grove Dictionary of Opera*, which should be corrected. My own article "Balfe in Italy' in *Opera Quarterly*, Vol. 18, No. 4, August 2002 also made the same error.
3. *The Musical World* (London) 29 March 1856, p. 197.
4. Ibid.
5. See *The Donizetti Society Journal* No. 7, London 2002, p. 552.
6. See *Donizetti and His Operas* by William Ashbrook, p. 33. Donizetti experienced the same disappointment.
7. See *Joséphine and Emilie* by Dudley Cheke, pp. 43–54.
8. *The Musical World* (London) 12 April, 1856, p. 229.
9. See the *Harmonicon* January 1831, p. 49 in which there is a reference that 'About three years ago he [Balfe] returned for a short time to London, and we heard him in private sing a cavatina of his own composition.'
10. Ibid.
11. *The Musical World* (London) 12 April, 1856, p. 229.
12. Ibid.
13. Ibid.

14. See *Giuditta Pasta: Gloria del bel canto* by Giorgio Appolonia, p. 302 .
15. See *English Opera from 1834 to 1864* by George Biddlecombe, p. 127, letter from Bellini to his friend Monteleone dated 17 September 1829 that mentions Balfe by name.
16. Ibid.
17. E-mail communication from Philip Gossett to the author, dated 9 December 2001.
18. The author has copies of both of these autograph scores.
19. The libretto for Balfe's first opera *I rivale di se stessi*, which was composed for Palermo, has a printed date of 29 June 1829 on its cover, which means that Balfe most probably arrived in Palermo around May 1829 or earlier and not in December 1828 as suggested by some of his earlier biographers.
20. The *New Grove Dictionary of Opera* needs to be corrected as the opera actually had its premiere in 1829 not 1830, based on the date printed on the libretto.
21. *Harmonicon* (London) July 1830, p. 310, reported on the performances of *La Straniera*, saying that much applause was bestowed on Madame Fink, and Messrs. Boccacini and Balfe. 'The latter gentleman, whose name is spelt Balf and Balph, is an Englishman, very young, and possessed of a remarkably fine bass voice.'
22. *Harmonicon* (London) January 1831, p. 49.
23. Ibid.
24. *Harmonicon* (London), December 1830, p. 522.
25. See, *Donizetti and His Operas* by William Ashbrook, p. 62–63.
26. Ibid.
27. *Harmonicon* (London), May 1831, pg 127.
28. Lina Roser had arrived in Milan *circa* 1829 from Berlin with her Viennese foster mother, Katharina Vogel. A copy of a document in the possession of the author written by one of Balfe's granddaughters states that Lina talked about studying in Milan with one of Mozart's sons, Karl Thomas Mozart (K.T. Mozart spent most of his adult life in Italy), it's possible that Lina only had music lessons, from Mozart's son and not vocal lessons which would still leave open the question as to whom her vocal coach may have been. Micheroux's name was never mentioned in the document referred to above. Whether Micheroux was in Milan during this period is not known.
29. *Harmonicon* (London), 'Emulating each other in the wish to display the merits of the opera, they were both equally successful; and those who participated in the delight of hearing them will never forget the magical effect of their execution, nor be ignorant of what constitutes the perfection of their enchanting science.   But, exquisite as they were, undoubtedly. Mad. Pasta's vocal exertions, her histrionic powers, if possible, surpassed them. That she stands alone in "sole dimension" in this branch of her art, is universally acknowledged, but her acting in *La sonnambula* places her beyond even the possibility of imitation.'

CHAPTER THREE

Milan and Venice – with Maria Malibran 1832–1835

The Italy of this period was vastly different from the unified country we know today. In the 1830s, the country was divided into a series of states and regions. So anyone endeavouring to pursue their chosen profession as a musician or singer had to move between various political regions, in order to participate in the opera seasons and earn an income.

In northern Italy, Lombardy and Venetia, as previously mentioned, were under Austrian rule. The Piedmont area and the Island of Sardinia were controlled by Italian Princes of the House of Savoy who were based in Turin. Parma, Tuscany and the Papal political states were all separate entities. Revolution was ripe, particularly in the Milan area where the Austrian elite and military controlled the daily lives of so many. All that came to a head in 1848.

For a singer to move from one region to another, it was necessary to have documentation and also a passport. Transportation was also primitive. No railways existed in the country. Naples got the first railway on the peninsula in 1839. To get from one town or city to another, the only methods of transportation were by horse-drawn coach, on horseback or on foot, as Verdi did in his early days.

The northern Italian circuit for opera during these years saw many small towns, such as Cremona, Pavia, Vincenza and Varese, involved in presenting opera. Towns with larger populations like Parma, Bergamo, Verona and Genoa were in the second tier and they usually had longer seasons because of their socio-economic structure. Genoa later became more important. The cities of Milan and Venice, and to a somewhat lesser degree Turin, were the top tier. Further south Florence and Naples also qualified.

Sometime singers who performed at La Scala Milan or in Venice were invited to sing at the Italian opera in Vienna which brought with it higher fees and great prestige and frequently a Habsburg, Royal audience. The Director at La Scala also managed the Italian opera in Vienna along with others.

The performances throughout northern Italy were generally controlled by a string of impresarios who had a network of arrangements through which the singers passed in order to gain a singing contract. Depending upon the location sometimes it was princes who controlled orchestras and the theatres, which added to the confusion. Some of the more important impresarios of the time, such as Alessandro Lanari (1790–1862), who started his career in the small town of Lucca in 1819 and later managed the Teatro Pergola in Florence and the Teatro La Fenice in Venice were continually on the verge of bankruptcy, which meant singers did not always get paid on time; the chorus sometimes not at all.

Another important impresario, Bartolomeo Merelli (1794–1879), who managed La Scala intermittently from 1829 to 1850 and later, was not above selling his singer contracts to one of his competitors if he thought he could make money on the deal. Merelli's La Scala also included a gambling operation in the theatre. A singer's contract generally held more leverage for the impresario than for the singer. If a singer violated their contract such as showing up later for a season or declaring illness they were liable to find themselves in court or perhaps in jail. The system was also fraught with favours. Regardless of contractual obligations, roles were often promised and dished-out based on personal favours. Those who objected found it difficult to get new roles due the impresario communications network. Frequently prima donnas were accompanied by their mothers or another family member as part of their protection.

The business of singing almost anywhere in Italy during the early years of the nineteenth century was certainly precarious at best, particularly at the secondary levels where the economics were forever unstable. Similar situations prevailed for operatic composers. The history of battles between Verdi and Merelli, which happened later, are legion. At one point Verdi refused to have any of his operas produced at La Scala. Bellini and Donizetti had the same problems at various theatres. Balfe also experienced insignificant fees for his compositions when compared to the money paid to some of the leading composers such as Bellini. So for Balfe, it would have been a difficult experience trying to earn a living. Being married possibly initially brought some level of stability to his earnings since if he was not employed at least his wife would be working, but fate would soon change that, at least for a while.

However, it is also important to remember that the years Balfe was in Italy, were some of the most productive times in terms of the major new works being introduced by Bellini, Donizetti, Pacini, Ricci and others. This was an enormously valuable learning experience for the twenty-two-year-old future composer as he continued to sing in the works of these composers while learning his craft.

In early November 1831 Balfe and his wife went west from the town of Varese near the lakes to the small town of Novara in the Piedmont region, a distance of maybe forty miles. They were a travelling troupe, as they were accompanied by some of the performers from Varese. The month of November was spent in Novara singing in two operas, Bellini's *Capuleti e i Montecchi* and Pacini's opera *Il falgename di Livonia*. This time Balfe sang the bass part of Capellio, in *Capuleti*, having learned his lesson the previous month. The reviews were satisfactory.

The tenor in the Bellini opera, Lorenzo Bonfigl[1] (1805–1876), had created the part of Tebaldo in the same opera at the Teatro La Fenice in Venice in March 1830.[1] Bonfigli would also appear in the premiere of a Balfe opera in Milan at a later date. Other cast members included Elisa Taccani, a mezzo-soprano who had sung the role of Romeo and had also created the part of Lisa in Bellini's *La sonnambula* at its premiere at the Teatro Carcano the previous year, when she sang opposite Pasta and Rubini. She later sang Adalgisa to Pasta's *Norma* in Bergamo with the composer directing the opera.[2]

The big event in Milan that season was the planned premiere of Bellini's new opera, *Norma* which was to open at La Scala on 26 December with Giuditta Pasta in the title role, Giulia Grisi as Adalgisa, Domenico Donzelli in the role of Pollione, and Vincenzo Negrini (1807–1840) as Oroveso.

However, Balfe had to be in Bergamo in December for rehearsals as he was scheduled to sing there in early January. Lina was engaged to open the season in Parma in a Bellini opera on 26 of December. Their contractual obligations prevented them from being in Milan for the opening night of what would become one of the century's greatest operatic works. It must have been a difficult decision for Balfe, and his wife not to be able to attend the historic premiere of a new Bellini opera. There was great excitement everywhere in Milan as the opening night approached. The composer Bellini was in town, and he had just celebrated his thirtieth birthday.

The new Bellini opera racked up thirty-four performances at La Scala that first season.[3] There can be little doubt that Balfe and his bride found seats for at least one of those historic performances, when they returned to Milan. The last performance of *Norma* at La Scala that season was on 20 March 1832.[4] Given the news that the new opera created, and the deep interest they had in the singers performing it; Pasta was a good friend of both of them, Balfe knew Grisi well and he had sung with the tenor, Donzelli in Paris, there is little doubt that they would have attended at least one performance.

Years later when Balfe would conduct one of Europe's great prima donnas in the title role of *Norma* in London, his handling of the orchestra for Bellini's masterpiece was greatly acclaimed by the critics. He was singled out for his precision, knowledge of the work and his overall direction of the orchestra. No doubt his early experiences in Milan contributed to him achieving such praise.

Meanwhile, the now pregnant Lina Roser-Balfe was due in Parma for the Carnival season at the Teatro Ducale, where she would sing the role of Adelaide in Bellini's *La straniera* on opening night, 26 December 1831. There were twenty-five performances of this successful opera.   This was followed by nine performances of Donizetti's *Alina, regina di Golconda*, a two-act buffa opera in which Lina sang the role of Alina. Her next performance was a premiere by Luigi Ricci, *Il nuovo Figaro*, on 15 February with the important tenor Francesco Pedrazzi in the cast.[5] Lina sang the part of Amalia, with some of the performances again shared with Margherita Rubini.[6] The opera ran for twenty-four nights, which tends to refute some of the reporting that said the opera was a failure.[7]

It was not unusual for singers in the nineteenth century to sing night after night, for four or five nights or even longer without a break. Towards the middle of the season, Lina had experienced some difficulties with the theatre management when they requested her to sing an unscheduled work, which did not suit her vocally or dramatically. She was also having some signs of exhaustion and had to bow out of some performances. While Lina did share her roles in Parma on a few occasions with the soprano Margherita Rubini, her schedule for a young woman now about four months pregnant still seems astounding by any standards. On the other hand, this is evidence that says that Lina's professional career was clearly on an upward trend. Later in life, when Lina was to occasionally sing in London or Paris, her professionalism was always greatly praised by the critics.

In December, Balfe had to part company with his wife for the first time since she was due at Parma by mid-December and he had to be in Bergamo a little later for rehearsals. It would have been too far and take too much time for him to travel with her to Parma before going to Bergamo. He was returning to sing at the Teatro Riccardi for several performance of *Il falgename di Livonia* during January 1832. It's possible that he also sang in other works during this period. Operatic management gave little attention to the needs or scheduling of two married singers working in the profession. Where and when they sang they had to work it out for themselves.

Immediately following this activity, Balfe went to Parma to be with his pregnant wife in mid-February. However, before leaving Bergamo he had composed a cantata for one of his friends there. The short piece was for tenor and bass with a dedication that said 'To Guglielmo Balfe's friend, Francesco Maria Zanchi'. It is an autograph score and more like a *Fanfare* than a full cantata. It's dated Bergamo, February 1832. See Appendix IX–6 for more details.

When Lina's season at Parma was over they immediately left for Milan. From March to December 1832 Lina did not sing again. Their first child, Louisa Catherine Maria Balfe, was born probably in the Milan area between June and August 1832. No birth or baptismal record has been located in Italy for Louisa. Data from a later census in England confirm that she was in fact born in Italy. Her age is shown in the census documentation, which proves that the year 1832 was correct, but no specific month was given. Louisa was affectionally known as 'Gigia' to her mother and father all her life. The name apparently was a colloquialism or nickname for

Luigia (Louisa/Luisa being considered more French) as used in Italy of that period.[8]

The arrival of baby Louisa, however joyful for the couple, must also have brought some concerns for their economic welfare. Since their marriage Lina had been working regularly and while her pay would have been modest in those days it was probably enough to support them along with Balfe's irregular earnings at that stage of their life. With Lina out of the market it must have been a difficult time for them. Balfe was always a high-energy individual. There can be little doubt that he probably did gain some income working as a music copyist in the Milan area, where the music publishers Ricordi and Lucca would have had a need for those services to support their score rental business. There were also a significant number of theatres in the Milan area that would have had a need to create orchestral parts for performances. Balfe was a skilled musician who worked fast, so he would have been in demand.

Whatever their circumstances they managed to survive until the start of the next Carnival season at the Teatro Carcano, Milan, which opened on 26 December 1832 with Lina in the role of Giulietta in Bellini's *Capuleti e I Montecchi* and mezzo-soprano Palmira Michel as Romeo. The tenor role of Tebaldo was performed by her partner from Novara, the role's creator, Lorenzo Bonfigli.[9] No doubt Balfe attended. Baby Louisa was probably being taken care of by a nanny by then, at least most of the day.

Balfe's friend, the buffo bass Carlo Cambiaggio had now turned impresario. He was the manager at the Carcano, so Balfe was assured of getting work. The future certainly looked brighter. Almost immediately, Cambiaggio had Balfe singing in Rossini's *L'inganno felice* with Bonfigli. He then gave Balfe an assignment to write a new opera for his theatre. This was an opportunity that Balfe had been waiting for.

Balfe had worked on a libretto some time previously based on an early historical tale relating to Enrico IV in Lombardy. The libretto was possibly given to Balfe by one of the monks in the Oratory of San Carlo in Milan. The poet or author's name is not shown on the libretto, which indicates that the music for the work was written especially for the Oratory of San Carlo. No date was given. Additionally, Balfe's name is written on the libretto in handwriting that is clearly from the period.[10] The part that would become the female lead role and sung by Lina Balfe at the later Carcano performance was written for a youth named 'Carlino'.

The performance at the Oratory of San Carlo was probably sung by novices in the monastery as there was no female role in their libretto. In view of Balfe's activity in 1832 it may have been performed at the Oratory in 1831. The text for the libretto was appropriately adapted for the Teatro Carcano performance with the addition of the female role of Cristina. In general though, when the libretto for the Carcano performance is compared with the *Oratory* libretto they are essentially the same, except that the Oratory performance was given in two acts while the Carcano was in one act.

How Balfe might have been involved with the Oratorio is unknown. Possibly Lina, who was a strong Catholic, may have had something to do with it. It's also possible that they had been married there and that would have been Balfe's way to pay for the ceremony? We don't know.

In any event, Balfe's opera *Enrico IV, al passo della Marna* premiered with some fanfare at the Teatro Carcano on 13 February 1833 with the tenor Bonfigli as Enrico IV, Balfe as Constantino, Lina as Cristina the soprano lead and Cambiaggio as Gervasio. The opera was quite successful. Balfe was featured in one of the leading Milan musical periodicals the following week with a very complimentary article that was about a column and a half in length.[11] The opera was performed again during the 1834–35 season in Milan at the Teatro Carcano.[12] Later there were other productions in Genoa at the Teatro Carlo Felice also in Lecco and in the Turin area in the town of Bra. Florence possibly also heard it.

The music from this opera had been deemed to be 'lost' by most of the current major music reference books, including the *New Grove Opera*. However, that is not the case. There's a significant amount of sheet music from the opera available. This appears to include most of the music for the arias, duets and trios the Sinfonia and other parts based upon the libretto. This sheet music is in libraries in Milan and Venice. There also seem to be sections of the autograph score in the library in Mantua which has not been examined by the author. For more details on this Balfe's opera and the location of the music, see Appendix II.3.

Francesco Lucca of Milan published *Enrico IV* in 1832. This was a major step-up for Balfe from his previous publishers. It was also to be the last new opera Balfe composed in Italy for many years.

The Cambiaggio connection paid off even more for Balfe. The impresario had decided to mount a production of Donizetti's delightfully sparkling new opera, *L'elisir d'amore* with Cambiaggio himself in the role of the quack, Dr Dulcamara, and Balfe as the braggadocio sergeant Belcore for 25 March 1833.[13] This was only eight months after the opera's premiere at the Teatro Canobbiana in Milan in May 1832. There can be little doubt that this was a role ideally suited to Balfe's talents. The swaggering sergeant Belcore would have been beautifully presented by the Irishman. Balfe sang in two other operas, with Lina joining him in the opera *Elisa di Montaltieri* by Antonio Granara (1809–1836), along with Bonfigli at the Carcano before his season ended. He would meet again with his friend Carlo Cambiaggio the following year in Venice.

Despite his recent success as a composer, his focus was now on singing. Strangely, as will be seen, it was a time when he appeared to receive fewer engagements not more, while Lina's career was taking off at a rapid pace. How they managed to care for their daughter Louisa is not known. Generally, there would have been someone available to them as a nanny or the equivalent during the time they had to go to the theatre. Possibly they may have had an arrangement with a family where Louisa would have been taken care of while they were performing. However, in general it is difficult to fully understand how they might have managed, given their activity and the need to rehearse and be at the theatre at various hours of the day and night. Other singers of their generation no doubt had similar problems, and like any generation they found solutions. Lina and her husband were always very close to their children, as time would demonstrate.

Over the next several months Lina sang leading roles in a number of operas by Donizetti, Bellini, Mercadante and others. In Piacenza she sang with baritone Giorgio Ronconi (1810–1890), in *La Straniera* and again with Ronconi in Mercadante's *I Normanni a Parigi*.[14] There were also reports that Balfe had gone on a tour with the horn player, Giovanni Puzzi who would later become one of Balfe's close friends in London along with Puzzi's wife, Giacinta. However, no documentary evidence has been found to support the fact that Balfe was travelling anywhere during this timeframe. Perhaps he helped his wife with learning the many new roles she was taking on?

Their next joint appearance was at the Carnival season opening on 26 December 1833 in Mantua. Here Lina sang in Bellini's *La Straniera* in the role of Alaide, a role she was quite familiar with. She later appeared in Ricci's *Chiara di Rosembergh* with her husband, after which she sang the title role in *Norma* with Teresa Brambilla as Adalgisa. Returning to Milan in the spring of 1834 she appeared at the Teatro Canobbiana for the first time in *L'orfano della selva* by Carlo Coccia (1782–1873). This was followed by *Un Episodio del San Michele* by Cesare Pugni (1802–1870), which had its premiere in June 1834 with Lina in the cast. She continued to push herself and sing wherever she could get work.

Balfe's friend from Paris, Maria Malibran, arrived in Milan in the spring of 1834. She was scheduled to make her debut at La Scala in Bellini's *Norma*. She didn't know it then, but Giuditta Pasta, the role's creator, would be in the audience for her debut.

Malibran and Balfe were the same age, twenty-six. As time would prove she liked Balfe and was attracted to his virtuosity and overall personality. By now Malibran had the equivalent status of a Maria Callas in the 1950s. It is interesting to note that one of the few pictures that Callas had in her apartment at the time of her death in 1977 was of Malibran, whom she seemed to identify with in some special way.[15] Throughout her career, Malibran, like Callas a hundred and twenty years later, was an extraordinary performer who packed the house every night, so she was paid fabulous fees and in demand at most of the major cities in Europe. Maria Malibran was the daughter of Manuel Garcia (1775–1832), who was legendary as a role creator, a friend of composers and a composer and teacher himself. Garcia had died in Paris just two years earlier at age fifty-seven in 1832.

In 1825 Garcia had crossed the Atlantic and brought his family to New York after negotiating a contract to bring Italian opera to America with a Dominick Lynch (1786–1857), an American from New York who was visiting London.[16] Garcia brought his family, including his wife, his daughter Maria, his son Manuel Patricio and his younger daughter Pauline, to New York in November 1825.

There they gave the first performance of Italian opera in America, Rossini's *Il barbiere di Siviglia* on 29 November 1825. Maria, a mezzo-soprano, sang the role of Rosina, Garcia sang Almaviva and son Manuel Jr. sang Figaro. It was a historic event.

Shortly after her arrival in New York, Maria met what she thought to be a wealthy French merchant, Eugène Malibran. She married him in March 1826, much to the consternation of her father, who saw one of the key members of his small operatic troupe about to disappear from service. Garcia and his family went on to Mexico in October 1826 where they stayed for several years. Maria stayed behind in New York with her husband.

As it turned out Malibran was in financial trouble and the marriage did not work for Maria who eventually returned to Paris accompanied by her husband's nephew in November 1827 to restart her European career.[17] Her own family was still in Mexico, so she stayed with her husband's sister in Paris. However, it was the arrival of her brother, Manuel Patricio, early in December that gave her the greatest pleasure and new hope.

The Garcia family was unique in the history of opera. While Manuel, the father, had pioneered the way as a vocal teacher and singer in Europe and America, his son Manuel Patricio (born in Spain on St Patrick's Day, 17 March 1805) was to become one of the most important singing teachers of all time in Paris and London. His pupils were legendary, Jenny Lind, Catherine Hayes, Mathilde Marchesi and Charles Santley being four of them. His *Treatise* on the art of singing is still used today. Manuel Jr. lived a long life, dying in London in 1906 at the age of 101. Pauline, the younger sister born in 1821 in Paris ,became one of the greatest singers of the nineteenth century. She was also a composer. Some of her songs were recently released on CD. She died at age eighty-nine in Paris in 1910. Maria born in 1808 in Paris, tragically she died at the young age of twenty-eight in Manchester in 1836 from the after-effects of a riding accident.

Balfe eventually knew all of the members of the Garcia family intimately. One of Balfe's daughters would study voice with Manuel Jr. Balfe would write a cantata for Pauline and others which she would sing in Paris at the height of her career. In his immediate future he and Maria were about to sing together at La Scala, where her influence had prevailed upon the management to hire Balfe to sing opposite her in Rossini's *Otello* in May 1834. He would later compose an opera for Maria which she would sing in London in the not too distant future.

For Balfe, performing at La Scala had been an ambition since he first talked with Glossop a few years previously. They gave two performance of *Otello.*, Balfe sang the role of Jago, which had originally been composed for tenor voice in 1816, but by its nature the role required a darker heavier voice and by tradition in the nineteenth century it was frequently transposed for a baritone. Maria sang Desdemona and Domenico Reina (1797–1843) sang the title role. Giuseppina (Josefa) Ruiz-Garcia, Malibran's half-sister, sang the role of Rodrigo, which was normally sung by a tenor.[18] The performances went well and Malibran was invited back with the same cast the following October.

After La Scala, Balfe and his wife went to Turin, where Lina was engaged to sing in three operas during the summer and autumn. All of the operas were local premieres. Malibran stayed on in Milan for about a month before going to Sinigaglia, where she was to sing in Bellini's *Capuleti e I Montecchi, Norma and La sonnambula* in July.

In Turin Lina was pared again with the baritone Giorgio Ronconi at the Teatro Carignano in Cesare Pugni's (1802–1870) *Il disertore Svizzero*, Ferdinand Hérold's (1791–1833) *Zampa* and Donizetti's *Parisina*. The tenor in the performances was Giovanni Bassadonna (1806?–1851), who created roles for Donizetti and others. Lina's career continued to be on the fast track. When Ronconi left Turin Balfe took over his part of Daniele in *Zampa*.

On 23 September Balfe wrote a personal letter in Italian to Giovanni Ricordi, the music publisher in Milan, detailing the performances in Turin mentioning the dramatic content of the opera *Zampa* and saying among other things that 'Ronconi and my wife received great applause in Hérold's opera.'

The tone of the letter indicated that he had a good relationship with the founder of the music publishing empire, who was now one of Milan's most important citizens. Balfe signed the letter, 'tuo amico G. Balfe'. It was also indicative of Balfe's learning skills that by now he was not only to speak Italian but also able to write it.[19] He and Lina returned to Milan in early October where Malibran was already performing at La Scala in various Bellini operas. On

14 October Malibran and Balfe again sang in Rossini's *Otello* for two performances.

Over the past few years, Malibran had been desperately trying to get a divorce from her husband, without much success, because French law did not permit it. Meantime, she was seeing the Belgian violinist Charles de Beriot (1802–1870), who came with her to Milan. Balfe had met de Beriot in Paris through his Irish friend, the pianist George Alexander Osborne (1806-1893).

By now the Balfes' daughter, Louisa, was two years old and probably requiring more attention. The parents took some time-off in Milan before proceeding to Lina's next engagement, which would be at the Teatro Emeronittio (now the Malibran) at year end in Venice, where Lina was due to open in Donizetti's *L'elisir d'amore* on 31 December 1834 in the role of Adina. Carlo Cambiaggio was scheduled to sing Dr. Dulcamara again and another future great Verdi baritone (Rigoletto, 1851, and La Traviata, 1853, creator, Felice Varesi (1813–1889), was slated for the role of Belcore. The Nemorino was Filippo Tati, a role creator for Donizetti. Another Donizetti work followed, *Torquato Tasso*, an opera which had premiered a year earlier in Rome with the same cast. Lina sang the role of Eleonora. There were about ten performances.

Just prior to arriving in Venice Maria Malibran had received word that her marriage to Malibran had been declared null and void by the French Tribunal hearing the case.[20] So she was elated with her situation as she made her entrance into Venice, which had anticipated her arrival for weeks. Carlo Cambiaggio, ever the promoter and opportunists, had written a booklet with verse to celebrate her arrival.[21]

Venice basically closed down at the moment of her arrival at the Grand Canal and her entrance from a gondola on to St Mark's Square, where she and her party were escorted to the Palace where she was staying. She made her debut in Rossini's *Otello* on 26 March. Balfe did not sing the role of Jago in Venice but performed Elmiro, a bass role, instead. There were three *Otellos*. Rossini's *Cenerentola* followed with Balfe as Dandini after which *Norma* was scheduled.

Lina joined Malibran in *Norma*, singing the role of Adalgisa in three performances. It was a remarkable culmination for Lina given all of the roles and places she had sung over the previous three years. While some of the audiences were critical of Malibran's portrayal remembering Pasta's of earlier times, it was a matter of personal taste, as Bellini was favourable to a Malibran interpretation. For Lina to be singing with Malibran in Bellini's *Norma* at La Fenice no doubt was to be a high point in her career.

The manager of the Teatro Emeronittio, Gallo, was introduced to Malibran possibly by Cambiaggio, who seemed to know everyone. Gallo asked Malibran if she would consider giving performances for his theatre, which had been feeling the financial impact on seat sales with her presence and her sold-out performances at La Fenice. Malibran, who was always generous with her time, after a slight hesitation agreed to sing a benefit performance for him, choosing Bellini's *La sonnambula* as the opera. A date of 8 April was set for the performance at the Teatro Emeronittio. In addition, she offered one performance of *Il barbiere di Siviglia*, which would be sung at the La Fenice with Gallo getting a percentage of the takings. Balfe was to be Figaro and Cambiaggio Dr Bartolo.

Gallo's theatre was completely decorated with flowers for the one and only appearance by the great Maria Malibran on 8 April 1835 in *La sonnambula*. Balfe was set to sing the role of Count Rodolfo. The level of excitement was very intense by all reports. As the evening progressed the audience threw flowers at their prima donna, so much so that the entire stage was covered. Maria at one point slipped; Balfe grasped her and saved her from falling. In the process, her slipper became dislodged and fell off into the pit, where it immediately disappeared. The pianist Franz Liszt, in the audience that eventful night, counted thirty-six curtain calls.[22] It was a night to remember for the Balfes, as no doubt Lina was in the audience or backstage too. Maria refused to take any money from Gallo for her performance that evening. Gallo, quite awed by the turn of events, renamed his theatre the 'Teatro Malibran' name that endures to this day.[23]

While with Balfe in Venice Maria, recalling his compositional skills from Paris, and hearing about his accomplishments in Italy, had called him the 'English Rossini' and had suggested that he compose an opera for her for London. There was some discussion of *Hamlet* as a subject but nothing seemed to develop on that front. He agreed to contact her when he found a suitable subject and libretto. She suggested that he hurry.

Neither the Balfes nor Malibran would ever sing in Venice again. The experience of that eventful evening at the Teatro Malibran was unique in their lives. Malibran left for London shortly after this, to perform *La sonnambula* again, this time in English, with Bellini in the audience. Balfe and his wife returned to Milan around the middle of April, and there they met Giovanni Puzzi, who was organizing some concerts in London.

With Louisa now going on three Balfe and his wife must have had thought about their future and what was best for the family. Puzzi's offer was attractive as it meant that he had an immediate opportunity to work when he got to London. So he made up his mind and he Lina and Louisa would move to London that April 1835. Since they now had some funds, most probably they sailed from Genoa to England towards the end of April, arriving in London sometime in mid-May.

The experience he gained in Italy would greatly influence his direction as a composer in London and elsewhere in the years ahead. His time in the operatic trenches also gave him a deep understanding of a singer's needs, which would be acknowledged by some of the leading singers who performed in his operas.

Within a short period of time after arriving in England in May 1835 his unique talents would dramatically burst forth on the London scene to create a whole new genre of English opera for what would soon become the Victorian age in Britain.

NOTES

1. See *Vincenzo Bellini: His Life and His Opera* by Herbert Weinstock, p. 247.
2. Ibid, pp. 269, 326,
3. See G. Tintori's *Duecento anni di Teatro alla Scala: Cronologia, opera-balletti-concerti 1778–1977*, p. 25.
4. See *Giuditta Pasta: Gloria del Bel Canto* by Giorgio Appolonia, p. 308.
5. *Stagione lirica carnavale* 1831–1831 (Parma) online database which can be found at Google 'stagione lirica1830+parma.
6. See the report in the *Harmonicon* (London), of August 1832, p. 186, which says '... the new opera has experienced a most brilliant reception ... the principal singers, and Signora Roser [Balfe] in particular, exerted themselves with great effect.'
7. *Grove* 1889 edition states under 'Luigi Ricci' that the opera failed, which appears to be incorrect. A 'failed opera' in Italy in the nineteenth century was generally was pulled after the third night. Additionally, the opera was also performed at La Scala during the 1833. Pedrazzi also performed in it at that time.

8. See *The Opera Quarterly*, Vol. 19 No. 2, spring 2003, correspondence section p. 319. Letter from Renato Baserga explaining the use of the name 'Gigia' in Italy.

9. *Harmonicon*, March 1833, p. 65. The Teatro Carcano opened with Bellini's *Capuleti e I Montecchi*, the part of Juliet by Madame Roser Balfe, Romeo by Mdlle. Michell, and Tebaldo (the tenor) by Bonfigli. Though this opera is far from being a novelty in Milan, it still retains a great share of popularity. The opera had opened the previous season at La Scala with Bonfigli in the cast.

10. I am indebted to Alexander Weatherson of the Donizetti Society (London) for bringing this to my attention and giving me a copy of the libretto of *Enrico IV. Al passo della Marna*, the Oratory of San Carlo work.

11. See the periodical *Il barbiere di Siviglia, Giornale di Musica, Teatri e Varieta* 21 February, 1833, No. 8, p. 1.

12. The opera premiered at the Teatro Carcano not at La Scala as stated in one of the early biographies.

13. Information provided by Giogio Appolina of Varese, Italy.

14. *Donizetti Society Journal*, No. 5, article on a chronology of Giorgio Ronconi performances by Tom Kaufman. See p. 183.

15. See *Maria Callas: The Woman Behind the Legend* by Arianna Stassinopoulos, p.39.

16. See, *Manuel Garcia (1775–1832) Chronicle of the Life of a bel canto Tenor at the dawn of Romanticism* by James Radomski. pp. 188–200.

17. See *Maria Malibran: A Biography of the Singer* by Howard Bushnell, p. 41.

18. Josefa Ruiz-Garcia was the daughter of Manuel Garcia and his first wife, Manuela Moralez.

19. Original ALS in the procession of the author.

20. See *Maria Malibran: A Biography of the Singer* by Howard Bushnell, pp. 188–189.

21. The title of Cambiaggio's booklet is: '*In te L'occasion chela celebre Maria Garcia Malibran canta a La fenice l'ano 1835*'. The author has a copy of it. It also available from the music library of Fondazione Giorgio Cini in Venice.

22. For a detailed account of Malibran's appearance at the Teatro Emeronittio in *La sonnambula* see *Maria Malibran: A Biography of the Singer* by Howard Bushnell.

23. The Teatro Malibran which is not too far from the Teatro La Fenice in Venice, was refurbished in recent years and operas are still performed there. There is a beautiful book on the Teatro Malibran, that gives a listing of all of the performances there over the years that was published in 2001. The editors were Maria Ida Biggi and Giorgio Mangini; the publisher was Marsilio in Venice. It was sponsored by Amice della Fenice. Copies are generally available from Internet book databases.

CHAPTER FOUR

London –
Balfe operatic composer
1835–1837

B alfe arrived in London accompanied by Lina and their daughter Louisa in May 1835, not 1834 as various references sources have stated.[1] Malibran was already in town preparing for the start of several performances of an English version of Bellini's, *La sonnambula*, first given on 18 May, and later followed by Beethoven's *Fidelio*, also with Malibran.

The concert season was already under way. The great bass Luigi Lablache (1794–1858), informed his patrons and the public in *The Times* that he would be performing in a benefit concert on 14 May at the King's Theatre.[2]

This was followed with the announcement by the French harpist and composer Nicholas Bochsa of a major concert to take place on 27 May 1835 at the King's Theatre in which most of the leading Italian singers in London would participate. These included Giulia Grisi, Maria Malibran, Giovanni Battista Rubini (1794–1854) Luigi Lablache, Antonio Tamburini (1800–1876) and a good friend of Rossini's, the young Russian tenor Nicola Ivanoff (1810–1880) who had made his debut in Naples three years earlier. Giuditta Pasta was also scheduled to join the group. Malibran's companion and lover, de Bériot was set to perform a violin concerto at the concert.[3]

The conductor was the Naples born, Michael Costa (1808-1884). The orchestra leaders were Tom Cooke, Balfe's old friend from earlier days at the Drury Lane Theatre, and the young English operatic composer Edward Loder. Balfe may have been in the wings for this concert or perhaps he had a back seat in the house, but not for long.

Balfe's name first appears in *The Times* of 25 May in reference to a concert under the patronage of Her Royal Highness the

Duchess of Kent in which a Mr P. Begrez (1783–1863) announced his Annual Morning Concert at the Great Concert Room at the King's Theatre on Friday 29 May.[4] Among others, Giovanni Puzzi (1785–1876) was featured to play [horn], 'a new fantasia composed for him by Signor Balfi (*sic*), who has just arrived in London'.[5]

Others participating in Begrez's concert included soprano Giulia Grisi, contralto Marietta Brambilla (1807–1875), soprano, Anna Bishop (1810–1884), Rubini, Lablache, Tamburini and Ivanoff. The harpist Bochsa and the pianist Ignaz Moscheles (1794–1870) were the instrumentalists. The conductor was again Michael Costa. Balfe and Costa would become lifelong friends in London, despite on occasions competing with each other.

The horn *Fantasia* which Balfe composed for Puzzi was dedicated '*l'amico Giovanni Puzzi – Guglielmo Balfe*' by Balfe. Balfe probably composed the piece in Milan as a 'thank you' to Puzzi for helping him with his planning arrangements to go to London the previous April. The composition was published in 1835, around June or July, by Cramer Addison & Beale of Regent Street. The music is not in the British Library; it appears it may be in the Puzzi collection in the library at Parma.

Puzzi had a long career as a horn player. He played a hand horn. The valve horn was only just beginning to be known in England during this period.[6] Puzzi was also an impresario and concert organizer. His wife Giacinta Puzzi-Toso was an excellent singer, having created the part of Elisabetta in Donizetti's *Maria Stuarda* with Malibran in the title roles at La Scala in 1834. Giacinta later offered vocal lessons and coaching in London. Balfe composed a remarkable cantata for a Giacinta Puzzi benefit concert in London in 1851; a cantata for nine female voices. See Appendix IX–27 for more details. This horn *Fantasia* for Puzzi was also probably the first piece of music that Balfe had published in London.

On 3 June, Bochsa announced another concert at the King's Theatre for 15 June with the title 'Novel Entertainment' and a reference as it being on a 'splendid scale'. This time most of the previous performers, Grisi, Lablache, Rubini, Tamburini and Ivanoff, were again present.

Malibran performed again, and there was an announcement that said, 'Mr Balfe, who is making his first appearance at the King's Theatre'. There were several other vocalists, including the soprano

Annetta Fink-Lohr, with whom Balfe had sung in Italy, and Signor Begrez, of one of the earlier concerts, was also a soloist at the event.

The 'Novel Entertainment' that Bochsa had promised included not only a work by himself, his, *Grand Concerto Sinfonique*, but also for the 'First and only time in London, [Carl] Czerny's (1791–1857), celebrated *Concert Stuck*, for 8 pianos and 12 harps to be performed by 16 eminent pianists and 12 harpists'.[7]

Once again Balfe's timing could not have been better, as all of London would have been in attendance, given the spectacular nature of Bochsa's concert. Balfe's presence with this distinguished group of singers placed him in the forefront of musical London.

It was during this time that Balfe also composed a 'cantata' for Luigi Lablache with the title, *Il Postiglione*, which the great bass sang at various concerts. The piece was afterwards performed by other soloists, such as Theodore Giubilei (1801–1845) and Giuseppe De Begnis (1793–1849). See Appendix IX–14 for more details and availability of the music.

Over the next several months Balfe continued to participate in concerts. One particularly important one occurred on 14 August at the Royal Gardens in Vauxhall when it was announced that by permission of Mr Laporte (1799–1841), the manager of the King's Theatre, that Grisi, Mme Kyntherland, Signora Brambilla, Rubini, Tamburini, Ivanoff, Lablache and Balfi (*sic*) and others would appear. Clearly Balfe was now in the inner circle with the leading Italian artists of the Italian Opera in London.[8] His position and his relationships would also open up other major opportunities in the not too distant future.

Shortly thereafter, an event occurred on the continent that would impact all of these singers one way or another. On 23 September the composer Vincenzo Bellini died just outside Paris, at the age of thirty-five. Most of the Italian singers who were now in London were his friends and several had also created roles in a number of Bellini operas, yet strangely no special concert was given in honour of their departed friend and associate. Malibran, also a friend and associate of Bellini's, was already in Italy at the time and she was shocked to hear the sad news. By a strange coincidence, exactly on the same day one year later, Maria Malibran would also die, but not before Balfe had fulfilled his promise of composing an opera for her for London.

Meanwhile, Balfe was making progress and feeling comfortable in his new environment and with his involvement in vocal concerts that included such distinguished international Italian artists. The concerts resulted in him achieving an initial flow of earnings while he was also looking for new opportunities to compose.

In an amusing comment made a few years later while attending a dinner in his honour in Dublin he made the following statement about these early days in London: 'After going through a difficult ordeal [in Italy] I tried my fortune in London and never can forget the kind manner in which I was received there, although at first I was called a 'foreigner,' or ...an Irish Italian!'[9]

It was obvious that during the years he spent in Italy he had integrated well. The London comment mentioned above possibly resulted from his acquired preference for Italian food and his overall demeanour and personal style, which must have been more Italian in manner than British based upon the comment. Of course he also spoke fluent Italian, which enabled him to freely socialize with the Italian artists and their associates.

Sometime around July or August 1835, Balfe's friend Tom Cooke introduced him to Samuel Arnold, who was the manager of the Lyceum Theatre.[10] Samuel Arnold (1774–1852), was a librettist and impresario. He was the son of Dr Samuel Arnold (1740–1802), the composer, and had been involved with Drury Lane Theatre before he became the manager of the Lyceum where he endeavoured to create a venue for the performance of English opera. After a series of fires in the theatre which were not uncommon in London during the nineteenth century, the Lyceum was rebuilt in 1834 and called the Royal Lyceum English Opera House. It opened with the opera *Nourjahad* by Edward J. Loder (1813–1853), in July 1834, with a libretto by Samuel Arnold. The opera was not particularly successful.

Following this venture into English opera, Loder's career got off track because of personal financial pressures. As a result, he mostly focused on composing songs and ballads, the majority of which had very little success. His one lasting opera that has had some performances in recent years was *Raymond and Agnes*, which premiered in Manchester in 1855.

In August 1834, Arnold presented another new English opera, *The Mountain Sylph*, by John Barnett, who was a second cousin to Giacomo Meyerbeer (1791–1864), through his father's family, who were of German origin and named Beer. The father had changed the family name when he came to Britain. Barnett had first studied music with one of Balfe's teachers, Charles Horn, and with others. As a young man he had become apprenticed to Arnold in the Lyceum Theatre. In the process, Arnold also taught him music and as part of the arrangement Barnett did various jobs for Arnold in the theatre, including acting, for a number of years.

Unlike Loder's work, Barnett's new opera was structured along the lines of the Italian model, with mostly sung recitatives instead of spoken dialogue between musical numbers. The libretto was in English. The opera *The Mountain Sylph* was truly the first English opera to be composed in the nineteenth century that attempted to break the English tradition in which drama usually dominated the music. Barnett was quite successful with his new work. The music was considered to be moving and to have dramatic appeal.[11] The work had a long run and it was considered to be the first English grand romantic opera of the period. Barnett later composed two other operas, *Fair Rosamund* (1837), and *Farinelli* (1839). By then he had moved on to the Drury Lane Theatre as he and Arnold had had a dispute over money that ended their relationship. Barnett eventually decided to give up operatic composition. He spent time on the continent, where he composed a symphony and some other works. He ultimately returned to London, where he became a singing teacher, which was his profession until his death in 1890.

Balfe and Barnett became good friends, and a few years later Balfe sang in Barnett's last opera, *Farinelli*, in London. He apparently enjoyed singing in the performances. The opera *Farinelli* was successful enough that sheet music from it was later published with Balfe's name featured as the singer.

Arnold was still interested in trying to mount an English opera that would be successful, when Balfe arrived on the scene. He met with Balfe and discussed librettos with him and the dramatist Edward Fitzball (1792–1873). There was a loose agreement between them on what they were looking for that eventually led to the three settling on an adaptation of a work by the French writer Mme Stéphanie de Genlis called *Le Siège de Rochelle*. An English translation of the work had been published and was in circulation in London from 1808. By a coincidence, Balfe had recently looked at it, as other composers had used de Genlis' material for librettos.

However, it wasn't long before the arrangements with Balfe fell apart when the composer found out that because of financial difficulties Arnold would not be mounting a quality production. Balfe had enough experience of shoe-string operatic productions in the small towns in Italy to fully understand what a bad production could do to a new opera. Despite his desire to premiere an opera for the London stage, he rebelled and refused to work with Arnold. He was not willing to compromise his position.

For once he was in a position of strength as he had been earning money regularly since his arrival in London and he had a number of concerts scheduled for the remainder of the year. He also knew that his connections with Grisi, Malibran and Lablache would eventually help him get an opera produced. However, this time the help came from a totally different source. The librarian and copyist James H. Mapleson (?1800–1850?) of the Drury Lane Theatre whom Balfe knew from his early years in the orchestra pit, got word about what was happening at the Lyceum and spoke to Alfred Bunn (1806–1860), manager at the Theatre Royal Drury Lane. Bunn apparently was somewhat vague about remembering Balfe and his early involvement at Drury Lane. Eventually, Tom Cooke intervened.

Balfe, Bunn and Fitzball met and after discussions Bunn agreed to put on an elaborate staging exactly as Balfe had wanted. Bunn's contract with Balfe agreed to a nightly fee for the composer of five pounds, five shillings (five guineas) for each performance of the *Siège of Rochelle*. The first night, 29 October 1835 catapulted Balfe to fame.

The extraordinary reception the opera received continued for seventy nights. It was an amazing success story that had London buzzing. The work represented a new phase in English opera. From the start, Balfe was clearly recognized by the critics as the new musician for London. The composer was in his element and loving it all. Timing once again was in Balfe's corner, as he was on the leading edge of what would become the Victorian age, a period of great expansion and growth in Britain.

Balfe reportedly completed the composition of the opera in about six weeks, probably working day and night. Or, perhaps he had used some of the music he brought from Italy because of the time pressure he was under. This was not an unusual practice for a nineteenth-century composer who was under time constraints. Rossini and Donizetti transplanted arias and other music when they found it necessary in order to meet a deadline. There is also evidence to show that Balfe would do the same later. In any event, his years in Italy in the theatres there had trained him well for the task of producing a score in record time, and under adverse conditions, apart from his own personal skills and capability to work hard and fast.

Balfe's Italian style, combined with his gift for melody and the English text, had great appeal for the audience and critics alike. It was probably a question of being in the right place at the right time, something that Balfe seemed to experience quite frequently during his lifetime.

While the opera was structured to the English style with spoken dialogue the main arias could have come right from a Rossini, Donizetti or Pacini work. One particular piece 'Trav'llers all', is modelled along the lines of the classical Italian buffo aria. Balfe later liked to sing this piece at concerts (the Australian bass-baritone Peter Dawson has recorded it) in London and in Dublin.

The day after the first performance, the *Times* critic opened his review, which ran more that half a column, by saying the following:

> The opera of *The Siege of Rochelle*, which has been for some time announced at this theatre was brought out last night. It is a composition of Mr. Balfe, a gentleman who is said to have gained considerable reputation by some works which he has produced on the continent, but who appeared for the first time, on this occasion, before an English audience. The unqualified success of his attempt will probably encourage him to pursue the course in which he has engaged, and if his future works shall be as deserving, and as well received, as this of which we speak, the public may congratulate themselves upon having a native composer who can fairly take his stand among the more distinguished living musicians.
>
> ... Mr. Balfe being loudly called for, made his appearance, and bowed his thanks for the applause which was bestowed upon him.[12]

Some of the critics initially claimed that Balfe had plagiarized Luigi Ricci's opera *Chiara di Rosembergh*. As it turned out, the comparison was primarily based on the fact that the story for the two operas comes from the same de Genlis novel about the Siège of

Rochelle. Balfe was quite familiar with the Ricci work, which had premiered in Milan in 1831. He had sung in several performances of it Mantua the year before. However, the Ricci opera was not performed in London until 1837. Bunn afterwards in his memoirs said that the critics eventually changed their minds. Possibly, Balfe's Italianate style and the opera's structure and story initially confused some of the critics.

During the run of the opera, Balfe on occasions sang the role of Michel, replacing Henry Phillips who sometimes was 'indisposed'. The vocal score was dedicated to Queen Adelaide and published by Cramer, Addison & Beale of 201 Regent Street at the corner of Conduit Street in London.

This area where the music publishers Cramer, Addison & Beale were located and the adjacent Hanover Square, St Georges Street and the Bond Street areas seemed to attract various musicians over the years in terms of their residences. Malibran and her new husband, Charles de Bériot, also made their London residence in Conduit Street in 1836. The Beale music publishing family initially lived over their premises at the corner of Regent Street and 67 Conduit Street. While the Balfes were living at an area close by, known as the Quadrant, Regent Street, they later moved to Conduit Street, where they lived for several years.

The success of Balfe's new opera resulted in the development of a strong personal friendship between the composer and Frederick Beale (partner in the musical publishing firm) and his family. The Beales' son, Willert Beale, who was born in 1828, was destined to become an important concert agent and manager in the years ahead. He also became a composer and through his association with various artists and his family's connections he became proficient in various languages. In his memoirs Willert Beale talks very affectionately about Balfe's visits to his father's home in those early days in London.[13]

While Willert was only a child of around eight at the time he first met Balfe, he vividly remembered the composer coming to their home and singing for them. His description of Balfe is quite fascinating. It gives us a first-hand insight into the youthful (twenty-seven years old) Balfe's jovial personality as a father, and for his feelings for young children. Referring to Balfe's visits to the Beale home he saw Balfe as:

A blue-eyed, handsome little fellow, the very embodiment of sunny smiles and laughter, he was the merriest playmate we children had yet known. We adored him. He romped with us, told us fairy tales, sang comic songs to us, until we were completely infatuated, and hopelessly fascinated by his exuberant good-humour and inexhaustible fun. 'Peep through the opera-glass' and see him seated at the pianoforte, surrounded by children. Our neighbours, the Powers [Tyrone Power the Irish actor] and the Bishops [Henry Bishop and wife Anna Bishop], have come in, and we are all laughing until tears run down our cheeks at Mr. Balfe's singing: 'our little pigs lie on very good straw, hee-haw.' He imitates pigs to perfection. We make him sing the song over and over again, until he jumps up, catches hold of me, and throwing me over his shoulder, carries me in triumph around the room while the rest seize his coat tails, and try with all their might to drag him back to the piano. He has children of his own, and his wife, Madame Balfe, a very handsome woman, can hardly speak a word of English. They are always with us.

Balfe's personal and business relationship with the Beales would last many years until the death of the father Frederick Beale, when the publishing passed on to others. He remained friends with Willert Beale all his life.

The success of this first opera for London reminded Balfe that his next obligation was to Malibran. Malibran was not around to see Balfe's new opera, having left London for Italy in July. However, before going she had spoken to Alfred Bunn at Drury Lane about her desire for Balfe to compose an opera for her for the following year. Balfe obviously had to find a suitable libretto quickly. He did have a subject matter in mind that was particularly popular at the time.

On 18 November Balfe wrote the following fascinating letter to Malibran, who was then in Italy. The relationship that existed between the composer and the prima donna was very close and friendly, as the tone of the letter clearly shows. The two were the same age, and the chemistry between them was always excellent. Apart from the contents and amusing sign-off of the letter the post-script is intriguing, with its multiple underlined exclamation marks, perhaps suggesting a closer more romantic relationship between the two?

London November 18th, 1835

Dear chére, Cara, Angelica, great Little Malibran!

I write you these few lines to express to you my gratitude for the manner in which you spoke to Bunn about me. Immediately after you left London he sent for me and engaged me to write an opera for the opening of Drury Lane. I have done honour to the very flattering recommendations you gave [of] me to him, and have written him an opera [*Siège of Rochelle*] which has [had] the most extraordinary reception. What is better [than that] which fills his house every night. This evening was the 18th representation and every night it is gaining favour. There is not one piece in it that is not highly delightful. Now Bunn has spoken to me about writing an opera for you when you come. I have thoughts of a subject which would please me exceptionally to write and of it meets with your approbation I shall set about it immediately. It is *Notre Dame de Paris* from Victor Hugo's romance and the part of Esmeralda I should compose for you. I suppose you know the subject, be good enough to write a few lines and let me know what you think about it. If you prefer some other to that, tell me and I shall do just as you like, but be quick as you can for there is not much time to be lost for I should like to write an opera worthy of my little idol Marietta Malibran.

Give my love to de Bériot [Charles de Bériot] and all friends that are good enough to remember me at Milan, and believe me your most dear friend.

Billy Balfe the
H'Irish Potato H'Eater[14]

P.S. Direct [response] to the Theatre Drury Lane and I beg of you write to me as soon as you can – God bless you – Take care of yourself.

I hope that you'll find my pistol short and sweet!!!!

In this moment a friend of mine brought me the news, that you are singing on crutches – I hope it is not true ... they say that you had a severe fall and that you are lame – I suppose it is all paper [newspaper] stuff and nonsense.

Meanwhile, with the success of the *Siege of Rochelle* working for him, Balfe confined his activity to composing his next opera, which would be called *The Maid of Artois* with a libretto roughly based on the *Manon Lescaut* story. Whether Malibran ever responded to the Balfe letter or not, we don't know. It appears that Bunn in his capacity as a poet decided he would write the libretto for Balfe's new opera, which Malibran would perform in May 1836. Presumably, the prima donna agreed with the arrangement, given the fact that Bunn had agreed to her outlandish fees for the season.

Maria Malibran, having at last obtained a marriage annulment, was now able to marry the violinist Charles de Bériot on 29 March 1836 in Paris. Two weeks later, the de Bériots departed for London for the opera season at Drury Lane. Maria continued to use the Malibran name professionally for the rest of her short life.

Balfe had a unique challenge in composing an opera for Malibran. At the time Malibran was one of the most sought-after singers in Europe. Her musical ability, command of languages (English, Italian, French and Spanish) and her theatrical drawing-power placed her foremost among operatic artists throughout Europe. Her level as a singer of importance was such that she really should have been singing with the Italian Opera at the King's Theatre and not at Drury Lane. Malibran was also perhaps the only leading continental prima donna in Europe who was comfortable with singing in English since she was fluent in the language. However, she had decided to sing at the Drury Lane Theatre under Bunn's management simply because he was prepared to pay her the highest fees. As with so many great singers a Malibran performance guaranteed a sold-out house, which meant that she commanded top fees. For Balfe it was an exceptional opportunity that would test all of his skills as a composer in an environment where the critics were highly sophisticated and ready to pounce on any minute slip-up.

Malibran's natural voice was mezzo-soprano; however, her vocal technique was such that no role was basically too difficult for her. Balfe understood her voice intimately, having sung with her in Italy and also seen her in some of the most demanding roles. The de Bériots moved into their new apartment at Conduit Street on their arrival in London in preparation for the opera season.

On 16 May 1836 Balfe signed two contracts with Bunn for *The Maid of Artois*, both of the same date. Since Bunn was providing the libretto for *The Maid of Artois*, Balfe agreed to pay Bunn one hundred pounds for the total publishing rights for the finished opera with Bunn's libretto. Balfe was required to pay Bunn the one-hundred pounds at the time of signing the agreement. This is an indication of Balfe's economic progress since he had arrived in England. A one hundred pound fee was an exceptionally large amount of money in 1836.

The second contract, similar to their previous agreement, required Bunn to pay Balfe five pounds five shillings (five guineas) for each night of the performance up to fifty-nights. This type of performance-based arrangement was not uncommon in London for English opera in those days. Balfe was confident in his ability and with Malibran in the cast the opera was assured success. These two contracts covered the entire arrangements between Balfe and Bunn for the publication and production of *The Maid of Artois* in May 1836.[15]

By way of contrast, Bunn had agreed to pay Malibran one hundred and twenty pounds *per night* for each of her performances. *The Maid of Artois* premiered eleven days later on 27 May 1836 after the signing of the Balfe–Bunn contracts. The opera was a brilliant success, primarily because of Malibran's presence. The production was lavish and artistically and financially very successful for its creators. Balfe afterwards did make some adjustments to the score following the first night's performance.[16]

The vocal score of the opera was published by Cramer, Addison & Beale in June 1836. At the same time it was also announced that various arrangements from the opera had been made by Nicholas Bochsa, Julius Benedict (1804–1885) and Ignaz Moscheles.

Within four months Malibran was tragically dead in Manchester. Following a concert she had given, she collapsed and never recovered. She was twenty-eight years old, the same age as Balfe. Most reports say that it was the result of an earlier horse-riding accident that created the problem that lead to her death. There were also controversial reports on what happened after her death in relation to de Bériot. The demise of such a singer at such an early age will always result in theories and concerns. Malibran was no exception. Ireland also never had the opportunity to see her. She had been scheduled to travel to Dublin for a first appearance there on 20 September 1836, which never happened.

One can't help thinking that perhaps Balfe might have had some influence on her decision to visit Dublin and the possibility that he would appear with her in his native city. However, fate destined otherwise. When Balfe heard about her death he was in a state of shock for some time. She had been his friend and had helped him more than anyone to create a new life for himself, Lina and their daughter Louisa, whom she had met in Italy. It was a sad day and moment for the Balfes and the whole operatic world.[17] Even the young Princess Victoria recorded the tragic event in her personal diary, quite shocked by the prima donna's death at such an early age.

The death of Malibran in September cast a sombre cloud over Balfe and his family. However, Balfe's ability to recover from adversity shows up many times in his career. With his optimistic outlook the singer and composer returned to the stage in the roles of Michel in a revival of *The Siège of Rochelle* in October 1836. Once again his popularity as a composer and performer was commented on and applauded by the press. Early in the New Year Lina Balfe was once again pregnant. They gave consideration to moving, given their possible need for more space for the new addition to their family. They also had added a housekeeper and a servant.

Their son, Michael William Balfe, was born in July or early August 1836.[18] Their new arrival was destined to live a long life, much longer than his father's. However, he was always in the shadow of his famous father. Ultimately, his actions would be a big disappointment to both of his parents, particularly his mother, in so many ways. Meanwhile daughter Louisa was now going on four years old.

Since their arrival in London, Lina had not been very visible. Perhaps her limited English created the problem for her. The majority of the Balfe's friends during this period of their lives were either English, Irish or Italian, so it would have been difficult for her in terms of socializing. It would take Lina a few years before she emerged to become more involved in her husband's business affairs and social life. She continued to have problems with the English language, both spoken and written. However, she also spoke French and Italian. Despite the drawback of her English later in life she did a considerable amount of entertainment and socializing. She also became her husband's score-keeper; keeping track of his autograph scores, payment of his fees and the sale of sheet music. After his death, she took over the responsibility of finalizing and launching his last opera, meeting with the Prince of Wales in the process. She also donated all of his autograph operatic scores and many other works to the British Library so that future generations would have open access to her husband's music.

Lina came from an outstanding Austrian musical family. Her grandfather, Johann Georg Roser, was Kapellmeister at Linz in 1787. Leopold Mozart (Mozart's father) had recommended him for the position.[19] Lina's father, Franz de Paula Roser, was born in Naarn in Upper Austria in August 1779. His early music training was received from his father. As a young man he initially entered a Cistercian monastery to become a priest. However, his musical interests eventually took over and he left the monastery. He pursued a musical career in Vienna during which he became a pupil of Wolfgang Amadeus Mozart (1756–1791) in 1789 for a brief period.[20] Roser claimed he receive over thirty lessons from the famous composer.

Roser subsequently became an impresario of sorts, taking travelling opera troupes to Paris, Verona and probably elsewhere. He also composed over sixty operettas for Vienna, to become one of its most important early nineteenth century composers of operetta. He also managed theatres there. In 1806, he moved to Pest (Budapest), then a part of the Habsburg Empire, where he became a musician to one of the local rulers. He left the area in 1811 and went first to Linz and then to Vienna, where he continued his career as a theatre manager at some of the leading opera houses there. In 1824 he returned to Pest to manage the German theatre there. He died in Pest in August 1830.[21]

When Roser was first in Pest his daughter Magdalena (later called Lina) was born, probably in 1810 and not 1808 as is frequently stated in most reference books. It would appear that her mother died in childbirth as Lina was taken in by foster parents, an Austrian couple from Vienna named Katharina and Dieter Wilhelm Vogel who were friends of her father's.[22] The Vogels had been involved in managing the important Teatre an der Wien in Vienna for some years. In addition they also did some acting.

Obviously Roser, then aged thirty, and in a situation where he was frequently moving from city to city or job to job, which was not uncommon in those days, was in no position to raise a young daughter, so he took the course of having his friends the Vogels take care of Lina since they had no children of their own. By all accounts they did a good job.

As Lina grew up, the Vogels brought her with them to Berlin, and to other places. In 1828 when they applied for passports in Vienna to go to Berlin Lina's age was given as eighteen at the time, making her birthdate 1810. The following year they obtained passports to go to Milan. On arrival in Milan Lina commenced study with one of Mozart's sons, Karl Thomas Mozart (1784–1858).[23] Karl Mozart lived most of his adult life in and around Milan and Como. Lina made her operatic debut at the Teatro Carcano on 30 December 1830. She was probably unaware of the death of her father in Budapest four months earlier, given the amount of time that the information would have taken to get to Milan from Budapest,

As the New Year arrived in 1837, the Balfes were now enjoying the fruits of success in London. The loss of Malibran was difficult to accept. The Balfe family now consisted of a daughter and son and the prospects looked bright economically, given the success of the composer's first two operas.

The year 1837 was also an eventful year in Britain. King, William IV would die on 20 June. Princess Victoria was the declared heir apparent. Her ascent to the throne of England would have enormous consequences for England and it Empire. On a personal level for Balfe the change in monarchy would also have highly significant benefits as a new era was ushered in with the new very young Queen Victoria. Balfe and his family would reap many benefits from it in the future, including the new Queen's patronage for his operatic endeavours in the early years of what was to become known as the Victorian era.

NOTES

1. Tyldesley, in his book on Balfe (p. 20) is incorrect when he says that Balfe and his wife arrived in London in 1834. They were both still in Italy in 1834 and only arrived in London in May 1835.
2. See *The Times*, newspaper theatre advertising section, 13 May 1835.
3. See advertisement in *The Times*, 15 May 1835.
4. Pierre Ignace Begrez was born in Namur, Belgium, in 1783. He studied at the Paris Conservatoire as a violinist. While working in the Opéra orchestra he became interested in singing. He was awarded first prize in vocal studies at the Conservatoire in 1814. He made his vocal debut as a tenor in 1815. Shortly afterwards, he went to London, where he performed in the Italian Opera at the King's Theatre for a number of seasons. While still quite successful he retired from opera in 1822 and took up teaching and singing at concerts, spending the rest of his life in London. Annually he organized a concert with the best Italian artists performing.
5. See *Times* advertisement, front page, 25 May 1835, 'Great Concert Room – King's Theatre'.
6. According to Dr Bradley Strauchen, Horniman Museum & Gardens, London, who did his

doctoral dissertation on Giovanni Puzzi, Puzzi played a hand-horn all his life. Strauchen also says that valve-horns did not gain popularity in England until much later in the nineteenth century. A number of Puzzi adaptations for horn of Balfe's music are apparently among the Puzzi collection in Parma.

7. Advertisement, 'Novel Entertainment – King's Theatre', *The Times*, 3 June 1835.
8. Pierre François Laporte was a French actor and impresario who came from a theatrical family in Paris. He arrived in London in 1826 as a theatrical performer at Drury Lane. He later became involved with the Italian Opera in London through a partner in Paris. Eventually he became manager of the King's Theatre and Italian Opera in London from about 1828 to 1842, when his lawyer and assistant Benjamin Lumley took over.
9. *Freeman's Journal* (Dublin) 27 December 1838.
10. There is some confusion about the timing of Balfe's relationship with Arnold. This is primarily caused by one of Balfe's early biographers (Kenny, p. 105), who says that Balfe was involved with Arnold for the 'opening' of the Lyceum/English Opera House. This of course is incorrect. While the rebuilt theatre opened in July 1834, Balfe was not in England at that time. Additionally, Balfe's first opera for London did not premiere until October 1835, so his relationship with Arnold initially had to start around July/August 1835. In addition the same error occurs in the Temperley's book the *Music in Britain: Romantic Age*, p. 308, where the timing of opening of the rebuilt Lyceum/English Opera House is confused with the year later discussions with Balfe about a new opera and Arnold's decision to open the theatre with the Loder new work. Again, Tyldesley's book on Balfe further adds to the confusion (p. 44) having picked up on the Kenny error by stating that Balfe's dealing with Arnold was in 1834 for the opening of the 'Royal Lyceum and English Opera House', which again is incorrect.
11. See, *Music in Britain: The Romantic Age 1800–1914* edited by Nicholas Temperley, pp. 313–314.
12. *The Times*, 30 October 1835.
13. See *The Light of other Days*, by Willert Beale, Vol. 1, pp. 9–12.
14. Letter from Balfe to Malibran dated 18 November 1835 in the Malibran collection at Koninklijk Conservatorium, Brussels.
15. Based on copies of the two contract dated 16 May 1836 in the possession of the author.
16. See Tyldesley book on Balfe pp. 61–69.
17. For details of Malibran's last days, see, *Maria Malibran: Diva of the Romantic* Age by April Fitzlyon and *Maria Malibran: A Biography of a Singer* by Howard Bushnell.
18. The 1841 English Census taken June 1841 shows that Michael William Balfe junior was a resident in the Balfe's home at Conduit Street, London and that at the time of the census (June) his age was four. This meant that he was born after June 1836, most probably between July or early August of 1836, since the Balfes' next child, Victoire, was born on 1 September 1837. Birth registrations in England did not go into effect until January 1837. Additionally, when Balfe junior died on 5 August 1915 his age was given as seventy-nine years old, which mean that he was born in July or the very beginning of August 1836.
19. E-mail to the author from Peter Clive of Ottawa, Canada author of *Mozart and His Circle*.
20. See *Die Musik in Geschichte und Gegenwart* (MGG), Germany, vol 11, 1st edition, pp. 922–925
21. See, *The New Grove Dictionary of Opera*, Vol. 4, pp. 48–49.
22. E-mail from Hubert Reitterer, Österreichisches Biographisches Lexikon 1815–1950, Vienna.
23. Document written by one of Balfe's granddaughters *circa* 1800–1810 in London, titled, 'Links with the Past' by Lina Jephson. In the document, Jephson is basically recounting discussions with Lina Balfe some years earlier, in which Lina Balfe reminisced about her early years and all of the people she and her husband had met. Towards the close of the document Lina Jephson states, 'One last memory forms a link with a still remoter past. She [Lina Roser Balfe] had studied with a son of Mozart, an admirable Master, though lacking the charm and fair exterior of his father. He had a curious habit whenever he was excited, of plucking a hair from his eyebrow, and turning it round and round on his cheek, till at length he had none left, but still the habit persisted, and he plucked out imaginary hairs, much to the enjoyment of his pupils.'

CHAPTER FIVE

London and Dublin –
More Operas
1838–1841

While Balfe recognized the progress he had made in the two years since his arrival in London, his actions somehow suggest that events were not satisfying enough, or not moving fast enough for him. He continually looked for new avenues to be able to demonstrate his skills as a composer. His competition in London still was not really that significant. Bunn's English opera seasons at Drury Lane didn't last long enough to offer him year-round employment as a composer, despite his early successes. The Lyceum, which was still being run by Arnold, was moving towards financial collapse. On the more personal side, he hadn't yet really moved into the role of conductor.

The Italian Opera at Her Majesty's Theatre run by Laporte was only interested in works by leading Italian composers. With Malibran gone he had lost perhaps his best and most important supporter. While his friend Giulia Grisi, who was also quite influential, was now spending most of her time split between singing in London at Her Majesty's Theatre and in Paris at the Théâtre-Italiens, which meant that he didn't always have direct access to her.

Early in 1837 Lina was once again pregnant.[1] Now with a five-year-old and a three-month-old and another baby on the way there was little doubt that they would soon have to move to a more spacious home. For now, however, Balfe's agenda was full, mostly with concert work, and as a result he probably could not, or logically would not deal with, the idea of a household move at that time.

On 30 January he performed in a concert at Drury Lane. The evening included a variety of singers and instrumentalists. Balfe was initially paired with the soprano Mademoiselle Blasis, whom he knew from his time in Paris; this time they sang a duet from a Rossini opera.[2] Later in the evening he sang 'The Light of other Days' from *The Maid of Artois*. The baritone Giorgio Ronconi participated and the instrumentalists included his friend Giovanni Puzzi and the double-bass player and composer Domenico Dragonetti (1763–1846). Another Balfe friend, Tom Cooke, conducted some of the pieces while the German musician Julius Benedict (1804–1885), who had also recently arrived in London,conducted the main concert.[3]

As the year moved on, Bunn had set a revival of *The Maid of Artois* for April with Mrs Wood (Mary Ann Paton) singing the title role.[4] The general consensus seemed to be that Wood was not quite suited to the part, despite her experience and talents. The revival perhaps came too soon after her friend Malibran's demise to be successful. Only a few performances were given. The opera was revived again in 1839 with Emma Romer in the title part; however, it wasn't until 1846 that it would have another successful season, this time with Anna Bishop and Balfe at the conductor's podium.

Balfe continued to appear at concerts. On 5 May he sang at a charity concert for 'widows and orphans' at the Hanover Square Concert Rooms. The programme was primarily made up of British artists, including Mrs Wood, Mrs Bishop, Clara Novello (1818–1908), and Arthur Edwin Seguin (1809–1852). A number of years later, Seguin would premiere one of Balfe's most important operas in New York.

Meanwhile Bunn had Balfe writing a new opera for Drury Lane. The title was *Catherine Grey*. The libretto was written by George Linley, an author and composer, and not by Bunn. It was Balfe's first and last collaboration with George Linley. The opera was said to be the first English opera to use sung recitatives throughout since Arne's *Artaxerxes* in 1762.[5]

The premiere occurred on 27 May, exactly one year after *The Maid of Artois*. The opera was structured along the Italian model with sung recitatives. It seems that during the first night there was some reaction from the audience to the overture, which the critics thought was too long and too loud. Balfe was actually singing one of the leading roles in the opera and not in the pit. The opera's success was limited despite experienced singers such as Mrs Wood and Emma Romer (1814–1868), in the cast. The work never received a revival.

The Times critic, while mentioning that Balfe's effort (as the composer) was 'most credible', went on to say that he thought that Balfe's 'act of offering an opera with the whole of the dialogue being in recitatives was in defiance of English prejudices'; he also mentioned that he felt taking that approach was extremely hardy [on the part of Balfe].[6] The acerbic critic at the *Athenæum*, Chorley, who was never a friend of Balfe's, felt that the new opera was not as good as *The Siège of Rochelle*; however, on the other hand, he said that it was not as bad as *The Maid of Artois*! Clearly, English-language opera constructed along the Italian lines was not for the British public or the critics.

The lack of success of the opera *Catherine Grey*, whether it related to the casting, as some of the other critics suggested, or to a bad libretto, obviously made Balfe reflect. It would be a long time before he again composed an opera to an English-language libretto with sung recitatives. In the meantime, he continued to take on concert work.

By mid-year most of England was focused on the young Princess Victoria becoming Queen. The death of King William IV occurred on 20 June. Within a short period of time the new Queen had already begun to entertain and engage in other events even before the customary one month of mourning was over. It was indicative of how the momentum of the new era got off to a fast start.

The name of the King's Theatre, the home of Italian Opera in London, was changed on 20 July to Her Majesty's Theatre in recognition of the new Queen.[7] About a year or so earlier a young Canadian-born son of a merchant named Louis Levey, who had immigrated to England, had joined Laporte at the Theatre – his assumed name was Benjamin Lumley (1811–1875). Lumley was a lawyer and former parliamentary agent who had recently been appointed to manage the finances at the theatre. Lumley would eventually replace Laporte in 1842 as manager of the Italian Opera at Her Majesty's Theatre. A few years after that, Lumley's actions would also have a significant influence on Balfe's career and life.

During the next several months Balfe was once again on the concert circuit. Early in July he was active in a charity concert at the great room at Her Majesty's Theatre, With Pasta, Grisi, Rubini, Ivanoff and Tamburini, Balfe sang a duet from *Don Giovanni*.[8] On 19 July he performed in another concert this one at Drury Lane to raise funds for a statue of Beethoven to be erected in Beethoven's home town of Bonn, Germany. Participants included Henry Bishop, the soprano Wilhelmine Schroeder-Devrient (1804-1860), the bass Henry Phillips (1801–1876), Balfe and others.

Shortly after this concert the Balfes left for Paris. Lina was now probably seven months pregnant. The purpose or reason for them going to France at that particular time is unknown. Presumably Balfe's restlessness had taken over and he was exploring some possible opportunities in the French capital. Perhaps the suggestion came from Giulia Grisi, who was still in London at the time. However, the season at the Théâtre-Italiens did not commence until October, so his reason for being in Paris must have been related to something else.

During their stay there Balfe managed to compose a scene and aria for the contralto Adele Cresini for possible insertion into an opera by Marco Marliani (1805–1849), called *Ildegonda nel Carcere*. This opera had premiered in Paris in March 1837. At the time Balfe arrived in Paris the opera was actually being performed in London at Her Majesty's Theatre with Balfe's friends, Grisi, Rubini and Lablache singing the leading roles.[9] The interesting piece of music, which runs just under ten minutes, has been recorded by Richard Bonynge and l'Orchestre de la Suisse Romande. (See discography at Appendix XI for details).[10] Whether or not it was ever actually interpolated in the Marliani opera we don't know.

While in Paris, the Balfes' second daughter, Victoire Balfe, was born on 1 September 1837. One would like to believe that the Balfes called her Victoire because it was the year that the young Princess Victoria became Queen Victoria. However, whether it was a coincidence or not, or just a whimsical act that caused their daughter to be called that, the fact is that the Balfes were actually staying in an apartment on the rue Victoire. Possibly it may have been a combination of both? Later when Victoire appeared publicly in London as a young woman she was somtimes referred to as Victoria, not Victoire.

On their return to England a few weeks later, Bunn had a new libretto by Fitzball which he wanted Balfe to work on immediately. It was titled *Joan of Arc*. Bunn and Balfe executed the contract for the opera on 11 October 1837. The contract also committed Balfe to writing another opera for Bunn, the subject matter of which was to be determined and based on a libretto to be written by Bunn.

Balfe's fee was to be five guineas per night per performance. It is interesting that Balfe had not been able to negotiate a better fee given his overall success. Of course one of the difficulties he was experiencing was the fact that Bunn was really the only source in town to perform English operas since Bunn controlled both Drury Lane and Covent Garden. Arnold, while continuing to offer English Opera at the Lyceum, was also continually on the verge of bankruptcy, so the fee he was liable to offer probably would have been much less than Bunn's.

The contract also guaranteed that Balfe would be paid each Saturday all the money then due to him for the performances of his operas. However, as part of the consideration Balfe also agreed that after the twentieth performance of either of his operas that Bunn would own the operas completely free from all charges. Balfe obviously was not a good negotiator.

Balfe, now under extreme time pressure once again, produced an opera within six weeks, since *Joan of Arc* premiered on 30 November 1837. Balfe sang one of the leading roles. The vocal score was published by Cramer, Addison and Beale. It was also dedicated, with permission, to Her Most Gracious Majesty, Queen Victoria.

The opera was not a great success, although one soprano number, 'Peace in the valley', and the duet for baritone and soprano, 'O'er shepherd pipe', were sometimes performed at various concerts.

The Times critic, in a short review of the work subtly touched on Balfe's style as a composer, tending to be critical of Balfe's approach. However, by now, Balfe in writing his operas was also clearly focused on the potential sale of sheet music of arias or ballads.

The following is a brief extract from the opening of the *Times* review:

> A new grand opera, called *Joan of Arc*, the music by Balfe, was produced last night. The merits of the composer are pretty generally known, namely, that he is a master of the mechanism of his art, and that he is often very happy in producing pleasing airs, of   which originality is not a leading characteristic.[11]

Balfe's new opera also experienced some serious competition from his old Dublin friend, O'Rourke, whose name was now anglicized as Rooke and who revived his opera *Amelie* at Covent Garden with much success. Rooke's work ran for fifty performances while Balfe's new opera was seen twenty-two times.

Early in November Balfe also completed the music for a historic play called *Caractus*, which aired a number of times at Drury Lane. At the same time he commenced work on a new opera for Bunn, called *Diadesté*, to a libretto by Fitzball. Presumably, Bunn was not able to come up with a satisfactory libretto himself. There also seems to be some confusion as to whether or not this opera ful-filled his contract with Bunn – to produce a second opera for Drury Lane to a Bunn written libretto.[12] The opera was planned to premiere during the spring of the following year.

After the year drew to a close, the Balfes moved to a new apart-ment in the more fashionable area of Mayfair. For the next sever-al years they were to live at 61 Conduit Street, just off Regent Street in London. Their family now consisted of five-year-old Louisa, one-year-old Michael junior and three-month-old Victoire. They also had a housekeeper, a nanny and servants. The Balfes had come a long way from their Spartan days in northern Italy.

In March 1838 the first English-language performance of Mozart's *Magic Flute* was mounted at Drury Lane. The all British cast generally got good reviews. Balfe had the role of Papageno, which should have been ideal for him. However, the *Times* critic indicated that he was not completely comfortable in the part.

More concerts continued and by May his new comic opera, with its strange-sounding name *Diadesté*, apparently called after a Venetian game, had its premiere. It was given a good review with particular references to Balfe's skills at composing opera buffa.

Balfe's association with Her Majesty's Theatre during this peri-od led to a discussion on possibly composing an Italian opera for the theatre. No doubt Balfe's relationship with Grisi and Lablache in some way influenced the Laporte decision. In any event, early in May a commission was extended to the composer. Almost immediately after the first performance of *Diadesté*, he set to work on a libretto provided by Manfredo Maggione (1810–1862?), which was based on Shakespeare's play *The Merry Wives of Windsor*. In a period of two months Balfe had completed the score. The opera *Falstaff* was in two acts.[13]

The title role was written for the great basso, Lablache, the role of Carlo Fenton for Rubini, Ford for Tamburini, Mrs Ford for Grisi, Annetta for Albertazzi and Mrs. Page for Caremoli. It was a remarkable line-up of the best operatic talent. Only three years earlier, in January 1835, what became known as the 'Puritani Quartette' (Grisi, Rubini, Tamburini and Lablache) had created Bellini's opera *I Puritani* in Paris, and now the same cast was about to create an Italian opera for Balfe in London. How the subject matter got selected is not known.

The librettist Maggione was a well-established London-based translator of operas into English or Italian. He completed translations of operas by Auber and Halevy. He also translated Donizetti's *Lucia di Lammermoor*. During most of the nineteenth century, French operas were translated into Italian to be performed in London and elsewhere in the provinces. Maggione later became a good friend of the soprano Giuseppina Strepponi (1815–1897), Giuseppe Verdi's (1813–1901), friend and future wife. They probably met while she was in Paris. She always spoke of him affectionately.

The London critics were amazed at this new Balfe venture. It clearly showed the composer's confidence in himself and his ability to compose music for the best operatic talent and probably the most sophisticated audience in Europe. His relationship with these leading artists who were in demand all over Europe and in Russia was unique and obviously had been achieved through great personal integrity and respect.

Notwithstanding the fact that he was under pressure to compose a major opera in Italian in the short period of six weeks, Balfe continued to participate in concerts. Early in June he sang at a major concert given by Julius Benedict at Her Majesty's Theatre. All of the leading Italian artists were present including Grisi, Rubini, Lablache, Tamburini, Ivanoff and several others. Balfe sang from his opera *Catherine Grey*. He also joined in the famous *Il Giuramento* scene from Rossini's opera *Guglielmo Tell* that closes the second act.xiv The scene was sung in Italian with Tamburini in the part of Tell, while Balfe would have had one of the secondary parts. Other performers included Rubini, Ivanoff, Lablache and his son Frederick, Castellan, Tamburini and Cantone.[15]

Falstaff premiered on 19 July 1838 at Her Majesty's Theatre. The *Times* critic gave a full column to his review. The following are some excerpts as they relate to Balfe and his work:

For the benefit of Signor Lablache, *Falstaff,* in an Italian
shape, was, last night presented. We had a full, bold, mascu-
line colouring of Shakespeare brought to a level with light
sketchiness of a modern Italian drama. The amalgamation
seems incompatible – almost impossible; and yet it is accomplished in Balfe's new opera in a way which cannot be pro-
nounced a failure.[16]

The *Times* critic goes on to say:

For the share of Mr. Balfe, the composer, in this production,
which may well be called the lion's share, great praise is to be
given. It is decidedly the best thing he has done. He writes
now like a man who is determined to found a great reputation, and is satisfied that he has the means of doing so. The
opera, as a whole, is even creditable to the state of the art in
this country. Not that it is faultless; on the contrary, it has
defects on which the severity of criticism, if it pleases, may
fasten; but it abounds in beauties, and some of them certainly of a very high order.
   ... We are not sure if Mr. Balfe does not stand alone as the
composer of an opera to Italian words by an Englishman; but
whether he is or not, it is quite safe to affirm that no English
composer now living could have made himself so completely
at home in such an undertaking. There may be defects in the
rhythmical part of it, as connected with that very beautiful
and musical language, on which it would be absurd to attempt
to pronounce at a first hearing; but general effect, as music, is
certainly good; and there is no risk in saying further, that
none of the modern race of Italian composers, Rossini
excepted, who is out of date [Rossini's last opera was composed in 1829] could have produced such a work.[17]

The house was well attended, all of the principals were well
praised, the encores were numerous and, according to *The Times*
critic – Mr. Balfe, with a certain reluctance, took a curtain call.
Unfortunately for Balfe, *Falstaff* was premiered at the tail-end of
the opera season, which meant that once August arrived there were
no more performances.
   Falstaff is a classic comic opera in the tradition of Rossini. Some

MR. BALFE,
TEACHER OF DANCING,

RESPECTFULLY acquaints the Nobility, Gentry and Public of WEXFORD and its Vicinity, that he proposes visiting that County early in *June*; and feeling grateful for the Encouragement he met with last Season, has arranged his Business in Dublin so as to be able to attend Six Months there, and Six Months in Wexford. He teaches the most fashionable and graceful Style of Dancing for Company, as also the much admired *Tambourine Dance*, the *Waltz's*, that were so fashionable in Dublin last Winter, and the most graceful *Fancy Dances*.

☞ Commands will be received for him at Miss O'BRIEN's BOARDING SCHOOL, where he will attend. Dublin, May 29, 1813.

(Wexford Herald 3 June, 1813)

1. Advertisement by Balfe's father in Wexford, June 1813.

2. The house at 10 Pitt Street, Dublin, where Michael W. Balfe was born in 1808.

3. Balfe's first published song, Dublin, *circa* December 1822, when he was fourteen years old.

4. Rotunda Concert Rooms, Dublin where Balfe performed during the early nineteenth century.

5. Renowned singer Maria Malibran, a friend of Balfe's.

6. Portrait of Balfe as a young man.

I RIVALI DI SE STESSI

Melo-Dramma Comico per Musica

DA RAPPRESENTARSI

NEL REAL TEATRO CAROLINO

La sera dé 29. Giugno 1829.

PER TERZA OPERA DELL' ANNO TEATRALE
1829. e 1830.

PALERMO 1829.

Dalla Società Tipografica.

UN AVVERTIMENTO
AI GELOSI

FARSA GIOCOSA

DA RAPPRESENTARSI

NEL TEATRO RE

IN MILANO

L'ESTATE DEL 1831.

Milano

dalla Stamperia Dova, Contrada dell'Agnello

N.° 962.

180567-A
MUSIK-8.

7. Libretto for *I rivali di se stessi*, Balfe's first opera, as performed in Italy in 1829.

8. Libretto for *Un avvertimento di gelosi*, Balfe's second opera, performed in 1831.

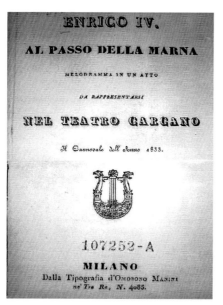

9. Libretto for Balfe's third work, *Enrico IV, al passo della Marna*, which had its premiere at the Teatro Carcano, Milan,

10. The soprano, Giulia Grisi, whom Balfe first met in Bologna in 1829.

LA SONNAMBULA

MELO-DRAMMA IN DUE ATTI

DA RAPPRESENTARSI

NEL TEATRO

M. F. G.

MALIBRAN

POSTO A S. GIO. GRISOSTOMO

La Quadragesima

1835.

Parole, del Sig. Felice Romani.
Musica, del Sig. Maestro Vincenzo Bellini

VENEZIA
NELLA EDIT. TIPOGRAFIA RIZZI

PERSONAGGI.

Il Conte RODOLFO , Signore del villaggio
Sig. Guglielmo Balfe

TERESA , Molinara
Sig. Marietta Bramati

AMINA , Orfanella raccolta da Teresa, fidanzata
ad
Mad. M. F. G. Malibran

ELVINO , ricco possidente del villaggio
Sig. Enrico Antonio Canali

LISA , Ostessa amante di Elvino
Sig. Rosina Ferrari

ALESSIO , Contadino , amante di Lisa
Sig. Nicolò Fontana

Un NOTARO
Sig. Lorenzo Lombardi

Cori - Comparse - Contadini - Contadine

La Scena è in un villaggio della Svizzera.

11. Malibran and Balfe in *La sonnambula* in Venice, 1835.

12. The Teatro Malibran in Venice, 2006.

13. Playbill of *The Siege of Rochelle*, Balfe's first London opera, 1835.

14. Malibran in Balfe's *The Maid of Artois* in 1836, London.

15. Balfe's *Falstaff* with Luigi Lablache in the title role, premiered in 1838.

16. Portrait of Balfe's young wife, Lina Balfe.

17. Portrait of the thirty-eight year-old Michael W. Balfe in Vienna.

18. Louisa 'Gigia' Balfe, the composer's first-born child.

19. Balfe's youngest daughter, Victoire Balfe.

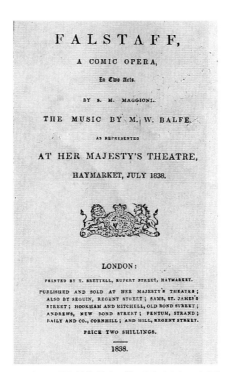

20. The libretto for the premiere of Balfe's *Falstaff* at His Majesty's Theatre, London.

21. Playbill of *The Bohemian Girl*, from 8 December 1843, Theatre Royal, Drury Lane, London.

22. Balfe's first composition, *Le puits d'amour*, composed for the Opéra Comique, Paris, in 1843.

23. A German version of the popular *The Bohemian Girl*, premiered as *Die Zigeunerin* in Vienna in 1846.

of the vocal music, while quite sparkling, is also quite difficult in terms of its florid style. Based on the libretto and autograph score the principal arias duets and trios are as follows:

Aria – Falstaff: *Ho bisogno dei danari*
Aria - Mrs Ford: *Ah, vecchiaccio scostumato*
Trio – Mrs Ford, Mrs. Page & Miss Page: *Vorrei parlar, ma l'ira*
Duet –Ford & Fenton: *Non credete poi chio sia*
Duet – Ford & Falstaff: *Voi siete un uom di spirito*
Aria – Fenton: *Ah! la mia mente estatica*
Duet – Mrs Ford & Falstaff: *Siete qui, caro amico*
Aria – Ford: *Che mai vedo?*
Aria – Annetta: *Una donna più felice*
Duet – Fenton & Annetta: *Ah! sì, tu m'ami, o cara*
Aria – Falstaff: *È l' ora stabilita, ardente nume*

The opera was never revived. Perhaps during Lablache's lifetime other singers may have been concerned about being compared to Lablache in the title role? In 1848, when Balfe was musical director at Her Majesty's Theatre,he did plan a revival. He had reworked some the music he had written for Grisi to accommodate the soprano Jenny Lind, who was then performing at the theatre. Lablache was again going to perform the part of *Falstaff.*

One of London's leading periodicals actually announced at the time that the revival would occur the following week.[18] However, nothing ever took place. The only conclusion that one can come to is that at the last moment Jenny Lind found she was not comfortable with her part as Mrs. Ford, and despite her close relationship with Balfe the revival had to be cancelled because of her actions. There was also a report in 1856 of a revival in Paris at the Théâtre-Italiens, with Balfe to present it, but that never seems to have occurred.[19]

Balfe's original autograph orchestral score of the opera, beautifully bound and in pristine condition, is held by the British Library. See Appendix III for details. Shortly after the opera's premiere, sheet music of the main arias, duets and trios was published by Cramer, Addison and Beale in London; in Paris by Chez Pacini and by Troupenas and in Milan by Francesco Lucca.[20] A vocal score was produced by the same London publisher. As far as it's known no full orchestral score was ever published.

One interesting factor is that Balfe introduced a soprano aria, 'Una Donna più felice', from his 1833 Milan opera, *Enrico IV*, into *Falstaff*. No doubt some of the time constraints placed on him to compose the *Falstaff* necessitated this action.[21]

In a reflective moment, the editor (James Davison?) of *The Musical World* (London) in 1848, wrote the following:

> *Falstaff* achieved a great success, and was considered by musicians as the *chef d'oeuvre* of the composer. Would that the present management of her Majesty's Theatre could be tempted to abandon something of its reverence for the works of 'young Verdi,' and turn its attention to this clever and effective composition, any piece of which is worth all of the 'gems,' as they are called, of the modern Italian 'phenomenon,' agglomerated into one mass! Would not the subscribers be thankful? – would not the public sing 'Io triumphie?" – would not the great Lablache rejoice from his inmost soul at being once more constituted the interpreter of Shakspere (*sic*) – made musically apparent through the medium of Balfe's melodies? Let us hope for the best. Meanwhile, we ask the reader's pardon seriously for bringing the names of Balfe and Verdi into juxta-position, even by contrast.[22]

It was shortly after this article appeared that the revival of Balfe's *Falstaff* with Jenny Lind in the Grisi role was announced. However, as mentioned above, the opera was never revived. The irony of the above article is that in 1848 Balfe was the musical director and conductor at Her Majesty's Theatre who was introducing all those Verdi operas premieres!

The pace which Balfe continued to keep up ever since his return from Italy was quite amazing, particularly for someone that was known to suffer from bronchial asthma. However, during these years he seemed to be relatively free of illness or if he experienced some problems his schedule was such that it never seemed to let it interfere with his work.

His singing commitments continued. In October he performed the title role in an English language version of Mozart's *Don Juan (Don Giovanni)* at the Theatre Royal in Drury Lane.

The Times critic had the following to say about his performance:

The libertine, Don Juan was represented by Mr Balfe. His consummate skill as a musician enables him, by judicious management to make the most of a vocal organ of very moderate power and capacity.

... the direction for the banquet (*Fin ch'an dal vino*), though demanding a voice of greater compass, were poured forth with buoyant heartiness. His acting was of too swaggering a character. He evidenced more that enough of the bold confidence of Don Juan, but we looked in vain for the elegance and polish of that accomplished rake who succeeds so well, with females of every rank, age and complexion.[23]

As it turned out, Drury Lane under Bunn's management was now having some financial difficulties similar to those of other London theatres and the season was shortened.

The timing worked for Balfe as he had plans to make a return visit to Ireland towards the end of 1838. He had received an invitation from John Calcraft (*c*1793–1870), who was then manager of the Theatre Royal in Dublin. Calcraft (his real name was John W. Cole) was lessee of the Theatre Royal, Dublin from 1830 to 1851. Probably Calcraft invited Balfe at the prompting of one of the composer's early Dublin friends; Richard Levey an excellent musician, who was then leader of the orchestra at the Theatre Royal.[24] The invitation was for Balfe to join a group of British singers who were coming to Ireland at year-end to perform a season of English opera. Balfe accepted the invitation.

He had not been to Ireland since his departure early in 1823. It would be an interesting experience for him. His mother and two sisters still lived there. He also had numerous friends who were active in music circles. Included among these was a former teacher, James Barton, his fellow student and friend, Levey, and William Conran (*c*1806–1857), a pianist and music teacher. Balfe travelled alone, taking the boat to Dublin at the end of October.

Musically, Dublin had changed considerably since the time when Balfe lived there. The Theatre Royal was now seeing regular visits by Italian opera companies, who mostly performed operas by Rossini. There were also visits by British artists who sang operas in English. The Rotunda Concert Rooms were still active with visiting artists. In another two years the thirty-year-old pianist Franz

Liszt would give his first Irish recital at the Rotunda as part of his extended concert tour of Britain.

On arrival in Dublin Balfe stayed at the fashionable Morrison's Hotel on the corner of Nassau and Dawson Streets. He visited his mother almost immediately. She lived just a short distance from the hotel. His mother was now in her late fifties and apparently still living in the same neighborhood, but not in the best of health. His younger sister Amelia was just sixteen. His other sister was probably in her later twenties and possibly married. She later advertised in Dublin as Mrs Dodd, a teacher of voice and music.[25] When Balfe saw the condition of his mother and once his singing engagement was over at the Theatre Royal, he immediately made arrangements for her to return with him to live in the family home in London.

For the next two months through the end of December Balfe performed the lead baritone roles in various operas by Rossini (*The Barber of Seville* and *Cinderella*) and in Bellini's *La sonnambula* and Beethoven's *Fidelio* (Rocco). He also sang in Cooke's *Amelie*, Auber's Fra *Diavolo* and *Masaniello*.

Early in December a notice appeared in one of the leading newspapers to say that a public dinner would be held at Morrison's Hotel on 28 December to celebrate Balfe's return. The attendance was limited to one hundred gentlemen at a cost of one guinea each. Balfe's former teacher and mentor, James Barton, took the chair to welcome the distinguished guest. The table was decorated with banners and medallions featuring Balfe's early Italian operas, *Enrico IV al passo della Marna*, *I rivale di se stessi* and *Un avvertimento ai gelosi*.

After the anthem was sung with Balfe taking the lead there was a toast given to the Queen. Balfe rose to give a speech making reference to the fact that he had been away from his native city for sixteen years and following with:

> I say my native city, for I believe that you are aware that I have the honour to be a Dublin man (cheers). I have traveled very far, and have brought out the first of my works in Italy. I was received with the greatest hospitality and encouragement and I am proud and happy to say that I have been most eminently successful. After going through a difficult ordeal [in Italy] I tried my fortune in London and never can forget the kind

manner in which I was received there, although at first I was called a' foreigner or... an Irish Italian!

After so long an absence, if I have revisited my native city (sic) and the friends of my youth, I have done so, on the liberal engagement of my friend, Mr. Calcraft; and by the kind and liberal permission of the lessee of Drury Lane [Alfred Bunn], at a time when my absence was a great personal inconvenience to him. I need not tell you how delighted I have felt by the overwhelming kindness of the reception I have met with in the theatre [Royal] of Hawkins Street [Dublin], (cheers). It was indeed a reception more than sufficiently complimentary to whatever talent I may possess. I feel that this is the proudest day of my life, and my most sanguine hope is that I may merit the honour, which you have bestowed on me.

Gentlemen, I sincerely thank you all, and before I sit down permit me to express the wish that lies nearest to my heart, that I may soon have the pleasure of seeing you all again. (Loud continuous cheering).

During the evening there was much merry-making and music. Balfe, accompanying himself, sang 'When I beheld the Anchor Weighed' from *The Siège of Rochelle*. He followed this with a duet for bass and baritone 'Voi siete un Uom di spirito' from his *Falstaff*. He was joined in this number by Antonio Sapio (c1897–1857) a London-born singer and teacher then residing in Dublin.[26]

Three of his friends, William Conran and Joseph and John Robinson sang a quartette with him from his opera *Catherine Grey*. Apparently one or two of the men were actually singing female parts! Balfe continued with the aria "What is the spell" from Rooke's *Amelia* in which Balfe was accompanied by W. C. Conran (1802?–1857), on the piano and Samuel Pigott (1797–1853), on the cello. (Pigott's beautiful instrument was the 1720 Stradivarius cello that later became famous as the Piatti cello.)[27] Balfe concluded the evening with his rollicking 'Travellers All' from the *Siège of Rochelle*. During this visit he also gave recitals after the opera in which he sang various arias from his operas.

Balfe returned to London at the end of the month. His mother accompanied him. However, she was quite ill. She had never met Lina or any of her grandchildren before. It must have been a good family gathering for her despite her condition. As the month of January progress, her condition gradually worsened, and on 24 January she passed away. She was fifty-seven years old.[28] It is also possible that Balfe's younger sister Amelia came to London to be with her mother during those final days. Amelia does show up in the census records of the Balfe home some time later.

In London, Balfe continued his career as a singer, performing in a variety of operas over the next six months. Bunn was not underwriting any new works given his financial position, so Balfe the composer became a full-time singer. He had no other option. There was a revival of *The Maid of Artois* at Drury Lane with Emma Romer in the title role and Balfe singing one of the other roles. This was a 'command performance' for Queen Victoria on 29 January. Despite very inclement weather Her Majesty arrived on time and seemed to enjoy the opera very much, according to the *Times* critic. Early in February he ventured into a new title role in the premiere of John Barnett's opera *Farinelli*. On the first night something very unusual happened to him, *The Times* reporting that he had a dreadful cold and that during the first act his voice began to fail. It was very awkward as he had the principal role. Balfe, embarrassed by his indisposition, turned to the audience and asked for 'forgiveness for his deficiencies'. The audience responded with a burst of applause. He endeavoured to continue but the audience cried out 'enough'. At the end of the opera Barnett appeared before the curtain with the cast, all of whom were well applauded by the audience.

In general, the *Farinelli* work was not perceived as being particularly successful. However, that did not stop Queen Victoria attending a performance some time later; fortunately Balfe's voice was back to normal by then. His need to keep active and generate income was further complicated by the fact that Lina was again pregnant.

Later Balfe returned to Dublin, this time he was accompanied by Lina and the pianist Thalberg. They gave a series of concerts at the Theatre Royal and at the Rotunda Concert Rooms, where Balfe had performed as a youth many years previously. It must have been a nostalgic time for him. In Dublin they were joined by Antonio Sapio and he and Balfe sang from *Falstaff* again. The group mostly performed solos and duets from Italian opera. This was Lina's first venture on the stage since she had arrived from Italy. Presumably, they had brought the children with them, although we don't know for sure.

Lina and Balfe sang a duet, 'Non fuggir', from Donizetti's 1836 comic masterpiece *Il Campanello*. This was followed with another Donizetti duet, from his opera *Il borgomastro*. Thalberg played some of his operatic variations. Lina closed out the first half of the concert with the finale 'Ah! non giunge' from *La sonnambula*.

The second half of the concert was primarily given to selections from Balfe's operas. He also performed in a number of operas including *La sonnambula*, *The Barber of Seville* and *L'elisir d'amore*, each of which was sung in English. They sang a trio from *The Maid of Artois* with Balfe, Emma Romer and tenor John Templeton (1802–1886). Later they also sang in *The Siège of Rochelle*. During this period, they may also have toured the provinces, possibly visiting Limerick, Cork and Galway.

The Balfes' second son, Edward , was born early in 1840 in London. However, there were complications at birth and Edward did not live long. He passed away from hydrocephalus (water on the brain) when he was only twenty-one months old in April 1841.[29] It must have been a heart-breaking time for the family.

Balfe, in London and forever driven to try to find ways to increase his income, reflected on the fact that he had not composed a new opera for nearly three years. His friend Bunn was in bankruptcy and Arnold was still struggling. Courageous and willing to accept risks, he agreed to take over the management of the Lyceum Theatre from Arnold and to create an English National Opera company. On the face of it, it seemed logical given his experience. However, whatever talents Balfe may have had as a musician, his skills at managing an operatic venture and theatre, although short-lived, would have the best backing. What Lina may have said to him about this we don't know. His primary concerns were his wife and three young children and the need to take care of them. There was no real opportunity for him to compose operas for any theatre in London at the time. So unless he was to create the opportunity for himself, he had to try something different and that's exactly what he did.

Balfe felt confident with his new endeavour as Queen Victoria was pleased to lend her name to the venture, which made him feel that it would be very successful. It was up to him to gather together the British talent which would create a series of new operas for a public that was now used to patronizing English Opera. In effect, he was looking to create a National English Opera Company.

His ambitions and the challenges he took on far exceeded his capabilities to control and manage the situation. The whole project came to a crashing halt in a very short period of time. The indefatigable Balfe, somewhat upset with himself, would again rise to the challenge by taking his talents to Paris where much opportunity awaited him in a totally different environment.

NOTES

1. Lina Balfe gave birth to a daughter, Victoire, in Paris on 1 September 1837.
2. Mdlle. Blasis was considered to be a good soprano by the London critic Henry Chorley. See *Thirty Years' Musical Recollections*, p. 4.
3. Copy playbill in the possession of the author.
4. See *A History of English Opera* by Eric Walter White, p. 270.
5. See *Henry Fothergill Chorley: Victorian Journalist* by Robert Terrell Bledsoe, p. 65.
6. See *Times* review, Monday 29 May 1837.
7. See *The Times*, 20 July, 1837; Announcement by Mr Laporte, the manager of the King's Theatre that the name would be changed forthwith to 'Her Majesty's Theatre'.
8. Concert details provided courtesy of Bill Ecker, Harmonie Autographs and Music, Inc. New York
9. See *Donizetti Society Journal*, No. 4 article by Tom Kaufman, 'Giulia Grisi: a re-evaluation', p.205.
10. See liner notes by Richard Bonynge on the recording cover.
11. See *The Times*, 1 December 1837, review of *Joan of Arc* by Balfe.
12. In Eric White's book, *The History of English Opera*, see p. 275; White seems to believe that Balfe may have worked on another libretto by Bunn's, possibly sometime in 1839, to fulfill the contract. He also feels that this may have been *The Bohemian Girl*, which is somewhat questionable.
13. Prior to Balfe's *Falstaff*, Antonio Salieri's *Falstaff* premiered in Vienna in 1799, while Otto Nicolai's *Die lustigen Weiber von Windsor* had its premiere in Berlin in 1849, Adolphe Adam's *Falstaff* in Paris in 1856, and Giuseppe Verdi's *Falstaff*, by far the most famous version, premiered in Milan in 1893. Each of these composer's versions of *Falstaff* has been recorded more than once. There is currently no recording of Balfe's *Falstaff* as of this writing.
14. It closes the second act in the Italian version of the opera.
15. Copy playbill in the possession of the author.
16. See *Times* review, by James Davison (?), 20 July 1838.
17. Ibid.
18. *The Musical World*, 1 July 1848, front page.
19. *The Musical World*, 27 September 1856, p. 615.
20. Tyldesley in his book on Balfe, p. 79, is incorrect when he says that 'none of the numbers were published separately'.
21. My thanks to Dr Valerie Langfield of Cheshire in the UK., for her help in identifying this interpolation. Dr Langfield has done extensive study of the Balfe *Falstaff* autograph score in the British Library.
22. *The Musical World* (London) 1 April 1848, p. 210.
23. See *Times*, *Don Juan* review, 2 October 1838
24. Richard Levey's real name was Richard Michael O'Shaughnessy (he changed his name while in London because of the difficulty the locals had in pronouncing it, taking instead his moth-

er's maiden name, which he used for the rest of his long life) Levey was an excellent violinist who was a member of the orchestra at the Theatre Royal for fifty years. He was also the co-author of the book, *The Annals of the Theatre Royal Dublin*, published in 1890 in Dublin.

25. There is very little documentary evidence available in terms of Balfe's two sisters. We know from the British 1841 census (which was conducted in June of that year) that Amelia Balfe was living with her brother and his family at 61 Conduit Street, London, and her age was given as eighteen years at the time of the census. This probably meant that she was born in the latter half of 1822 and would have turned nineteen in 1841, since the father died in January 1823. As far as we know Balfe's other sister, whose first name we do not know, stayed in Dublin and married and her name changed to Mrs Dodd. How old she might have been at the time of Balfe's first return visit to Dublin at the end of 1838 is difficult to say, except that she had to be younger than her brother, Michael who was then thirty years old, since the parents were married in 1807 and Michael, was their first child.

26. Sapio late, became the first vocal teacher of the Irish international prima donna Catherine Hayes. See *Catherine Hayes: The Hibernian Prima Donna* by Basil Walsh.

27. This famous cello is now in the possession of the Mexican cellist. Carlos Prieto, who has written a book on the history of the instrument's owners, including Pigott. The title of the English-language version is *The Adventures of a Cello* by Carlos Prieto. This version was published in 2006 by the University of Texas Press.

28. Death certificate shows that she was residing at 61 Conduit Street in London and age fifty-seven at the time of her death.

29. Death certificate of Edward Balfe, son of Michael William and Lina Balfe aged twenty-one months died on 23 April 1841. Cause of death shown as hydrocephalus.

CHAPTER SIX

Paris (Opéra Comique) and London (1842–1843)

Balfe's venture into opera management at what was now called the 'Theatre Royal, English Opera House', got off to a bad start in March 1841. He had composed a new opera, *Keolanthe*, for the opening night which was delayed three days because of the 'indisposition' of the baritone Henry Phillips, who had gone to Dublin and was late getting back for the opening night, claiming he had some sort of a virus. Phillips' action permanently severed his relationship with Balfe. About two months later he walked out on the production, leaving Balfe in the lurch.[1]

Lina Balfe was making her London operatic debut in the lead role of *Keolanthe*. The opera was well received. The audience initially showed some resentment with Phillips over his 'indisposition' because of the delay. However, Balfe spoke to the audience at the end of the performance, trying to smooth over their concerns – according to the *Times* critic, Balfe, with great good humour, begged the audience to look over the imperfections since we all get "influenza'.[2]

The evening was an interesting debut for Lina Balfe since the opera was in English. The *Times* critic stated that

> ... she deserved great praise for her constant effort to realize her conception of what was good. Apparently her notes weren't always distinct [?], nor did she have great flexibility; it is evident that she does not come up to her own standard of excellence, but she has the most intense feeling, and when an opportunity is given, is capable of really outbursts of passion.[3]

There was no mention about Lina's diction or her handling of the words. So presumably she had made strides in terms of her accent.

There were several encores throughout the evening. The critic stated that the opening night promised well for the enterprise. There were several performances into April. Lina later took a benefit performance on 5 May 1841.

Loder's opera *The Deer Stalker* followed *Keolanthe*. It did not achieve much success. Balfe's Irish friend, Samuel Lover (1797–1868), novelist, painter and musician, wrote a type of buffa operetta for the venture called *Il Paddy Whack in Italia*, which premiered mid-April.[4] The music shows that Glover, not Balfe, actually wrote it. However, one can't help believing that Balfe personally must have had some influence on the piece, given its theme and his sense of humour along with his experiences in Italy.

In an interesting comment about Balfe's character, Glover, who knew Balfe personally from his early days in Dublin and again when the friendship picked up with Balfe's arrival in London, stated that 'I never once met him out of temper, out of spirits, or out of charity. He had a kindly word for everyone and a helping hand for many, and among his other attractive qualities I may add, he had some little humour ...'[5]

Balfe agreed to sing the part of O'Donnell, the '*Il Paddy Whack* character!' The critics treated the piece as trivial, which it probably was.[6] The most famous piece of music that came from it was a ballad called; 'Molly Bawn', which Balfe sang with great credibility, so much so that there was quite a demand for it, and sheet music was published by Duff & Stewart of London featuring Balfe as the soloist of the piece.[7] It is fortunate that the music was published because it meant that more than a half-century later, the great Irish tenor John McCormack was able to record the charming song, 'Molly Bawn' by Glover. It was during this period that Samuel Glover also wrote three different librettos for Balfe to help him with his new venture. Balfe never used any of them, much to the surprise of Glover, who was an experienced writer.

In creating a National Opera, Balfe had discussions with a number of his contemporaries, such as Barnett, Loder, Benedict, Macfarren, Lover and others, about writing new operas for the venture. However, it seems that the other composers were not too speedy in answering the call, which added to the already emerging problem of a shortfall in cash-flow and the fact that some of the singers had not been paid. Balfe was criticized and the blame for the bad management was clearly on his shoulders. To fill in some of the season Balfe gave his wife a benefit performance of the *Siege of Rochelle* in early May in which he sang the part of Michel.

In his usual forthright manner Balfe, came before the curtain to speak to the audience about the problem and the lack of singers due to defections. He announced that it was the last night of the English Opera House under his management. He apologized for his indiscretions and the fact the he was "such a fool" to take on the venture. He made the commitment that he would never again take on the role of theatre management. The audience expressed their concern by responding sympathetically to him. On 13 May 1841 his tenure as an opera house manager ended. He never again became involved in that end of the business.[8]

His bankruptcy was announced in *The Times* on 10 July, 1841. The judge considering the case declared his assets to be small.[9] He spoke with his friend Giulia Grisi, who was on the verge of departing for Dublin for a two-week opera season starting on 30 August 1841. She promised him that on her return to London, she would set up a benefit concert for him at Her Majesty's Theatre in September and that she would perform. Afterwards she would be departing for Paris for the opening season at Théâtre-Italiens. Grisi arranged the benefit concert for 22 September; in addition to Grisi and others, Balfe and his wife also participated.[10]

His prospects in London were bleak. He had no contracts for operatic compositions. Bunn was out of business for the time being having declared bankruptcy in 1840. Arnold had discontinued his activity. Balfe must also have had some concern about the fact that Queen Victoria had given her name to his venture; however, no mention was made of that fact.

The Balfes were still living at 61 Conduit Street when the new census was accomplished in June 1841.[11] In addition to their three children the composer's younger sister Amelia Balfe was also resident there on the date the census was taken. It also appeared that they were housing at least four servants and possibly a teacher for the children during this period.

The pressure for an income had to be acute. Giulia Grisi had departed for Paris immediately after the benefit concert as planned. Earlier she had also insisted on him coming to Paris to write an opera for her for the Théâtre-Italiens. She had already made an announcement about it to the management of the Paris theatre. One of the Parisian musical periodicals had picked up on the situation and making mention that Balfe, "the Auber of England" would be arriving in Paris to compose an opera for the Théatre-Italiens for Grisi, Tamburini and Mario.[12]

Balfe felt Paris was his best option given that lack of opportunity in London. He and Lina departed for Paris at the end of September. They took their eldest daughter, Louisa "Gigia" with them. She was now almost ten years old. Their other children they left at their home with Balfe's younger sister, Amelia who would take care of them together with the servants and their housekeeper. For Balfe it was the start of a journey that would eventually take him to meet new people who would significantly influence his career and future.

One of Balfe's early biographers states that when Balfe arrived in Paris "one of his first calls was to see Rossini" who was immediately sympathetic and indignant over the way the English had treated their composer.[13] However, this cannot be correct, as Rossini had spent most of 1840 and 1841 in Bologna where he had been quite ill.[14] He was still in Italy when Balfe arrived in Paris at the end of September 1841.

Balfe's key contact in Paris was Giulia Grisi, who was about to open the season at the Théâtre- Italiens in Rossini's *Semiramide* early in October, along with Balfe's other friends, Albertazzi, Tamburini and Morelli.[15] One of his other contacts there was Cherubini; however, the Italian was now into his eighties and he was no longer associated with the Conservatory, so he was really not an option.

Grisi's had all of the arrangements made when Balfe arrived in Paris. She provided him with a libretto which he would use to compose a new opera for her for the Théâtre-Italiens. The name of the work was to be *Elfrida*. It has been suggested that Manfredo Maggione had written the libretto and given it to Grisi before she left London.[16] However, Giovanni Paisiello (1740–1816) had also written an opera with the same title, *Elfrida*, which premiered in Naples in 1792. In any event, Balfe set to work immediately. However, before long, fate was to play a hand again with Balfe's tenuous situation.

Giulia Grisi had married Vicomte Gérard de Melcy in London in 1836, no doubt attracted by the title. Apparently, de Melcy, who was impoverished, knew that on his marriage, legally he would get access to Grisi enormous annual earnings. Grisi was now one of the highest-paid singers in Europe. For Grisi the whole arrangement turned into a disaster when she realized the mistake she had made. She quickly broke from him, but was not able to get a formal divorce as both of them were Catholics.

Two years later Grisi met the young handsome tenor Giovanni Mario (1810–1883) in Paris, at the very beginning of what would become one of the most illustrious operatic careers of the nineteenth century. Grisi and Mario were immediately attracted to each other. They partnered for life. They were never able to get married because she could not get a divorce. She eventually settled financially with de Melcy, who outlived her.

Mario and Grisi had three children. They were two of the most successful singers of all time, primarily singing in London, Paris, Dublin and St Petersburg. They made one trip to New York in 1854, where they opened the season at the new Academy of Music on 14th street. They almost always sang together.[17] Both had outstanding voices. Balfe and his wife were life-long friends with both of them.

Having started his new assignment with his usual enthusiasm and gusto, Balfe was suddenly shocked to be advised by Grisi in a very private conversation with the prima donna that she would not be able to fulfill her commitment to perform the opera before the season was over as she was now pregnant. The season was scheduled to end on 30 March so Balfe in his inimitable style would have had more than enough time to produce the opera. However, he wouldn't have a prima donna to sing it.

Grisi would have been around seven months pregnant by the time the new Balfe opera would have been produced at the end of the season. According to some reports, she was already experiencing some difficult moments on the stage that necessitated her resting, much to the disapproval of the audience who were not aware that she was pregnant. No one would have understood the situation better than Lina Balfe who had gone through the very same experience in Parma before her first child was born a number of years previously.

Perhaps endeavoring to compensate in some small way for the disappointment, Grisi also arranged for both Balfe and his wife to join her, Lablache, Tamburini and Mario in a major concert to be conducted by the composer, Auber and performed at the Royal

Palace in early February. The Balfes were scheduled to sing a duet from Donizetti's 1837, *Pia de'Tolomei,* an opera that neither of them had ever sung.

While the Balfes were devastated over the change in events, they fully understood Grisi's predicament and were left with no alternative but to cancel the work. The opera was never produced. It's possible that some of the music from it may have made its way into *The Bohemian Girl* which Balfe would premiere about two years later. Balfe's current dilemma was what to do next. He suggested to Lina that perhaps she should return to London but Lina decided to stay on to try to help him resolve their difficulty.

He did have another friend in Paris, and he did the most logical thing. He contacted his Limerick born friend, George Alexander Osborne (1806-1893) whom he had first met in his early days in Paris when he was training to be a singer. Osborne was an excellent pianist and teacher, who was a friend of most of the leading musicians in Paris at the time including Chopin and Berlioz, and others. Osborne would have welcomed him.

Osborne introduced Balfe to Pierre Érard (1796–1855), the nephew of the founder, Sebastian Érard (1752–1831), of the famous Érard salon which Liszt, Chopin, Moscheles, Thalberg and even Osborne had used for concerts. Érard became very interested in Balfe and suggested that he give a concert of his music at the salon, which he would organize and promote. It was a remarkable gesture on the part of Érard and says a lot for Osborne's friendship with the salon owner.

Balfe, initially somewhat surprised and hesitant at the suggestion, eventually was persuaded probably by Osborne and Lina that the visibility would be very valuable. Érard, true to his word, set about having the music the Balfes had brought with them reworked to a French text; no doubt Osborne and Balfe worked together on it. They also agreed that music by Rossini would be included. Érard organized the singers and set a date of 16 March 1842 for the 'Grand Concert Balfe' at the salon in Paris.

Osborne performed opera variations on the piano. The singers included Balfe and his wife Lina, the mezzo-soprano Pauline Viardot Garcia (1821–1910), Malibran's younger sister, Willoughby Weiss (1820–1867), a baritone and a pupil of Balfe's who apparently was in Paris at the time, and the soprano Henrietta Nissen

(1819–1875). Viardot sang the famous rondo-finale from Balfe's *The Maid of Artois* which her sister had created in London. Lina Balfe sang from *La sonnambula*, Balfe sang Rossini arias including the 'Largo al Factotum' and he and Weiss sang excerpts from *Falstaff*.[18] Balfe and Osborne also performed as the accompanists.

The concert was a remarkable success with a full house, much to the surprise of the Balfes. Most important, the next day Balfe was paid a visit by the renowned writer and librettist Eugène Scribe (1791–1861), who had been in the audience. Scribe's talents were very much in demand. He had created librettos for Auber, Donizetti, Halévy, Meyerbeer and others. He was the most important librettist in Paris at the time.

Scribe was so favourably impressed with Balfe at the concert that he wanted to meet him personally and to extend an offer to him of collaborating on a new opera for the Opéra Comique. Balfe, initially dumbfounded; immediately accepted. Over the next several weeks Scribe forwarded Balfe, who remained in Paris, the various sections of the libretto as it was developed. Scribe's collaborator on the libretto was André de Leuven, who would work with Balfe again in the future.[19]

The name of the new opera was *Le puits d'amour*. It was to be a three-act opera, appropriately set in London. It was scheduled to premiere early in 1843. There was also some indication that if Balfe had been anything else but Irish-born this opportunity may not have been extended to him. However, on that subject we will never really know the facts.

Meanwhile, Balfe was also active in another area. In April 1842 he composed a new cantata (35 pages), with an Italian text, for seven voices. He appears to have written the text himself. The accompaniment was for pianoforte, violin and violoncello. The violinist for the premiere was Henri Vieuxtemps (1820–1881), a pupil of de Beriot, and the cellist was Alexander Batta (1816–1902). The primary singers who premiered the work were some of the best in Europe. They included Gilbert Duprez, Pauline Viardot Garcia, Henrietta Nissen, Alexander Dupont, Willoughby Weiss, Balfe and his wife Lina. Strangely the music for the cantata was never published but the signed original autograph score is held by the Pierpont Morgan Library in New York. See Appendix IX–17 for full details.

Balfe with his new commission now secure had time to spare. He and the family left Paris and returned to London.[20]   A short time later he went to Dublin, where he had been engaged to sing in a short season of English opera at the Theatre Royal, with the soprano Adelaide Kemble (1814–1879).[21] Kemble was an English-born dramatic soprano from an illustrious theatrical family. She had studied singing with Giuditta Pasta in Italy, where she had made her debut as *Norma* in Venice in 1838. She was a major pro-tagonist in the role of *Norma*. Sometimes she was compared to Giulia Grisi in her dramatic and vocal skills in the title role.

The conductor for the Dublin performances was J. L. Hatton (1809–1886), pianist and composer, who was a good friend of Balfe's from Drury Lane. Balfe performed in *The Marriage of Figaro*, and in *La sonnambula* in the part of Rodolfo. Kemble sang Amina. Kemble also sang several performances of *Norma* with great success. Willoughby Weiss, who also joined the company, was the Oroveso in these performances.

It is interesting to note that early in July, Kemble gave her last performance of *Norma* – Balfe was the conductor. It was Balfe's first venture into conducting since his return from Italy in 1835. It was also a significant moment for him, and perhaps he felt it was best to first try it out in Dublin, where most of the orchestra mem-bers at the Theatre Royal were his friends, rather than in London. The move gave him new possibilities as far as his future income was concerned, in addition to new self-confidence. Balfe and Kemble also gave a morning concert at the Round Room in the Rotunda before returning to London. The whole period went very well for Balfe and it was a relief to be able to come out from under the financial pressures, even if was only for a brief period.

Balfe was now thirty-four years old, with a wife and two daugh-ters aged ten and five years old respectively, and a son who was going on six. Order seemed to be returning to his life, with the future brighter that it had been during the past few years in London. He had composed six operas for London since his arrival, and now he was about to embark on a new venture for the Opéra Comique in Paris. He must have had the distinct feeling that his life was beginning to change and be more focused and that he was possibly on the threshold of success as a composer.

On leaving Dublin, he first returned to London to his family and after a short period went on to Paris to finalize the music and plans for *Le puits d'amour*, which was now scheduled for its premiere on 20 April 1843 at the Opéra Comique.

The prima donna selected for the main role was Anne Thillon (1819–1903), a British soprano who had studied in France and had created a number of operatic roles in the provinces and in Paris. The other members of the cast were also experienced singers. See Appendix IV for more details.

The opera was a complete success. It had twenty-eight performances. The critics hailed Balfe as an Irishman, not British, and more akin to his French brothers. It was truly a remarkable entry for Balfe 'the Auber of England' into the Opéra Comique world of such paragons as Adam, Auber, Boieldieu, Hérold and others, some of whom were no longer on the scene; however, their music, spirit and style lived on. Paris was also a very overcrowded marketplace for a new composer or musician.[22]

It is a great credit to Balfe's intellect and ability to grow and to have learned enough to understand the French musical idiom which was quite different from that of London, or for that matter from his Italian learning experience. No doubt his outgoing personality, his style and fluency in the language all contributed to his success.

The Opéra Comique management was delighted with the new opera, so much so, that they offered Balfe a new contract for another opera for the following year. It was an auspicious start to 1843, a year that had so much more in store for the composer and his family. Returning to London, he found a new opportunity awaited him at the Princess Theatre in Oxford Street, where F. M. Maddox was the manager. He wanted Balfe to provide him with a new opera and in the meantime invited Balfe and his wife to perform in a revival of *The Siege of Rochelle*, at his Princess Theatre.

Maddox was in the business of running a theatre which presented Italian and French operas and performing them with an English libretto. Balfe suggested that they create an English version of *Le puits d'amour* for his theatre. Maddox agreed. On 14 August 1843, Balfe's new opera, *Geraldine; or, the Lover's Well*, premiered with Eugenia Garcia (sister-in-law to Pauline Viardot Garcia) in the title role. The audience liked it and it had a relatively successful run. It finished up in September.

By then, Balfe was pleased to find that his old friend Alfred Bunn, now extricated from bankruptcy, was back in business at Drury Lane.[23] Bunn, remembering that he and Balfe had an agreement to produce another opera for Drury Lane, prepared a libretto for Balfe.

The new libretto was based on an adaptation from a French ballet pantomime called *La gypsy* by Joseph Mazilier and Jules-Henri Vernoy de Saint-Georges (1799–1875), which had been produced in Paris in 1839.[24] The writer Saint-Georges was an associate of Eugène Scribe.

There has been much discussion on when Balfe might have started composing what would become his most successful opera, *The Bohemian Girl*. One of Balfe's early biographers says that Balfe was actually working on a new opera for Bunn as early as the time immediately after *The Maid of Artois* (1836) and by then Balfe had already composed some of the music for *The Bohemian Girl*.[25] However, this does not quite seem logical, as Balfe produced two other operas for Bunn, (*Catherine Grey* and *Joan of Arc*, both in 1837) after *The Maid of Artois* and surely whatever music he had on hand he would have tried to use it for one of those, given the time constraints he was under, particularly for *Joan of Arc*.

Additionally, it was the *Joan of Arc* contract of October 1837 that obligated him to produce a second work for Bunn, and this may well have been satisfied by *Diadeste* in 1838, even though its libretto was prepared by Fitzball and not by Bunn as required by the contract.

There is also some speculation that the composer was already working on a new opera for London when he had the visit by Scribe and the request to compose a work for the Opéra Comique. Others are of the opinion that the music Balfe used for *The Bohemian Girl* clearly had French origins as the music was more suited stylistically for a French text instead of the archaic libretto with the bad word-settings provided by Bunn, which has been heavily criticized.[26]

However, there is one definitive voice on this, which appears to help settle the debate. In preparing a new libretto for a famous Sir Thomas Beecham (1879–1961), new arrangement of the opera at the Royal Opera House, Covent Garden for the *Festival of Britain* in 1951, the experienced writer and musician Dennis Arundel had done extensive study and editing of Balfe's French and Italian

Bohemian Girl scores in preparation for Beecham's new musical arrangement of the opera.

Beecham was incorporating music from these two foreign, differently structured scores into his new arrangement of the English opera. He was also replacing the spoken dialogue with recitatives. It was, in effect, virtually a libretto rewrite, except for some of the more prominent well-known lines. Arundell obviously had to work very closely with Beecham and his assistant, Norman del Mar (1919–1994), on their thoughts on the musical structure, as he worked on his libretto.

In answer to questions posed to him about the opera's origins, Arundell made the following statement about the possibility that Balfe may have started working on *The Bohemian Girl* while in France:

> I think this is true – if for no other reason than that a large portion of the vocal score as we know it, is obviously written so as naturally to fit to French words. One has only to look at the air, 'I dreamt that I dwelt' in the French version [of the score] to see how perfectively the melody expresses the rise and fall of the words and how clumsily the English [Bunn's text] keeps pace with it; Bunn was known in his day as a sort of hack poet and most of his libretto is in poor English, even from the uncritical Victorian point of view. It would be strange, to say the least, if this crude writing inspired Balfe to some of his finest work, which happens to fit the French version like a glove.[27]

In arranging a lavish revival of the opera in 1951, Sir Thomas Beecham and his assistant, Norman del Mar, created his new arrangement of the opera with the addition of music from Balfe's French and Italian scores. This augmented the opera considerably, making it more than three hours, while maintaining the three acts format of the original.[28]

The opera was broadcast by the BBC Third Programme on the evening of 18 August 1951, after 'cliff-hanger' negotiations between Beecham and the BBC on what he should be paid for the broadcast. The BBC had initially offered Beecham twenty guineas (twenty-one pounds), which he indignantly rejected, publicly. The BBC eventually agreed to seventy-five pounds the night before the broadcast was scheduled, which Beecham accepted, so the broadcast went on.

Back at Drury Lane, Bunn, anxious to get active again in the business of presenting English Opera, immediately appointed Julius Benedict as his musical director. A revival of Balfe's popular work *The Siège of Rochelle* opened Bunn's new season. *The Bohemian Girl* followed on 27 November 1843. For Balfe it was an enormously eventful evening. Balfe initially conducted several of the early performances, before handing the baton over to Benedict. Clearly Balfe was now moving himself into the role of a conductor in addition to that of composer.

The opera was a huge success, eventually running for more than one-hundred nights. The main numbers, the soprano aria, 'I dreamt I dwelt in marble halls' was loudly applauded, as was the tenor aria, 'When other lips [Then you'll remember me]'. Both were encored. The *Times* critic said of the opera after the final curtain:

> The delight which the audience has exhibited from time to time during the performances now broke out with increased force. They called for the actors [singers], and they called for Balfe, whom they had already greeted when he had first entered the   orchestra to conduct. The opera has every appearance of being a decided 'hit,' for the house was full, and the applause really seemed honest. The success was certainly merited ...

The son of William Harrison (1813–1868), the tenor who created the role of Thaddeus in the opera, in his memoirs states that he recollected, even though he was only a boy that first night and that when his father had sung 'Then you'll remember me [When other lips]'

> ... there was 'a prodigious uproar occasioned by his singing.' The majority of the audience insisted on hearing the song a second time. To this there were numerous opponents, and the noise made by the rival factions was deafening. Balfe laid down the baton and folded his arms; ... some minutes elapsed, after which the dissentients gave way, and the song, destined to become a national melody, was sung again.[29]

Within a year the sheet music of the main numbers from *The*

Bohemian Girl were racking up incredible sales. The tenor song was reported to have sold over 80,000 copies alone.

For details of the premiere cast and other information see Appendix III. Also Tyldesley in his book on Balfe provides good background information on the musical construction of the opera and the various scores.[30]

The Balfes, in a joyous mood, took the night of Thursday 7 December 1843 as a benefit night. After the opera they gave a gave a short concert which included Balfe and his wife singing 'Non Fuggir', a duet from Donizetti's *Il Campanello*, something they had previously sung. This was followed by Balfe singing the cantata 'I Postiglione' which he had composed for Lablache some year's earlier. Lina then sang a number very suitable for the occasion, appropriately called 'La Speranza' by her husband, and they completed the evening with a duet from Donizetti's *L'elisir d'Amore*. Benedict and Madame Dulcken also played variations from the opera *Norma*.[31] A few days later, the Balfes left for Paris, where they were to get started on his new work for the Opéra Comique for 1844.

The significance of the sheet music sales was indicative of emerging cultural changes in Victorian Britain. It was brought on by the advent of industrial growth, the railway networks and steam. All of these forces, along with the expansion of the Queen's Empire, would eventually create large somewhat affluent middle classes in cities such as Birmingham, Manchester, Liverpool and many other places throughout Britain.

In addition, an explosion in the growth of piano makers in London and the provinces occurred by mid-century along with the distribution of upright pianos. This greatly helped to contribute to an increased demand for sheet music. Balfe was very conscious of the opportunity and as a result, he spent endless hours reworking his operatic ballads in order to ensure they became 'hits' because of the potential sheet music sales.[32] His desire to 'get it right' the first time around, was a perennial driving force for him, no doubt primarily economically based.

For Balfe, *The Bohemian Girl* success would continue many years into the future. His new opera truly was the pioneering musical work by which future success would be measured at Drury Lane and Broadway for over a century.

Over the next ten to fifteen years virtually every major city in

Europe, America and Australia had heard it. Dublin heard it first in 1844. This was followed by the east coast cities of America. New York heard it in 1844. Sydney, Australia heard it in 1846.[33] It was an incredible success story; however, financially Balfe didn't always reap the benefits of its broad circulation, as copyright laws were not in effect in many countries during those decades. The only other opera in the nineteenth century which came close to it in terms of broad-based success was Verdi's 1844 opera *Ernani*, which had a similar acceptance level around the world.

Because of *The Bohemian Girl*, it wasn't long before Balfe was setting off on an arduous journey that would take him to cities such as Vienna, Trieste, Bologna and Berlin to personally conduct the opera. His name spread far and wide – his music always ahead of him in terms of his travels. Some of his letters talk fondly about 'the girl' and her success, which is how he referred to what would become his all time most successful work.

As mentioned earlier, the opera took on a life of its own even into the twentieth century where its music became the background for a silent movie of the same name in London in 1922, and later it was adapted for a Broadway show. Even, later still, Hollywood used it for the comedy team of Laurel and Hardy in the 1930s and the first Lassie movie in 1943 used some of the music. See Appendix XI for details of recordings of the opera and excerpts.

NOTES

1. See *A History of English Opera* by Eric W. White, p. 276.
2. *The Times*, 10 March 1841.
3. Ibid.
4. Copy libretto in the possession of the author.
5. *Life of Glover* by Bayle Bernard, p. 125.
6. See *Times* review, 21 April 1841.
7. Sheet music of the song, "Molly Bawn" featuring Balfe as the soloist in the possession of the author.
8. *A History of English Opera* by Eric W. White, p. 277.
9. *Times* 20 August, p.142.
10. *The Times*, 22 September 1841.
11. Copy of Balfe household at 61 Conduit Street, London as shown in the British census of 1841, which took place in June of that year.
12. According to Eric W. White in his book, *A History of English Opera*, p. 277, a notice to this effect appeared in *La France Musicale* towards the end of August 1841; no doubt Giulia Grisi had already set the wheels in motion for her friend to come to France.
13. Barrett in his biography of Balfe makes this statement on p.137. It was obviously fabricated. Eric W. White also references this fact in his book *A History of English Opera*, p. 278, attributing his source to Barrett.
14. See Herbert Weinstock's *Rossini*, pp. 206–214, describing Rossini's life and illness in

Bologna during 1840–1841 and a referenced letter written by Rossini from Bologna in September 1841.

15. Article by Thomas G. Kaufman "Giulia Grisi; A Re-evaluation" in the *Donizetti Society Journal*, No. 4, pp. 208–209.
16. See Eric White, *A History of English Opera*, p. 278.
17. For a detailed account of the lives of these two great singers see the excellent biography *Mario and Grisi*, by Elizabeth Forbes.
18. See *Second Empire Opera, The Théâtre Lyric Paris*, by T. J. Walsh, p. 262.
19. Both Eric White in *A History of English Opera*, p. 278, and Tyldesley in his Balfe book, p. 88, state incorrectly that Scribe's collaborator was Vernoy de Saint-Georges on this occasion. The vocal score in the possession of this author also verifies the fact that it was de Leuven who prepared the libretto. White and Tyldesley probably took their information from Kenny's anecdotal biography of Balfe which is also incorrect.
20. There is a reference in Eric White's book that Balfe actually went to Norwich on his return to Britain. However, this seems to be an error, as Balfe was in Dublin by mid-May of 1842 singing in opera.
21. *Annals of the Theatre Royal Dublin*, by R. M. Levey, p. 33.
22. See *The Keys to French Opera in the Nineteenth Century* by Hervé Lacombe.
23. See *Theatre Royal Drury Lane* by W. McQueen Pope, p. 279.
24. *The New Grove Dictionary of Opera*, Vol 1, p. 521.
25. See Kenny biography of Balfe, p. 183. His information is based on second-hand facts culled from the entry in the *Dictionary of Universal Biography* by George Macfarren.
26. See T. J. Walsh's book, *Second Empire Opera: The Théâtre Lyrique, Paris 1851–1870*, pp. 262–265 for another discussion on this subject.
27. See document 'The Bohemian Girl' – Dennis Arundell on his new version [of the libretto], Royal Opera House Archives, Covent Garden, London.
28. There is no complete score of the Sir Thomas Beecham arrangement among his papers at the University of Sheffield in England. The Beecham production was quite lavish and funded by Beecham himself. It was broadcast on the evening of 18 August 1851 by the BBC Third Programme in London. Interestingly, the three principals for the broadcast were Americans, the very young Roberta Peters, on the brink of a long and wonderful career, the London-based baritone, Jess Walters from Brooklyn, New York and the tenor Anthony Marlow, who was from Detroit. Next to Beecham, Roberta Peters was considered the star of the performances. After the English premiere of the opera in London in November 1843, Balfe created at least five other versions of the opera; one for Vienna in 1846 with a German libretto by J. Kupelwieser, a version for Trieste in 1854 with an Italian libretto by Riccardo Paderini, another for Rouen, in 1862 to a French libretto by Saint-Georges and a revised and extended French version also by Saint-Georges for Paris in 1869, which seems to have been translated into a new Italian version by Giuseppe Zaffira, also in 1869. See Appendices II-4, IV-4 and 5 and V-3 for more details of the foreign language versions of the score.
29. *Stray Records*, by Clifford Harrison, Vol. 1, p. 103.
30. *Michael William Balfe: His Life and His English Operas*, by William Tyldesley, pp. 88–115.
31. Details taken from an original Drury Lane playbill for the night of 7 December 1843 in the possession of the author.
32. *Stray Records*, by Clifford Harrison, pp. 104–105.
33. For a list of the many cities in which the opera was performed seem Loewenberg, *Annals of Opera*, year of 1843.

CHAPTER SEVEN

Paris (The Opéra), London and new operas 1844–1846

The news of Balfe's new London opera, *The Bohemian Girl* had already reached Parisian music circles by the time the composer and his family reached the city. With his earlier success in Paris and now this new London excitement Balfe was in demand. He immediately set to work on the new opera for the Opéra Comique.

Scribe was not available as he was preparing new librettos for Auber, Adam and others, so Balfe worked with two other experienced librettists associated with the Opéra Comique, Léon Brunswick (aka Léon Lévy) and André de Leuven. The latter had worked with Balfe on his previous opera for Paris.

While Balfe was in Paris the success of *The Bohemian Girl* roared on in London. The opera by now almost had a cult following. The London street barrel-organ players were rolling out the best of tunes from *The Bohemian Girl*. Sheet music from the opera was in strong demand everywhere. This momentum would almost continue until the end of the century and, to some degree, beyond.

On 24 June 1844, the London cast took time out to bring *The Bohemian Girl* to Dublin, where it was performed at the Theatre Royal with equal applause and acclaim for almost two weeks. Meanwhile, Balfe was seeing his personal economics beginning to take a strong upward turn. He had just received five hundred pounds from his music publishers for the rights to publish the score.

Back in Paris, the new comic opera *Les quatre fils Aymon* was scheduled for July. There were casting problems, as the prima donna Anne Thillon, who was originally intended for the principal role of Hermine, became unavailable due to the fact that she had received a contract to make he debut in London at the Princess

Theatre, in an English translations of an Auber opera arranged by Maddox. In time the casting difficulties were sorted out and the premiere of Balfe's new opera was set for Monday 15 July 1844. The libretto for the opera was based on an early French fable from around the time of Charlemagne which was a popular story at the time, both in France and Germany. The opera was quite successful for the Opéra Comique, with sixteen performances which were given before the season close.

However, when compared to the twenty-eight performances of the previous Balfe opera it possibly was somewhat disappointing for the composer but could probably be attributed to a timing issue, as the premiere was late in the season. Another factor could have been the casting, as Thillon was a great favourite in Paris at the time and her inability to perform may have impacted the run. Mlle. Darcier (1818–1870), who did sing the lead soprano role, had made her debut at the Opéra Comique four years earlier. She was experienced and had created operas for leading composers in France. The tenor Chollet, who took the part of 'Oliver', was also a well established performer in the French capital.

The important French composer and writer Hector Berlioz (1803–1869), who was a close friend of George Alexander Osborne and who knew Balfe through Osborne, was then doing reviews for one of the musical periodicals in Paris. He made the following amusing comments in reviewing *Les quatre fils Aymon*:

> There are people who are amazed that an Englishman could have written this pretty music, but first of all Balfe is not English, he is a son of Ireland, the green Erin, the sweet country of the harp as Tom Moore calls it. The Irish are all improvisers; they improvise whether it be their verse, their prose, their music or their miming. The only thing they do not improvise, is revolutions ... besides why should not an Englishman make good music? There are plenty of Italians, French and Germans who make bad music ... M. Balfe's music, it is easy to see is improvised à l'Irlandaise; full of vivacity and verve ... it is expressive and dramatic and only needs occasionally a little more originality.[1]

Berlioz was considered to be a powerful outspoken critic. He was married to an actress, Henriette Smithson (1809–1854), from

County Clare in Ireland. He also had other Irish connections, as George Osborne was a very close friend, so he probably felt somewhat partial to the Irish; in particular to his fellow musician Balfe, with his charm and likeable personality.

Word of Balfe's Paris and London successes had already reached Vienna. His latest French opera, *Les quatre fils Aymon*, had a certain appeal for the German-speaking world given its story. The manager of the theatre in the Josefstadt, a secondary theatre in Vienna, Franz Pokorny obtained a copy of the score probably from Balfe in Paris and had it translated into German with the title of, *Die vier Haimonskinder*.[2] It received its first performance in Vienna in November 1844.[3]

The Balfes returned to London from Paris in the early autumn. The composer would have two obligations on his arrival in London, one of which he was totally unaware of.

Almost immediately on Balfe's arrival in London, the manager of the Princess Theatre contacted him with a contract for an English version of *Les quatre fils Aymon*. They quickly reached an agreement as Maddox's needs were immediate. Maddox arranged for the translation and the opera premiered on 20 November 1844. The cast included singers who had performed in Balfe's opera *Geraldine* at the Princess Theatre the year before. The son of Balfe's old friend and mentor from his early days in Dublin and London, Charles Horn, played one of the Aymon brothers. Balfe conducted the performances.

The *Times* critic was quite favourable about the entire opera, particularly mentioning the scenery and the quality of the backdrops. He felt that in general the two French librettists had done a good job with the story even if they distorted the fable somewhat in the process. The soprano Helen Condell was making her debut. After a nervous start she gradually gained confidence and gave a strong powerful performance. While the rest of the cast was quite adequate, and performed well, Charles Horn junior was singled out for his acting and professionalism in his role of 'Allurd' one of the brother.[4]

The *Times* critics went on to say: "The opera was as successful as could be. Everybody was called for, including Mr Balfe, who had been warmly greeted as he entered the orchestra; Miss Condell received a bouquet or two."[5]

Once again we see Balfe broadening his skills in his arena, and shifting away from singing to conducting. It was a move that would create greater stability for him economically, apart from being a better use of his skills. Lina must have been pleased to see this. As time progressed he continued to conduct more and sing less. Within two years he would have shifted completely to the role of conductor and composer. Balfe was now thirty-six years old and moving towards his peak productive years.

Earlier in the year Balfe had committed to Bunn for a new opera for Drury Lane for the winter season. He had been working on a libretto in Paris based upon a story by Vernoy de Saint-Georges called, *La Reine de Chypre*. He finalized the music on his return to London and Bunn scheduled the new work, now called *The Daughter of St Mark*, at Drury Lane for 27 November 1844. For this opera, he reverted to the Italian model with recitatives, no doubt a reflection of his most recent continental sojourn and the librettists he was working with in Paris, such as Sainte-Georges, de Leuven, etc. At heart, Balfe probably preferred the Italian recitative style over the spoken dialogue given his early training and despite the risks, wanted to try out that structure every so often to see if the attitude of audiences was changing. The opera was quite successful. It has some stirring music including a rousing tenor baritone duet, almost in the early Verdi style.

Our industrious composer now had two new operas being performed in London, in addition to *The Bohemian Girl*, which was still a part of Bunn's season at Drury Lane. Balfe had also just completed a new opera in Paris and a new German version of this work was now premiering in Vienna! He also had two new operas being talked about in the musical press.

The Bohemian Girl had now also reached New York. On 25 November 1844, the English opera troupe the Seguins performed the American premiere of the opera at the Park Theatre in downtown New York.[6] The opera was an immediate 'hit'. The score was published locally by Atwill of 201 Broadway. It's interesting that the music published by Atwill refers to the opera as 'Balfe's Celebrated Opera' on the cover sheets, not as by 'Michael W. Balfe', as if the name 'Balfe' was now a household word and recognized in New York and America.[7]

It wasn't only the music that had such appeal; it was also the story, where 'good triumphs over evil', which had special emotional qualities for New World residents. Over the next several years, the Seguins went up and down the east coast of America, to Boston, Philadelphia, Washington, Baltimore, Charleston, Savannah and lots of other places performing English opera and Balfe's music in *The Bohemian Girl* always stood out as one of their best attractions.[8]

Balfe was closing out one of his best years ever, with the one-hundredth performance of *The Bohemian Girl* taking place in December 1844. The event was celebrated with a special presentation of a silver tea set to Balfe on the stage at Drury Lane.

Early in January 1845, a short feature appeared in one of London's leading musical periodicals to the effect that:

> Another New Opera by Balfe – This mercurial composer has returned to Paris, and is now busily engaged in the composition of another new opera, the libretto of which has been written by M. S. George [Saint-Georges], the author of *La Reine de Chypre*, and forwarded to Mr. Bunn, for translation into English. The principal part is intended for Madame Thillon, whose engagement at Drury Lane commences in May next. It is also said that an Italian opera, by Balfe, called *Elfrida,* will be brought out at Her Majesty's Theatre, in May next.[9]

Balfe's opera *Elfrida,* written for Grisi in 1842, had never been performed as planned. However, the opera score still appeared to be intact with the potential for being performed. This would suggest that Balfe had never used the music from *Elfrida* for any of his more recent compositions, including *The Bohemian Girl*; otherwise there would hardly have been talk of it being considered for the next season at the Italian Opera. As it turned out, *Elfrida* by Balfe was never mounted at the Italian Opera for whatever reason, or anywhere else.

Back on the continent, the strong appeal of his *Die vier Haimonskinder* in Vienna, where it ran for several performances with Vienna's own soprano, Jetty Treffz (1826-1878), created a demand in other German-speaking cities.[10] The first to mount it was the city of Pest (Budapest) where a performance was given on 10 March 1845, at the German theatre.[11] Several other cities, including Leipzig and Stuttgart, followed shortly afterwards. It opened again in Vienna, this time at the prestigious Theater an der Wien later in the year, with Jetty Treffz again appearing in the lead soprano role. The Josefstadt Theatre also restaged the opera at the same time. Both theatres ran the opera through the end of the year.

The libretto which Bunn received from de St Georges was for a new Balfe opera called, *The Enchantress*, with the virtuoso soprano Anne Thillon scheduled in the title role. It had its premiere on 14 May 1845. Some of the critics complained about the length of the work, which ran for four hours! Despite its length, it was very well received by the audience. The *Times* critic reported as follows:

> The house was crowded to suffocation, and as Balfe entered the orchestra there was the usual amount of cheering on the part of the audience. The Parisian dramatist, M. de St Georges, wrote the libretto on purpose for this theatre, and came over here to superintend its production. The whole conception and structure of the piece is completely French [the opera had dialog not recitatives]...[12]

The critic further stated:

> Mr Balfe in adapting his music to a work of this description, has exerted himself most creditably, as he has caught much of the dramatic spirit of the *genre*, and has introduced some of his happiest melodies ... The audience at the conclusion raised a hearty shout for Madame Thillon, then for Balfe, then for the remaining vocalists...

Balfe's energy and incredible output and the rate at which he was composing must have had him active twelve to fourteen hours daily. He was certainly unique among British composers of the period in this respect. While Loder, Barnett and other Balfe contemporaries continued to compose various works no other British composer had the same vitality at home or abroad. Balfe was in the mould of Rossini and Donizetti when it came to opera output.

However, in a short time Balfe's first real competitor, fellow countryman William Vincent Wallace (1812–1865), would arrive at Drury Lane, where he had been introduced by Edward Fitzball to Bunn. Fitzball, impressed with Wallace's music skills, had given him a libretto of *Maritana* for review. With Balfe active in Paris and elsewhere Bunn was eager to have a new opera to premiere so he gave Wallace a contract and *Maritana* was first performed at Drury Lane on 15 November 1845. It had immediate success. Some of the cast had sung in the premiere of *The Bohemian Girl.*

The following year *Maritana* was also heard in Dublin and New York and eventually it made it to Vienna a number of years later where Wallace supervised its production. The opera became the first true competitive work that could be compared to *The Bohemian Girl* in terms of popularity throughout the nineteenth century.

The early 1840s now saw Balfe, with his astute sense of the marketplace, also starting to focus on songs. He had a remarkable ability to understand and grasp the sentiment of his times in much the same way that Charles Dickens (1812–1870), did in writing. Perhaps he and Dickens had discussed ideas?

Balfe in a way was the Charles Dickens of Victorian music. Dickens was also one of his good friends. Dickens and Balfe's paths paralleled each other in many respects. They were born around the same time. They had children of a similar age, although Dickens had more than Balfe. Careerwise, both came to the fore around the same time. They mixed in the same circles. Each had spent time in Italy, albeit at different times. Both were London-based, so it was quite logical that they came to know each other well.[13] The fame of both of them also spread to America around the same time. While Dickens visited America, Balfe never did cross the Atlantic, for reasons which will be discussed later.

By the mid-1840s Balfe was composing songs at the rate of almost one or two a month in addition to his new operas. Generally he was paid around fifteen to twenty pounds for each song, while he normally received five guineas for each nightly performance of an opera by Bunn. His earnings were growing rapidly. What he may have been paid on the continent for an opera is unknown.

The focus of his songs was the new Victorian middle class, who were the owners of the mills in the Midlands, brewers, factory owners, railway contractors, ship builders, coal and corn merchants and various other occupations that combined to make up this new social class. The two most common measurements for the new middle-class was income and occupation. Their income had to be steady and progressive and be received generally from a non-manual job in business or possibly a profession.[14]

As their wealth grew, they tended to want to emulate the landed gentry by endeavouring to adopt certain social styles and graces. Generally, they were very socially conscious particularly as it related to the working class who engaged in manual labor. A consistent annual income of around five hundred pounds is what some writers felt was required in order to maintain a household, servants and a horse and carriage for a Victorian middle-class family.[15]

As the industrial revolution took hold in Britain there was great growth in the number of individuals who now had the money to be able to occupy new larger homes, travel in style on the new railways, go to the theatre and purchase an upright piano (which cost twenty pounds) and have their wives and daughters taught music.

When at home in Britain, Balfe never lost focus of this new emerging phenomena and its potential for new music sales. Lina in the process kept track of what was selling in terms of ballads from his operas or just songs. It wasn't too long before Balfe started to make trips out of London given the convenience of the railways to places such as Birmingham, Liverpool and Manchester to conduct concerts there.

Balfe was also stretching himself between London and Paris. He arrived in the continental city with Lina and probably the family early in November 1845. It was fortuitous, as the music of the new rising young Italian composer Giuseppe Verdi made its first entry into Paris in November that year. Verdi's first great La Scala success of 1842, *Nabucco*, now reached Paris and had its local premiere at the Théâtre-Italiens. This was the first performance of a Verdi opera in Paris. It is certain that the Balfes would have attended its local premiere. Apart from their interest in the new Italian composer's music, their friend from the early days in Italy, the great baritone Giorgio Ronconi, who had created the role at La Scala, was again singing the title role in Paris.[16]

In London, the musical press, ever alert to the news value of Balfe's activities, announced that the British composer was working on two new operas in Paris, one, with Scribe as his librettist, called *Le jour de Noël*. However, as it was to turn out, this work was never produced for some reason or other. The second opera was *L'etoile de Seville,* with a libretto by Hippolyte Lucas, who was associated with the Paris Opéra and who had previously worked on Donizetti translations for Paris. Balfe's new opera was scheduled to be performed at the most prestigious venue in Paris, the Académie Royale de Musique (the Paris Opéra) in December 1845.

It was quite an honour for Balfe as an 'outsider'" to have been invited to compose a new work for the prestigious Paris Opéra. No other British composer had ever been invited to submit a new work for the Académie Royale .

Some of the musical community in Paris was somewhat surprised, or possibly resentful at Balfe's new visibility. One in particular the pianist Frédéric Chopin (1810–1849) had some critical comments to make about Balfe in a series of letters he wrote to his family in Warsaw in December 1845.[17]

> Today see the first performance at the Grand Opéra of Balfe's new opera. He   wrote *Les quatre fils Aymon* (I think we saw it together at the Opéra Comique). Today's work is called *L'Etoile de Séville?* the story of Le Cid, not Corneille's, but following Calderon's version. The libretto is by Mr. Hippolyte Lucas (a mediocre writer, a journalist). Little is expected of it. Balfe is an Englishman who has been in Italy and is now passing through France.

He then continues...

> Since I wrote you the above lines I have been to see Balfe's opera: completely disappointing. The singing, of course, is as good as can be, so much so that I regretted to see such resources wasted, while Meyerbeer (who sat quietly in his box and followed the libretto), has two operas completely ready for performances, *Le Prophete* and *L'Africane*. Both are five acts, but he refuses to let the Opéra have them unless he gets fresh singers. However Madame Stolz (*sic*) who has influence over the director, will not allow anyone better than herself to have a part ... the scenery in Balfe's opera is   handsome and the costumes very lavish.

The comments are interesting for various reasons. First of course the comments are in a private letter to his family with the assumption that they would not necessarily ever appear in public. Chopin seems to be playing off the fact that 'no Englishman can compose', which was a common view on the part of continentals in the early nineteenth century. Berlioz had made a similar comment, somewhat in jest, when reviewing an earlier Balfe opera.

However, Chopin would have met Balfe through Osborne as Chopin and Osborne were close friends and had even given concerts together. Chopin surely would have known of Balfe's successes and his emerging position as a composer not only in Britain but also in Vienna. Most of the musical periodicals of the time in Paris had profiled Balfe and talked about his new opera and his background. So it seems strange that Chopin would have wanted to 'write-off' Balfe in such a cursory manner. Additionally, Chopin was an ailing man with only a few years to live and was known to be irritable and cranky, so Balfe's success may have irked him.

Chopin and Meyerbeer weren't the only composers in the audience that night. Auber, Adam, Halévy and others were also in attendance. We don't know what their thoughts were. It is fairly safe to assume that most of the elite came out to see the British composer's new work, and to witness its success ... or failure.

Balfe's opera, which premiered on 17 December 1845, had an exceptional cast. Rosine Stoltz, who had the title role, was thirty years old at the time had created operas for Donizetti, Auber, Halévy and Berlioz. Paul Barroilhet was in his thirties and he too had created roles for Donizetti, Adam and others. The young Italian tenor Italo Gardoni (1821–1882) was twenty-four years old but had been singing leading roles for five years and would go on to a very successful long international career. Maria Nau (1818–1891) was New York born, and had made her Paris debut in 1836 and already had created a role in a Meyerbeer opera. The sets were lavish along with the costumes, as some of the contemporary colored illustrations of Gardoni, Nau and Barroilhet demonstrate.[18]

The opera, which ran for fifteen nights, was well received by the critics. Apparently, it was intended to continue the run but somehow Rosine Stoltz, in a capricious moment for which she was noted, decided to leave the cast. The opera has never been performed again, although, excerpts from it, have been sung in various places. The London critics picked up on their composer and his activities in Paris, saying about his new opera 'its reception was highly flattering to the composer … at the conclusion the names of Mr. Balfe and M. Lucas were cited amidst tumultuous plaudits.' [19] See Appendix IV-3 for more details about the premiere of the opera and the location of librettos and the availability of scores.

While in Paris during these months, the Balfes went to see the Italian composer Gaetano Donizetti, who was in seclusion at Ivy. The forty-eight-year-old Donizetti was dying from an incurable disease that had affected his brain. When Balfe and his wife were in Milan in the 1830s, it's possible that they had met Donizetti, particularly during the period when Anna Bolena had premiered there. However, there is no known record of any meeting between them in Italy during that period.

In a document written by one of Balfe's granddaughters she records a discussion with Lina Balfe in which Balfe's wife talked about the time she and her husband visited the dying Donizetti in Paris and what transpired. Lina Balfe spoke to her granddaughter as follows: 'He [Donizetti] was out of his mind, and how he wept and repeated "Povero Bellini, povero Bellini" under the impression that it was his friend and fellow Composer who was thus afflicted.' [20]

The visit left a lasting impression on Lina Balfe and her husband. Donizetti died three years later in 1848.

While still in Paris, Balfe had a visit from a stranger from London. He was approached by the stranger as he was discussing his new opera with the tenor Gardoni and the baritone Barroilhet. It turned out that the stranger was a representative of Benjamin Lumley from Her Majesty's Theatre in London. Lumley had become manager of the Italian Opera at Her Majesty's Theatre on the death of the existing manager, Laporte, early in 1842. Lumley now wanted to talk with Balfe about a new proposition for the upcoming season at the Italian Opera at Her Majesty's Theatre in 1846. Balfe was intrigued; not knowing whether he was going to be asked to compose an opera or perform some other function.

The current musical director at Her Majesty's was Michael Costa (1808–1884), who had been in that position for many years, and as far as Balfe knew he still held that position.[21] However Balfe was unaware of what was going on in the local press. During November one of London leading musical periodicals had the following to say: 'Although nothing has, as yet been finally settled in regard to the conductorship of the   Philharmonic concerts next season, we believe that we may venture to state, that Signor Costa will wield the baton, and no mistake.'[22] Balfe's absorption in his work in Paris had left him unaware that Costa was being offered a new job as director of the Philharmonic Society orchestra in London for the 1846 season, much to Lumley's concern and irritation.

Balfe was reluctant to leave Paris with his new opera in full swing. Additionally, Lumley's representative was reluctant to reveal any of the details of the proposal, whether or not he actually knew them. However, Balfe knew Lumley, and considered him to be a smart astute 'no nonsense' businessman. Lumley's philosophy as far as management was concerned was very focused, and he believed that, 'the manager must be sole master of his theatre, ostensibly and positively'.[23]

Lumley had had financially successful seasons since he took over the management in 1842. He also felt confident about the future. As a result, in 1845 he raised the money through various channels and purchased the ownership of Her Majesty's Theatre, for one hundred and five thousand pounds.[24] The theatre had been administered by the Courts for more than fifty years because of debt problems and receivership. Logically Balfe knew that if Lumley wanted him to quickly come to London there had to be a good reason which he was not prepared to reveal except in person. Balfe reasoned that it might be best to pay Lumley a visit and so he departed for London in January 1846, leaving Lina and the family in Paris.

By the time Balfe arrived in London the row between Lumley and Costa was public knowledge. In his frustration with Costa, Lumley apparently had gone public with a letter to the newspapers. Costa responded in kind, and there was a further exchange publicly between the two. Their differences were obviously too great at that point in time for any reconciliation, so Costa resigned.[25]

Balfe's meeting with Lumley went well and he signed a one-year contract to become musical director and conductor at the Italian Opera at Her Majesty's Theatre on 20 January 1846.[26] He afterwards went to Drury Lane, where a new English opera, *Don Quixote*, by one of Balfe's contemporaries, George Macfarren (1813-1887), was being performed.

While Costa was initially contracted to conduct the Philharmonic Society concerts, rumours now began to circulate that a new Italian Opera Company was being organized at the Covent Garden Theatre, possibly with Costa as musical director. For over one hundred years, Her Majesty's Theatre and its previous designation The King's Theatre had exclusive rights to operate as the Italian Opera in London by law under the Licensing Act. As a result, it had had no serious competition since its inauguration in the eighteenth century. Now, all of that had changed with the repeal of the Licensing Act in 1843, and anyone with the right backing basically could become the owners of an Italian Opera Company and Theatre in London.[27] Within a year, this change would have a drastic impact on Lumley's operation for a variety of reasons.

Meanwhile, his agreement with Balfe gave the musician the control of artistic matters, the orchestra and singers. The season of 1846 proceeded along normal lines except that Balfe was now the conductor. Balfe personally knew many members of the orchestra, which consisted of over seventy experienced players. Under his contract with Lumley, Balfe was not allowed to compose any operas for Her Majesty's Theatre. This was a clause that Lumley had also previously imposed on Costa which the Italian had objected to during their differences. However, Balfe could continue to compose for other theatres and in fact he would continue to do so.

The season at Her Majesty's normally ran from around March; with a break during Easter week it continued into August, after which Balfe was free to engage in other affairs at other opera houses once the season was over. Balfe returned to London from Paris with his family almost immediately to get started with rehearsals at Her Majesty's in February. His new arrangement with Lumley must have pleased Lina because it meant he had a regular salary along with the fact that he would be based in London for most of the year. Their children were now growing up. Louisa 'Gigia' was almost fourteen years old, Michael junior was eight and Victoire was seven.

The planned season opening at Her Majesty's was on 3 March 1846 with the local premiere of Verdi's *Nabucco*. In London the opera was given the title of 'Nino [Rè D'Assyria]' because of the relationship of the Italian title to biblical history and the sensitivity to British Victorian religious morals.[28] A short time later he also gave the local premiere of another Verdi opera, *I Lombardi*. In total during the season Balfe prepared and conducted fifteen different operas, each of which was performed several times. Some of the singers were Balfe's long-time friends, Giulia Grisi, her partner the tenor Mario and Luigi Lablache. See Appendix VIII, year 1846, for full details and casts and performances.

Some of the critics (*Morning Chronicle*) apparently 'jumped the gun' and reported that 'so violent was the resentment about the Costa resignation that one of the oldest and most esteemed members of the band [orchestra], Mr Lindley, the cellist was reported to have thrown up his engagement.' However, others elected to wait until the first full rehearsal to report about Lindley's action, which gave quite a different impression:

> the superb veteran, Mr Lindley was observed among the foremost in his place and among the foremost to shake the new conductors warmly by the hand.

This was followed with a report that said:

> Mr. Balfe made his appearance, and was received with three spontaneous, enthusiastic, and unanimous cheers, which at once set at rest all anxiety on the matter.[29]

At the end of the premiere of *Nabucco* it was reported that:

> So well pleased was the audience that at the end of the opera Mr. Lumley was loudly called for from all parts of the house. Afterwards the same honor was conferred on Mr. Balfe, who was brought forward by Mr. Lumley, and received, with flattering demonstrations of approval.[30]

However, it wasn't all plain sailing for Balfe as one of the newspaper's (*Morning Chronicle*) critics continued to point fingers at the opera's loss of Costa as its director. The following appeared in the leading musical periodical in early May 1846 in defence of Balfe:

> It is absurd and unfair to attack Mr Balfe because the orchestra did not go so well under his direction, as under that of his talented predecessor [Costa]. How can it be expected? Signor Costa with the labour and experience of many years, brought

the orchestra to a condition of faultlessness that was universally acknowledged ... The orchestra at Her Majesty's Theatre is
new to Mr Balfe – who, besides though an excellent musician
and a highly popular composer, has not and cannot be expected
to have as much acquaintance with the art of conducting as one
[Costa], who has for years made it his principal and assiduous
study. We say with confidence that Mr. Balfe has supported his
novel position most effectively and we have little doubt that the
same experience would raise him to the same eminence as that
acquired by his predecessor. It must also be kept in mind that Mr
Balfe is not a Mr Nobody. Mr Balfe – and to this distinction
even the Morning Chronicle will not lay claim for Signor Costa
– is a composer of European fame. His school may not be one
of our predilections, but we cannot deny his popularity. The
orchestra is in no way humbled by the authority of its new
director, who is certainly a person of twice the eminence of his
predecessor ... The attacks of the Morning Chronicle are readily explained. The critic is an intimate friend of Signor Costa,
an implacable enemy of Mr Lumley.[31]

During all of this public exchange, Balfe and Costa remained close
friends, as they always did throughout their respective lives, much
to the credit of the two men.

By the time the season had ended in August, Lumley in appreciation of Balfe's efforts, extended his contract for another two
years.[32] It was also announced that Balfe would be departing immediately for Vienna for a period of two months, after which he
would return to London in time to introduce a new opera at Drury
Lane. The new opera, *The Bondman*, premiered at Drury Lane on
11 December 1846. It was considered one of Balfe's best operas,
musically. Balfe had been busy! While he was arriving in Vienna,
there was also a revival of *The Maid of Artois* at Drury Lane in
October 1846 with the English soprano Anna Bishop in the title
role. During the summer Balfe had written some new music for the
opera for the revival with Anna Bishop.

Meanwhile, Balfe's visibility elsewhere continued to broaden.
The Bohemian Girl in a German translation with the title *Die
Zigeunerin* reached Vienna in July 1846.[33] It was very successful, so
much so that it moved to another theatre, the prestigious Theater

an der Wien in September, with Balfe invited to conduct, a remarkable achievement. The principal singers included the great bass, Josef Staudigl (1807–1861), and the soprano Jetty Treffz, who would later become the wife of Johann Strauss junior. The opera was immensely successful. It was announced that the opera was scheduled to be performed at Munich, Hamburg, Brunswick and Limberg. In Vienna it was followed by another Balfe work, *Die Belagerung von Rochelle* (*The Siège of Rochelle*), with performances into October. There was also an announcement that a performance of Balfe's *Die vier Haimonskinder* was being revived at the German theatre in Pest (Budapest).

This was Balfe's debut in Vienna. He was thirty-eight years old and looked extremely affluent and handsome, as a painting of him from this period shows. After the first performance of his new opera, he became the 'toast of the town' and was invited to several important functions. The Viennese composer and orchestra leader Johann Strauss (1804–1849) senior reportedly called the British composer 'the King of melody'. Later, Strauss produced a special series of dance Quadrilles from several Balfe operas which became very popular in Vienna and other German-speaking cities. This music was so popular that as late as New Year's Eve 2003 some of this music was performed in Vienna, for the New Year's Eve festival concert!

During Balfe's stay in Vienna, Lina would have been proud of her husband, whom she accompanied to her father's city. She spoke the language, and as the daughter of Franz de Paula Roser, composer of Viennese operettas, she would have been very well received.

Another new arrival in Vienna around this time was the sensational soprano Jenny Lind (1820–1887), who it was reported was going to sing in Balfe operas. This was an important meeting for Balfe. Lind and Balfe would become good friends and work closely together in the years ahead in London and Dublin. As it turned out Lind did not sing in any Balfe operas in Vienna.

The Balfes had a great year. His single-minded focus and hard work had paid off significantly. However, his real challenge in his new job at Her Majesty's was in the future. It would start at the beginning of the next season when there would be a large number of defections from the orchestra and in the singer ranks as the new

Royal Italian Opera announced its plans for an inaugural season starting early in 1847.

NOTES

1. See *Second Empire Opera: The Théâtre Lyric Paris 1851–1870* by T. J. Walsh, pp. 261–263.
2. Tyldesley, in his book on Balfe, refers to the name of the German production as, '*Die Vier Haymenssöhne,*' which is incorrect. The name of the opera in German based upon the programmes issued at the time was *Die vier Haimonskinder.*
3. *The Musical World* (London) 9 January 1845, p. 18
4. *The Times,* 21 November 1844.
5. Ibid.
6. *Opera on the Road: Traveling Opera Troupes in the United States, 1825–60* by Katherine K. Preston, pp. 219–224.
7. Original Atwill, New York vocal score and music in the possession of the author.
8. Ibid.
9. *The Musical World,* 9 January 1845, p. 18.
10. Copy of programme in possession of the author.
11. RIPM Index – *Allgemeiner Wiener Music Zeitung* of the period.
12. *Times* review/report, 15 May 1845.
13. Charles Dickens visited Balfe on a number of occasions, and they also dined together occasionally. On one occasion Dickens presented the composer with a silver snuff box according to Balfe's granddaughter Lina Jephson in a family document she wrote called 'Links with the past' circa 1910, a copy of which is in the author's possession.
14. See *The Early Victorians 1832–51* by J. F. C. Harrison, pp. 98–105.
15. Ibid.
16. See *Verdi and His Major Contemporaries* by Thomas G. Kaufman, p. 268, *Nabucco* chronology.
17. See *Selected Correspondence of Fryderyk Chopin* by Bronislaw Edward Sydow: translated and edited by Arthur Hedley, pp. 256–261.
18. Copies of these contemporary illustrations are held by the author.
19. *The Musical World,* 1 January 1846, 'Foreign Intelligence', p. 4.
20. Copy document in the procession of the author, '*Links with the past*' by Lina Jepson, grand daughter of Michael and Lina Balfe. Alex Weatherson, Chairman of the Donizetti Society in London commented (*Donizetti Society Newsletter,* No. 92) about this visit as follows: 'Lina Roser-Balfe's moving testimony is of real value to his [Donizetti's] unhappy and confused state of mind.' It is not inconceivable, however, that poor Gaetano's [Donizetti] reaction to the appearance of his Irish colleague brought to his mind the fact that Balfe had sung (as a baritone) in many of Bellini's stagings and that this indeed may have precipitated the touching account (above) related so movingly so many years later.
21. *The Musical World,* 30 October 1846, p. 526 makes mention of a rumor that Michael Costa may have been engaged as the 'perpetual director at the Philharmonic – we know not how true it may be'.
22. *The Musical World,* 13 November 1845, p. 549.
23. *Musical Recollections of the Last Half-Century* by C.T. Cox, Vol. II, pp. 129–131.
24. See, The King's Theatre [Her Majesty's Theatre] 1704-1867 by Daniel Nalbach. pp. 103–106.
25. *The Musical World,* 7 February 1846, p. 60. Note: this issue of *The Musical World* is incorrectly dated on the front cover as 1845, which should be 1846.
26. *The Musical World* 7 February 1846. reference to this contract signing date by Balfe is contained in the Costa response letter.
27. See, The King's Theatre [Her Majesty's Theatre] *1704–1867* by Daniel Nalbach, pp. 103–106.

28. *Reminiscences of the Opera* by Benjamin Lumley, p. 146.
29. *The Musical World*, 7 March 1846, front page.
30. *The Musical World*, 7 March 1846, p. 106.
31. *The Musical World*, 2 May 1846, p. 190.
32. *The Musical World* 15 August 1846, p. 390.
33. Eric White, in his book *A History of English Opera*, p. 282, states that *The Bohemian Girl* reached Vienna 'early in 1846'. The correct period for the first performance of the opera in Vienna is summer; 24 July 1846, to be exact.

CHAPTER EIGHT

London (Lind and Verdi), Dublin, Frankfurt and Berlin 1847–1850

For Lumley the closing months of 1846 brought major challenges for the year ahead and for his overall business. The newly announced Royal Italian Opera at the Covent Garden Theatre, with Frederick Beale, the music publisher, among its directors, had declared open warfare against him, with Michael Costa as its musical director heading the charge in terms of building the orchestra as well as the chorus.[1] As far as Lumley's organization was concerned there were many defections from among his star performers, chorus and instrumentalists, and no doubt several were encouraged with special incentives.

For Lumley this was initially catastrophic, as it meant that he was losing his best sopranos, Grisi and Persiani, and the best tenor, Mario, and the baritone Tamburini, all of whom had been stalwarts at Her Majesty's Theatre for years. There were also others. Only the bass, Lablache, decided to stay. It wasn't just the singers; defections also included many members of the long-established orchestra who were departing for the new organization, including the veteran Lindley, the cellist.

Lumley had to scramble to get things organized in time for the opening season in February 1847. He reasoned that in order to survive he had to maintain the 'star' system, some way or other, and that the Swedish soprano Jenny Lind, who was making sensational news on the continent, was the answer whatever the cost. Lumley had endeavoured to sign up Lind while in Berlin earlier in the year, but to no avail. Since then, Lumley's needs had become far more urgent. He reached the conclusion that the best way to get Lind signed up was to offer her a package she could not afford to refuse.

He planned to influence Lind by offering her two operatic premieres at Her Majesty's for the coming season. The first was to be an opera written for her by her mentor, Felix Mendelssohn, which she would premiere during the season. Mendelssohn and Lumley had already talked about a new opera for Her Majesty's based on Shakespeare's *The Tempest*. The second was to feature Lind in the new opera that Giuseppe Verdi (1813–1901) had agreed to write for London for Lumley's 1847 season. Verdi also planned to come to London to supervise the rehearsals and to possibly conduct the first three performances.

However, there was one major block as far as Lind was concerned – she had previously signed a contract in 1845 with Alfred Bunn to sing in London at Drury Lane. She had to renege on the Bunn contract for personal reasons. In defence of her actions, Lind claimed that at the time she signed the agreement with Bunn in Berlin she was unaware that she was expected to sing in English, at Drury Lane, something she was not prepared to attempt. Bunn's response was that she would never sing in England unless she first met the terms of her contract with him. The situation was more or less a stalemate.

As all of this unfolded, Balfe was still in Vienna with three of his operas being performed there and another opera in preparation at Drury Lane for its premiere in December. While Balfe may have heard of some of the problems, most probably he was not fully aware of how serious the situation had become for the Lumley organization, and he was one of the key players in it.

Towards the end of September 1846 Lumley set off for Milan ,where he had arrangements to meet with Verdi early in October 1846. He planned to discuss the details and timing for Verdi's new opera for London, the singers, and to get Verdi's approval on Lind as the prima donna for the premiere.

Verdi's student and assistant, Emanuele Muzio (1821–1890), in a letter to Verdi's father-in-law Antonio Barezzi in September, had indicated that the composer was interested in Catherine Hayes [Caterina Hayez], the Irish soprano, for his new opera.[ii] Hayes was then the reigning *prima donna assoluta* at La Scala. However, after the Lumley meeting with Verdi all of that changed and Verdi, aware of the benefits of having Lind, agreed to accept her for the premiere, although he only knew her by reputation, never having heard her sing.

Lumley immediately departed first for Frankfurt where Lind was, but unable to get a decision from her there, he followed her to Stuttgart and eventually to Darmstadt, where he was at last able to spend time with Lind on 13 October 1846.[3] He had with him a long personal letter from Felix Mendelssohn addressed to Lind suggesting that she consider signing a contract with Lumley to sing in London.[4] Lumley also mentioned the new opera Mendelssohn was going to compose and he advised her that now Verdi also wanted her for the new opera he was writing for London.

As Lind said afterwards, the Mendelssohn letter was the deciding factor for her. She agreed to come to London provided Lumley would 'protect' her against Alfred Bunn so that she was not involved with any legal issues over her earlier contract. Lumley agreed and so Lind signed the contract on 17 October 1846 to come to London in April 1847 to sing at Her Majesty's Theatre. Lumley also agreed to pay Lind four thousand eight hundred pounds – an enormous amount of money – for the season, which, for her, would include April to August 1847. Lumley was elated. He also included added incentives such as a house, a carriage, and a form of a signing bonus. It was a very costly package he gave Lind, but his stakes were high.

Lind, then twenty-six years old, had never sung in Paris or London or in Italy for that matter. She had built her career initially in her native Sweden, and then in the German cities of Berlin, Dresden and Leipzig. Most recently she had appeared in Vienna, where she and Balfe met. After an initial debut in Sweden, and after a period of acute vocal problems, Lind had spend almost a year of hard study with Europe's most renowned vocal coach, Manuel Garcia in Paris. At the end of 1842 she returned to Sweden to take up her career again in Stockholm.

Her international career started shortly after that. In Berlin her mentor became Giacomo Meyerbeer, while in Leipzig it was Felix Mendelssohn (1809–1847). Her career had moved at a rapid pace because of her unique talents and incredible vocal skills. Her repertoire primarily included operas by Donizetti, Bellini, Mozart, Weber, Meyerbeer and others.

So on Balfe's return to London, where he thought his only immediate concern would be the premiere of his new opera, *The Bondman*, at Drury Lane on 11 December 1846, he found that there were far greater challenges ahead for him if his job as music director at Her Majesty's was to survive. He conducted the first night of his new opera and then immediately handed the baton over to Signor Schira after that. The state of affairs at Her Majesty's required his total attention with the ensuing chaos that was emerging on all fronts. Balfe in his inimitable style jumpted right into it.

He learned that fifty-three members of the normal seventy- five-member orchestra had indicated that they would not be available for the next season at Her Majesty's in 1847.[5] While Balfe concurred with Lumley's decision that the news and arrival of Lind in April for the commencement of the post-Easter season would greatly help shore up their situation, as far as the public was concerned, the problems with the orchestra were far more serious. Without an orchestra there would be no opera.

Lumley had created an exposure for himself that he had not foreseen. Apparently for several years he only offered orchestral members a seasonal contract, renewing it at his option as the season closed. While this may have worked well for him during a time when the Italian Opera at Her Majesty's had no competition it had the reverse affect when suddenly a major new competitor such as The Royal Italian Opera appeared on the scene. The new organization gave the orchestral players other options, some of which included potentially longer contracts which had much appeal.[6]Lumley had not anticipated such an event, and as such he had misjudged the situation, to his own detriment.

However, with his 'star' under contract his immediate problem was the job of replacing numerous orchestral players and developing them into an ensemble in time for the season opener on 16 February 1847. Balfe knew who the best players were in the orchestras in Paris, Milan, Turin and Venice and of course in London and other places in Britain. However, the task of contacting these people and making the arrangements for them to come to London in time for rehearsals and the opening night in February was monumental. Somehow or other, Lumley and Balfe did it with the help of a Henry Panofka (1807–1892?), a newly engaged Lumley assistant who was a trained musician. He had studied in Vienna and Paris and Lumley had assigned him to seek out orchestral members in foreign cities with a view to them joining the orchestra at Her Majesty's.

Fortunately by now the new railway systems throughout Europe made travel between major cities much faster than previously. A number of the new members arriving were also personal friends of Balfe's, including the outstanding cellist Piatti, who was replacing Lindley.[7] Between Panofka and Balfe they were able to fill the orchestra seats in record time. Additionally, London by then was a desirable place to work for a musician, given the political unrest emerging in major cities on the continent which would eventually come to a head in 1848 in Paris, Milan, Vienna and elsewhere.

The season opened on schedule on 16 February with *La Favorita* by Donizetti. As far as the principal singers were concerned, in addition to Lind, the very capable handsome young tenor Italo Gardoni from the Paris opera, whom Balfe knew well, replaced the popular Mario in leading roles. Others joining the company for the season included the spinto tenor, Gaetano Fraschini, a Verdi favourite, two sopranos from the previous season, Sanchioli and Castellan, and a new soprano, Mlle. Fagiani. Also part of the company were the two experienced baritones Filippo Coletti (1811–1894) and Signor Superchi. The great Luigi Lablache and his son the bass-baritone Frederick Lablache and the German bass, Josef Staudigl, were also in the company.

Of course, all London anxiously awaited the star of the new season, Jenny Lind. Her arrival was scheduled in April. However, there was continued anxiety on the part of Lumley as the time got closer and he still did not have a confirmation from Lind as to exactly when she would arrive in London.

The 'war' between The Royal Italian Opera and Her Majesty's continued to heat up. It was rumured that Bunn had sold his Lind contract rights to the Royal Italian Opera. No doubt the intent was to thwart Lumley and create a barrier to Lind's potential arrival in London. It was also further inflamed by two daily newspapers taking sides, the *Morning Chronicle* for The Royal Italian Opera, and the *Morning Post* for Italian Opera at Her Majesty's Theatre. *The Times* tended to stay neutral and the periodical *The Musical World* endeavoured to referee the conflict in a judicious manner. Balfe and Costa each personally kept a low profile and concentrated on the jobs at hand and remained friends. In the background, Balfe worked long hours to get his players working as an ensemble.

Towards the end of January, *The Musical World* had an extensive feature article starting on its front page about the turn of events at Her Majesty's. In terms of the orchestra, they said that Lumley had overcome one of his chief problems relating to building back up the orchestra by getting experienced players from, Milan, Turin, Paris and Brussels. The article went on to say:

> That Balfe continues to occupy the post of conductor of the orchestra is a fact on which we congratulate the Opera frequenters, in the teeth of the *Chronicle* [the *Morning Chronicle* continued to keep up the negative articles about Lumley and his organization]. We consider him [Balfe] eminently qualified for the position, and nothing we have heard or seen has had any influence in persuading us to the contrary. Moreover, Balfe is a zealous and conscientious artist and labours hard in his vocation. And, to conclude Balfe's name is European [recognized throughout Europe], and would confer honour upon any lyrical establishment whatever.[8]

Lumley, forging ahead, announced his season programmes in *The Musical World* on 6 February 1847, with Jenny Lind heading the list. He also mentioned that his chorus would consist of eighty qualified individuals who have been chosen from Italy, Germany and Britain, replacing those who had gone over to the competition.

As the New Year progressed – a number of socialites, Lady Palmerston, Lady Clarendon. Lady Clanricarde and Lady Ailesbury, arranged with Lumley for a special benefit concert to be performed 'For the relief of the distressed Irish because of Famine' which opened the evening of 27 February 1847. The proceeds of the benefit amounted to two thousand pounds, which was distributed in Ireland. The Queen and her party attended the evening. The concert was immediately followed with a performance of Verdi's *Nabucco* with Coletti in the title role. Balfe conducted as usual.

This was Balfe's only involvement in anything remotely related to a benefit for the Irish during the difficult Famine years. Throughout his career, Balfe was always very single-minded in relation to his professional activities. As far as is known, he never got involved with any religious or political groups or humanitarian causes. He never composed any religious music except for one piece in his early days in Bergamo, Italy. Likewise, he never composed anything of a political nature, even during his time in

Ireland in 1848 when there were very active political organizations such as the Young Ireland movement or the Fenians.

Most of his songs were classical Victorian ballads with sentimental lyrics, such as 'One smile from thee', 'Come into the garden, Maud' and Sweet words of love." He only wrote a few songs that were Irish-related, such as 'Killarney', 'Kathleen Machree' and 'Norah, darling! don't believe them', and these seemed to be more directed at the Irish abroad, not the Irish at home. Neither did Balfe ever compose an opera for Ireland. It does seem strange; however, given his activity in so many other places, one must come to the conclusion that most of his decisions were economically driven and that sentiment didn't play a role. Financially, Dublin would not have been able to compete with London, Paris, Vienna or Berlin in the 1840s and, later, for his services. In a way it's not too dissimilar to the decisions made a number of years later by famous Irish-born playwrights who were London-based.

In his role as musical director during the 1847 opera season at Her Majesty's Balfe prepared and conducted a number of operas by various composers. The initial series of performances were highly praised with a particular mention of Balfe's efforts with the orchestra and chorus as follows:

> Balfe, we repeat, has done wonders; and every night's perform-
> ance manifests an increased command over the forces he has
> collected from all parts of the world – like the armies of the
> Goths and Visigoths of old. Attila, king of the Huns never man-
> aged a motley multitude with more rigid discipline and perfect
> order than Balfe his newly gathered orchestra. Our applause
> and that of the house was for Balfe and his followers.[9]

Balfe's progress was continually being monitored, in view of the rawness of his orchestra and the potential for nightly disasters given the newness of the ensemble. In the middle of March *The Musical World* had this to say:

> There are points in Mr Balfe's orchestra that cannot be too
> much commended; and none of them is more worthy of note
> than the precision and unanimity with which the recitatives
> (the most fidgety part of modern Italian opera) are accompa-
> nied. Much of this no doubt is to be traced to Mr. Balfe's

being himself an admirable musician, and one thoroughly acquainted with all the exigencies of recitatives; but great credit, nevertheless, is due to his men for the care and attention with which they follow his directions.[10]

Balfe obviously had worked long and hard to bring the orchestra together and he was making good progress. He continued to add new members and make changes in certain sections where performers were not up to standard. He still had almost eight months of operatic performances to contend with before the season would be over. His determination and professionalism continued to drive the results. Details of his season and the operas being performed and the casts are provided in Appendix VIII.

Meanwhile the competition, the Royal Italian Opera, on 6 April had commenced its season with Rossini's *Semiramide* with Grisi and Alboni, at Covent Garden, with considerable success. The Italian Opera at Her Majesty's opened its post Easter season on 10 April, by substituting the scheduled opera with the English premiere of Verdi's opera *I due Foscari*, with Coletti and Fraschini. Donizetti's *L'elisir d'amore* was scheduled for the opening night, but at the last minute Lablache, who was to sing Dulcamara ,was suffering from a cold and alas too hoarse, so Balfe had to substitute Verdi's *I due Foscari*.

Opera management in nineteenth-century London did not normally provide for understudies. If a principal singer was indisposed the planned opera was usually cancelled and a substituted work was performed. As a result, with the last-minute cancellation of *L'elisir d'amore*, there was serious concern among the critics about the ability of the management to mount a substitute opera, particularly when the work was also a premiere that had never before been performed in London. However, *The Musical World* had the following to say: '...the instant that Balfe entered the orchestra, it was evident from the air of confidence that played upon his good-humoured countenance that all was right, and that he and his new-formed band of Huns and Vandals were ripe for mischief.

The Times had the following comments about the conductor:

> To be in such a state of forwardness with one work as to produce it directly the chance of another fails, is an instance of good generalship that might everywhere be imitated with

advantage. Let a special meed of praise be awarded to Mr. Balfe, who, at the shortest notice, was able to summons round him all the persons under his direction. From the commencement of the present season, the conduct of Mr. Balfe amid circumstances of unprecedented difficulty has been distinguished by an ability and indefatigable zeal, perhaps without parallel.'[11]

With the start of the season, Balfe's management of the orchestra once again became the focus of the critics:

> Mr Lumley was, as it happened? and it might easily have happened otherwise? very lucky in his choice of a successor to Signor Costa. Perhaps no artist in the country better qualified for the post, by education, taste and ability, could have been selected that Mr. Balfe. The sequel has guaranteed his efficiency no less than his fidelity and zeal. By judgment and energy, little short of magical, in an incredibility brief time, Mr. Balfe has filled the empty seats of the orchestra with an army of instrumentalists more numerous than his predecessor and if less used to discipline, scarcely less complete and efficient.[12]

However, despite the concerns about the orchestra, the arrival of Jenny Lind, which was now scheduled for the following week, was really the big news for everyone. Lind at last arrived on 16 April 1847, much to Lumley's relief and pleasure. Her planned debut date was Tuesday 4 May 1847 in the role of Alice in Meyerbeer's *Roberto il Diavolo*. Lind's presence in the opera house shortly after her arrival caused a great stir. Her long-awaited presence had been so keenly looked forward to by the public and opera management alike.

Balfe, who had met Lind in Vienna, had a good relationship with her. He had attended some of her performances there so he was familiar with her style and temperament. In the following weeks during rehearsals Balfe worked closely with her as her debut drew near. The Meyerbeer work she had chosen for her debut was an opera she had sung several times previously, so she was comfortable with her role. It was not an opera that Balfe was particularly familiar with.

Her partners for her debut night were Fraschini as Roberto and

Staudigl as Bertram, a role in which the great bass had distinguished himself in Germany. Lind was in the role of Alice, the soprano, Castellan as Isabella and Gardoni as Rambaldo. Balfe was the conductor.

The frenzy which broke out around the opera house the day before her debut was unprecedented in the Italian Opera house's history in London. Crowds lined the streets hoping to get a glimpse of the prima donna as she arrived for rehearsals and later for her debut. Lumley had increased ticket prices considerable yet the house was immediately sold out. On the night of her debut the house was overflowing. Queen Victoria and the Prince Consort and their party, which included the Duke of Wellington, were in attendance in the Royal Box.

The tension in the house was extraordinary. It was to reflect on the singers and the orchestra alike. When Lind made her first appearance on the stage, there was and immediate reaction from the audience:

> ...one shout that burst spontaneously from three-thousand throats made the roof of the edifice vibrate and tremble. It was a multitude of insensate madmen (*sic*), in a sea of hats and handkerchiefs. We never recollect such a sight within the walls of a theatre, or without.[13]

For Balfe in the orchestra pit, who no doubt waited for the calming down of the enthusiasm before continuing the music, it must have brought back vivid memories of the eventful night with Malibran in Venice, in April 1835 and made him glad to be a part of the 'Lind mania' that was about to permeate London, and beyond.

The critics praised Lind for her vocal quality and technique, which were perceived as quite unique. Lumley achieve everything he had hoped for, and Her Majesty's was saved for the time being. The other singers that night appeared to give somewhat nervous performances and indeed the orchestra had its moments under its indefatigable conductor. By the third performances of the opera, most of the first night nerves were gone and the future performances continued with great éclat.

Lind followed the Meyerbeer work with Bellini's *La sonnambula* and *Norma*, and later she sang Donizetti's *La Figlia del Reggimento*, all with great success and excitement.

On the personal side, Balfe also had another activity going on which required his attention. Lina Balfe had apparently organized a grand *Soirée Musicale* to take place on 9 June 1847 at Musical Hall in Store Street. The concert would be under the patronage of H.R.H. the Duchess of Kent, which would ensure good attendance.[14]

One suspects that Lina was concerned that Balfe was not composing operas because he was fully engaged with his work at Her Majesty's Theatre. Bunn continued to produce English operas at Drury Lane; however, they were mostly the works of Balfe's main competitor and friend, William Vincent Wallace.

In any event, in announcing her concert Lina advised that the programme would be made up entirely of music from Balfe's *Falstaff* and *L'etoile de Seville*. She announced that the artists performing would include herself, Madame Castellan, Italo Gardoni, Gaetano Fraschini, Filippo Coletti, Luigi Lablache, and Josef Staudigl, all members of Her Majesty's Italian Opera. Her husband would conduct the concert. The concert went off very well with a large attendance. A quartet from *L'etoile de Seville* was considered 'very beautiful, and entirely different from anything that we have heard from the pen of this fertile composer'.[15] Gardoni and Castellan also sang a duet from this opera. Lina Balfe elected to sing only one ballad, in English no less, 'Oh! Chide me not'. Lablache and Coletti sang a duet from *Falstaff* and Fraschini sang from *Keolanthe*. Apparently arias from Balfe's *Les Quatre Fils Aymon* were also sung during the evening. Balfe conducted the orchestra and assisted at the piano.

Meanwhile, at Her Majesty's, the next big event was the announced arrival of the thirty-four-year-old Giuseppe Verdi in London on 5 June. It was his first visit to London. The composer still had to finish his opera *I Masnadieri*, which was scheduled to premiere later in July. Lumley had given Verdi a box at the opera so that he could attend any time he wished. Verdi's assistant Emanuele Muzio had arrived ahead of Verdi and had already seen Lind in a number of performances of which he was very complimentary.

Verdi frequently went to the opera, where various ambassadors and members of royalty were introduced to him. Balfe would also have met him during this period. It would have been the first time that the two composers had actually met as during the period Balfe spent in Italy Verdi had not yet emerged on the scene.

Muzio worked with the singers in terms of teaching them their parts, while Verdi continued to work on the score and orchestration. There can be little doubt that Balfe would have been involved in some way in this activity, as musical director at the theatre. Additionally, Verdi did not plan to conduct the opera, which meant that Balfe would have had that responsibility; therefore he would have had the need to understand the score and the musical structure of the opera.

At the direction of Queen Victoria the date of Thursday 22 July was set for the premiere, as she was planning to leave town shortly thereafter. Verdi continued to work long hours in order to meet the deadline. Lumley had requested him to conduct the opera or at least some of the performances. As late as 18 July Verdi was still saying that he did not want to conduct the opera; however, under pressure from Lumley, he finally agreed.[16]

The premiere was a gala night with the Queen and her royal party in attendance in addition to the aristocracy and many diplomats and politicians. While the evening was a success the opera itself did not have lasting power. Shortly after the premiere Verdi sent Muzio back to Milan to have the score published by Francesco Lucca. Verdi, anxious to get back to Paris where his lover Giuseppina Strepponi was in residence, left London shortly after the second performance of the opera. He passed on his baton to Balfe, who conducted the remaining performances.

While Muzio thought Lind was excellent, particularly at the upper ranges and the flexibility of her voice, Verdi has a somewhat different opinion, he was heard to say 'Canta ma non incanta', meaning that she sang but she didn't enchant, or perhaps that she didn't have the right temperament for the music.[17] It was the only opera that Verdi wrote for London and while he came back to visit London again in the future it was not a place he liked because of the weather, the food and the language difficulty.

Around the same time as Balfe was conducting the final performances of Verdi's new opera *I Masnadieri* in London, his *Die Zigeunerin* and *Die vier Haimonskinder* were being performed again at the Theater an der Wien in Vienna with new casts and continued success.

Balfe' season at Her Majesty's ended in August. At Lind's request he joined her on a concert tour to Manchester, Birmingham, Liverpool, Hull, Bristol and Brighton and other places. Gardoni and Frederick Lablache and his wife were also in the party. Lind reportedly requested Balfe to compose a concert aria and duet for her for the tour. Balfe composed the duet 'M'offrian cittadi e popli' for Lind and Gardoni. He also composed the aria 'Qual Fior novello' for Gardoni. The concert aria he wrote for Lind had the title of 'Ah, forse in tal momento'. It was in three movements, *a largo, a cavatina and a cabaletta*. For details of this music sung by Lind and Gardoni, see Appendix IX–20 and&21.

During this tour, Balfe is reported to have been working on a new opera based on a Victor Hugo play, *Le roi s'amuse* (later used by Verdi for *Rigoletto*) it is not known if the music he offered Lind and Gardoni may have been from his work on this opera which was never produced. In addition to this activity, Balfe was also working on a new opera for Drury Lane, *The Maid of Honour*, which was scheduled to premiere there on 20 December. The opera season at Drury Lane was now being managed by M. Jullien, who was providing a season of Grand English Opera there. The French composer Hector Berlioz had been engaged by Jullien to be a conductor for the season. Berlioz was the conductor for Balfe new opera. Early in February in the New Year, the Queen, Prince Albert and their party added increased interest when they went to see Balfe's new opera at Drury Lane.

At the end of the Lind tour in the provinces in late September the composer went to Paris to be with his wife and family, where they planned to stay until late January 1848 since he had to return for the start of the new season in February. One report from Paris mentions that Balfe was already hard at work finishing an opera (*The Maid of Honour*) for M. Jullien at Drury Lane, and another opera for his friend, the writer and librettist de Saint-Georges for the Opéra Comique. Apparently, Balfe had also received a libretto for another opera for the Académie Royale, but the writer says that even with Balfe's rapidity he could not possibly complete all in the period of months he's going to be in Paris.[18]

Indeed, it was a very good year for Balfe, since he had an income virtually the entire year. He also managed to mould the orchestra into an efficient ensemble along with the chorus and to get through the season without any major disasters. On the personal side, his children were now truly growing up. His daughter Louisa was fifteen, Michael junior was eleven and Victoire was ten. Balfe was thirty-nine years old.

In London Mr Bunn, now manager of the Surrey Theatre, was performing *The Bohemian Girl* nightly to overflowing houses.

For the next several years Balfe continued to conduct at Her Majesty's. The crisis that he faced early in 1847 did not loom again. The seasons continued from February or March with a two- week break at Easter, after which the season ran through August. He continued to introduce new works by Verdi and other composers that had not previously been seen in London. He also conducted a major concert during which he performed, Mendelssohn's 3rd Symphony in A. The critics gave great praise to his overall execution, spirit and enthusiasm in the performance. He later followed this with Beethoven's 2nd Symphony.

Jenny Lind returned in 1848 for Lumley's new season and Balfe continued his work as musical director and conductor. In July there was talk of a revival of Balfe's comic opera *Falstaff* at Her Majesty's Theatre, with Jenny Lind in the role that Grisi premiered and with Lablache in the title role. It was announced that Balfe had reworked the main soprano role for Lind's voice type and that he had also added a new music for her. The performance was scheduled for late in July; however, at the last minute it was dropped. Most probably Jenny Lind was not comfortable with her role and decided not to perform the opera. Details of Balfe's seasonal activity and the casts that performed the operas can be reviewed at Appendix VIII.

Early in the New Year his opera *Die Zigeunerin* was performed for the first time at the Stadttheater in Pressburg in Bohemia, which was rather an interesting coincidence. The story of the English version of the opera (*The Bohemian Girl*) had been set in Pressburg. However, for the German version of the opera, the location was changed to Scotland for political reasons. In Vienna the opera also continued to be performed on a regular basis. It was also during this period that Vincent Wallace's *Maritana* had its premiere in Vienna at the Theater and der Wien.

After the1848 season in London was over Lind and Balfe and other members of the company went on tour, eventually ending in

Dublin. Lumley, Balfe and Lind all stayed in the fashionable Morrison's Hotel at the corner of Dawson and Nassau Streets, where Balfe had stayed previously. Balfe close friend from his early days, Richard M. Levey, who was the leader of the orchestra at Dublin's Theatre Royal, was glad to have his friend back in town. In his book about opera at Dublin's Theatre Royal during the nineteenth century, Levey paints an interesting picture of Balfe the conductor from personal observations as follows:

> Several eminent composers have failed in wielding the conductor's baton; but Balfe possessed all the qualities? great decision, 'an eye to threaten and command,' a faultless ear, ready to discover the slightest inaccuracy, and, above all, and intelligible and decisive beat, without which all the other attributes are nothing.[19]

Levey also mentions that during this visit by Lind, Lumley and Balfe that they had some free time on their hands and Levey was invited to some fun and games at the hotel. He mentions that Jenny Lind could dance almost as well as she could sing and that Balfe of course inherited the art (his father having been a dancing master). They set up a mock ballet with the prima donna performing the part of the Maiden and Balfe that of the Lover. The 'corps de ballet' consisted of other members of the company and one of the hotel waiters.

Lumley was placed on a throne to decide the merits of the aspirants, charged with deciding who was the most accomplished. Levey and another musician present provided the music. Lumley could not decide who was best so he felt that it required a vote among all. Balfe led off and danced like an 'angel'. Lind followed with the airs and graces of the great Taglioni to the point that she astonished all the onlookers. After a round of applause Lind was declared the winner. The evening concluded with songs, music and laughter with Balfe in the middle of it all.

The opera season lasted two weeks and included Lind's usual roles in *La sonnambula*, *I Puritani*, *La Figlia del Reggimento*, and *Lucia di Lammermoor*. Lind created as much a sensation in Dublin as she had in London.[20] Balfe conducted all operas. Her performances were truly spectacular and "Jenny Lind mania" arrived in

Dublin. They also gave a concert at Balfe's old haunt, the Rotunda Concert Rooms, to a packed house. Lind returned once more to Dublin a few years later to fulfill a promise she had made on her first visit: to give a charity concert for one of the Dublin Hospitals. Balfe only made one more visit to Dublin and that was many years later when his daughter Victoire would make her Dublin debut in opera.

After the 1848 Dublin season they all returned to London. At the end of November Lind performed in a concert at Gloucester with some other singers and Balfe as the accompanist. They continued to some other places before concluding their tour in early December. At the end of the tour, Lind declared a benefit concert for the orchestra members who were in her party during the tour. Balfe received a bonus of one hundred pounds while the orchestra leader received sixty-five pounds, and each of the members, thirty-two pounds. It was announced afterwards that Balfe left for Paris, where he was going to join his family and continue to work on a new opera for that city.[21]

Before departing Jenny Lind told Balfe that she was so appreciative of his work that she wanted to perform a benefit concert for him on whatever date was convenient for him at whatever venue he wished to select. Balfe chose Exeter Hall just off the Strand in central London, which was the largest concert hall at the time.[22] It had a capacity of three thousand seats. The date for the concert was set for 29 January 1849.

Balfe, by way of saying 'thanks' to Jenny Lind, composed a song for her, 'The Lonely Rose', which she planned to sing at their concert. Balfe's music publisher's paid him one hundred guineas for the right to publish the song. When Cramer and Beale published the music they set a charge of two shillings for the sheet music, which meant that they expected to immediately achieve sales in excess of one thousand copies of the music in order to break even based on the copyright fee alone, without the publishing and printing cost.

In addition to Lind singing at the Balfe concert, Luigi Lablache had offered his services along with the pianist Thalberg and the baritone Belletti, Frederick Lablache and a Miss Durlacher, a pupil of Balfe's, and a Mlle. Sophie Vera and a Miss Bassano. There would be an orchestra and Balfe would conduct. Most of the principal singers from Her Majesty's were in Paris and elsewhere as they were engaged in seasonal activity.

For the Balfe concert it was reported that Exeter Hall drew one of the largest crowds ever. The hall was virtually filled to suffocation point. Receipts amounted to over sixteen-hundred pounds which was considered a very good 'harvest' for Balfe. Additionally, the Editor of *The Musical World* added his comments by saying: 'May the shadow of his fortunes never be less, and may his next windfall overwhelm him ...'

As far as arranging the concert programme, Balfe was reported to have:

> ...provided a capital programme for his visitors; just such a one as would suit a mixed audience? for Balfe's admirers include aristocrats and underbred, artists and artisans, amateurs and connoisseurs, rich and poor, simple and wise, a true compound of the good and the brilliant, the solid and the taking.[23]

After various arias and duets, Lind commenced Balfe's 'The Lonely Rose' – she created a sensation with it, partly because she sang it in English, her pronunciation being marked with great distinction and clarity. The Balfe song was considered to be one of his best. Lind encored the song. The overall concert was a great success. Balfe conducted the orchestra in his operatic overtures to *The Bohemian Girl* and to *Le puits d'Amour*. The Duke of Wellington, a great fan of Jenny Lind's, was in attendance, as were many aristocrats.

The new season at Her Majesty's Theatre was scheduled to open on 15 March 1849. Rumours were rife that Lind would not be returning as she was engaged to be married. Lumley did produce a new 'star' without making any announcements about Jenny Lind. His new singer was the rather large Marietta Alboni (1823–1894), who was an outstanding experienced singer who had performed at Milan, Paris and even London, at the competition, the Royal Italian Opera.

Lumley had confirmation that Lind would be with the company; however, she was in Sweden and did not want to travel during the winter months so Lumley could not get a firm arrival date from her.[24] Balfe proceeded with rehearsals with the rest of the company and the opening night started on time but without Lind. The great soprano did eventually show up toward the end of April and sang in her first performance of the season in *La sonnambula*, shortly afterwards.

The new season included several new singers and operas. Balfe did the conducting of the orchestra which the critics now said was a remarkable ensemble. The opera season continued through August, as usual.

While his activity as musical director and conductor at Her Majesty's Theatre provided Balfe with a regular income it was also very time consuming. Since his last new opera in December 1847, he had not composed any new works, other than songs. The same pattern would prevail until August 1851. Lind's presence had been good for him. However, it had now been announced that on 4 May Jenny Lind would sing in her last operatic performance, after which she would only sing in concerts. The departure of Lind with her last operatic performances in May 1849 had to make him consider his own options as there was little doubt that the loss of the prima donna would most probably affect Lumley's business financially. For Lumley and Balfe it was the end of a unique era. The Lind decision came as a shock to both of them even though they were aware of the rumours.

Lumley, endeavouring to stabilize his situation with the departure of Lind, had recently extended Balfe's contract for three years. So while Balfe felt no immediate need to change he recognized that with the competition across town at Covent Garden and no Jenny Lind the whole business of Italian opera management would become less viable. Lumley later brought in Henriette Sontag from retirement in order to shore up his situation; however, she was not able to create the interest of a Lind. Even the press was now questioning the need for two major Italian opera houses in London and whether or not there was the audience to support them.

For Balfe the options weren't great. Bunn was no longer at Drury Lane. Jullien, who had been managing the theatre, was now virtually bankrupt. The possibility of doing something in Paris was quite limited and the three operas he had premiered there had not resulted in any long-term options to compose for one of the theatres there. Vienna and the German cities appeared to offer the best opportunistic for him. Early in October 1849 Balfe's *Die Zigeunerin* had its local premiere in Frankfurt, with Balfe conducting the opera.[25] The fourth night was a benefit night for Balfe. Jenny Lind travelled a significant distance just to attend one of the performances of her friend's most successful opera. She arrived in time for the opening night. *The Musical World* reported as follows:

The houses were great every time. The performance created the utmost pleasure, and Balfe was *féted* and honoured as though he had been in his own country. At the first performance Jenny Lind was present, and very conspicuous in applauding the best *morceau*. Our correspondent informs us that she had come nearly 100 miles out of her way, to be present at the *début* of her old *chef d'orchestre*, whose zeal and ability rendered her, as she is quick to acknowledge, so 'comfortable' during her London engagements.[26]

In addition to Lind a number of others attended, including the Rothschilds and various members of the visiting British aristocracy. At the same time in Vienna, the Emperor went to see *Die Zigeunerin*, which received an excellent reception, with many encores.

The following is a brief extract of one of the Frankfurt reviews:

Balfe's music unquestionably leans towards the Italian school, and resembles Bellini in style. His instrumentation is brilliant and characteristic without overpowering the singer. Balfe belongs to the original nature (*Künstlernaturen*), marching in his own path, and producing nothing which does not of itself issue from healthy individuality. We may accuse him of doing homage to the popular taste, but this will be, doubtless easily forgiven him ...[27]

After he was finished in Frankfurt at the end of 1849, he went to Berlin for the local premiere of his opera *The Bondman*, with the German title of *Die Mulatte*, at the Royal Grand Opera. Jenny Lind had arrived in Berlin ahead of Balfe. Perhaps it was her influence that created the opportunity for him. Shortly after arrival Lind gave a concert for the Queen's birthday at Potsdam. Balfe came to Berlin later in January to conduct his opera, which was announced at the same time as Lind's concert.[28] The first night took place on 25 January and the opera had an extraordinary initial reception.

The King and Queen and the Princess of Prussia, the Prince and Princess Karl, the Princess Charlotte and her royal bridegroom, the Duke of Saxe Meinengen, all attended the theatre. Balfe was not unknown to them as his reputation from Vienna had preceded him. Balfe conducted the orchestra. He was congratulated and invited back during the evening as the King expressed his desire to see the *Die Zigeunerin*. The composer felt very pleased about his reception and the possibilities Berlin offered. It wasn't too long before the King's wishes were fulfilled. Berlin saw several performances of his *Die Zigeunerin* later in the year in October 1850.

On Balfe's return to London in early February 1850 from Berlin, to take up his duties as musical director at Her Majesty's Theatre, *The Musical World* quoted the following report they had received from their representative about his success in the Prussian Capital:

> During his stay in Berlin Mr. Balfe has succeeded in obtaining the universal popularity which awaits him wherever he appears. With the splendid orchestra of our Grand Opera he was perfectively at home, and though he does not speak German fluently he soon found means to make his wishes known to the members of the Band [orchestra] and chorus, as well as to the principal singers.[29]

The report finished up by saying: Mr Balfe was delighted with the orchestra, and the orchestra was delighted with Mr Balfe."

In March 1850 in London, Balfe was active in a fundraising concert for The General Theatre Fund at which the novelist Charles Dickens was also present. Balfe and Dickens became good friends. The novelist at one point in time presented Balfe with a personalized snuff box as a gift. Dickens was also known to visit the Balfe home. Dickens also became quite friendly with the composer's wife, who kept a photograph of the writer in her family album.

NOTES

1. *The Musical World*, 2 January 1847, p. M10.
2. See, *Catherine Hayes: The Hibernian Prima Donna* by Basil Walsh, pp. 63–65. Also see *Giuseppe Verdi nelle lettere di Emanuele Muzio ad Antonio Barezzi* by L. A. Garibaldi, p. .274.
3. *Reminiscences of the Opera* by Benjamin Lumley, p. 164.
4. See *Memoir of Madame Jenny Lind-Goldsmidt*, Vol. 1, by Holland and Rockstro.
5. *The Musical World*, 9 January 1847, p. 17.
6. Ibid.
7. Ibid., p. 26.
8. *The Musical World*, 23 January 1847, p. 47.

9. *The Musical World*, 6 March 1847, p. 151.
10. *The Musical World*, 13 March 1847, pgs. 173–174.
11. *The Times* 12 April 1847.
12. *The Musical World*, 10 April 1847, front page.
13. *The Musical World*, 8 May 1847, p. 308.
14. *The Musical World*, 22 May 1847, front page.
15. *The Musical World*, 24 July, 1847, p. 481.
16. See *Verdi: A Biography* by Mary Jane Phillips-Matz. p. 217.
17. *The Musical World*, 6 May 1848.
18. Report from J.W. Davison, editor of *The Musical World*, issue date 16 October 1847, pp. 662–663.
19. *Annals of the theatre Royal Dublin* by R. M. Levey and J. O'Rorke, p.135.
20. For details of the operas that Balfe conducted in Dublin featuring Jenny Lind see *Annals of the Theatre Royal Dublin* by R.M. Levey and J. O'Rorke, pp. 135–142.
21. *The Musical World*, 9 December 1848, p. 799.
22. *The Musical World* 30 December 1848, p. 843.
23. *The Musical World*, 3 February 1849, p. 69.
24. *Reminiscences of the Opera* by Benjamin Lumley, p. 207.
25. *The Musical World*, 6 October 1949, front page.
26. *The Musical World*, 17 November 1849, front page.
27. *The Didaskalien* (Frankfurt) as reported by *The Musical World*, 24 November 1849, pp. 740–741.
28. *The Berlin Zeitung*, 8 January 1851, No. 6.
29. *The Musical World*, 16 February 1850. Front page.

CHAPTER NINE

London, St. Petersburg, Vienna, Trieste and New York 1850–1861

The year 1850 on the personal front for the Balfes had much to offer. His daughter Louisa, now about eighteen, had originally met a young man in Paris whom she was attracted to. He was Maxmillian Behrend (1823–1890), a wealthy twenty-six year old, the son of a corn merchant from Danzig. The family business was the Behrend Corn Trading Company. The family had been in the commodities business since before the Napoleonic wars. They also traded in timber and other commodities. Max did business in Britain, which he visited quite frequently since some of his financing came from the London Rothschild banking family.[1]

The relationship between Louisa and Max had developed quickly as he was very acceptable to the composer and his wife. He was also a Catholic, which was important to Lina. It also helped that the Behrends had an interest in music and theatre; possibly that was how Maxmillian first met Louisa. The romance developed and they became engaged some time in 1849 with plans to marry early in 1850 in London.

For the Balfes it was an important personal time. Louisa and Max were formally married at the Catholic Church at Warwick Road, London on Monday 15 April 1850. For some reason, perhaps because of Church of England laws relating to the residency within a parish, they also had to go through a ceremony at the fashionable St Georges Church in Hanover Square, before the marriage would be properly recognized.[2] A notice of the marriage appeared in *The Times* a few days later.

The day brought a lot of happiness to their small family. In the years ahead, Max would also prove to be a great asset to the Balfe family in many ways. He and Louisa would have eight children and many grandchildren. In time, the Behrends eventually moved to England with all of their children to be nearer the family, which would bring great joy to the Balfes. Their descendants live today in Britain, and elsewhere.

Meanwhile, the Italian Opera at Her Majesty's Theatre commenced its 1850 season in March with Mayr's *Medea in Corinth* with Giuditta Pasta's pupil, Teresa Parodi (1827–1887?), singing the title role and Balfe conducting. The new season progressed with a bigger roster of singers performing. The main new addition to Lumley's theatre was Catherine Hayes (1818–1861), the Irish prima donna who had made her debut at the Royal Italian Opera the previous season. She was partnered with the English tenor Sims Reeves (1818–1900) in *Lucia di Lammermoor,* an opera they both had performed at La Scala with phenomenal success.[3]

Hayes later became somewhat dissatisfied when Lumley assigned most of her primary roles to the aging soprano Sontag, who in Lumley's view was his 'star' replacement for Jenny Lind. Hayes left shortly afterwards. However, before her departure Balfe composed a song for his Irish friend, 'The Joy of Tears', with words by Fitzball, which the prima donna sang at various concerts.

While Balfe had a full season of opera ahead of him he still found time now to start composing more songs. The industrial revolution was very much in full swing . The growth of the middle classes had been continuing at a rapid pace and now as the country entered the 1850s the affluence created by the expansion became apparent, particularly to those in the music profession.

There was great demand for sheet music which encouraged Balfe to take advantage of the situation. His relationship with prominent Victorian era poets such as Fitzball, Morris, Kingsley and Tennyson and the Americans, Henry Longfellow (1807–1882) and Jessica Rankin would reach fruition by the end of the 1850s. His most famous song compositions such as, 'The Arrow and the Song', Come into the Garden Maud', 'The Sands of Dee', 'Trust her not', 'Excelsior', and 'The Village Blacksmith' all came from this period. It was also during these years that he received an assignment from the music publishing house Novello & Co. to provide a new arrangement of his friend Thomas Moore's, Irish Melodies. It was a task which he enjoyed very much. The Balfe arrangements were published in 1859. They were reissued many

times over, right into the twentieth century. There are eighty-five
songs in the arrangement album.

One of the highlights of the 1850 operatic season at Her
Majesty's was a visit to London of the great internationally
renowned soprano Giuditta Pasta. Pasta had been in retirement for
a number of years after a long career in which she created many
operas. Balfe knew her from his time in Milan twenty years previously. Initially, it was Pasta's intension to include attendance at
some of the performances of her pupil Teresa Parodi at Her
Majesty's that season. However, Lumley saw an opportunity to
make news, so he invited her to sing during her visit. Pasta, in
the true tradition of the great prima donna, eventually agreed,
but apparently insisted that it be a 'private farewell' concert with
only selected invitees. So she and Balfe went into rehearsal for a
concert which would be given on Monday 15 July 1850 in the intimate 'music room' of the theatre, in which she would present
scenes from some of her most famous roles.

Pasta gave two programmes which included scenes from
Rossini's *Tancredi*, Mayr's *Medea*, Gluck's, *Orfeo ed Euridice* and
Donizetti's famous *Anna Bolena*. Pasta was assisted at the concert
by leading artists from the opera company. It was an evening of
nostalgia for the audience, and Balfe included, in which the prima
donna, now fifty-three years old and after a career that lasted
twenty-five years at the top in places such as, Milan, Naples, Paris,
London, Berlin and Vienna, sadly was just a shadow of herself
according to the critics, who mostly declined to comment fully on
the evening. For Balfe it must have been an experience, as he now
had been directly involved musically with the five greatest prima
donnas of the age, Malibran, Sontag, Grisi, Lind and Pasta.

In addition to his opera season, Lumley had initiated a series of
major concerts which were given on Wednesday mornings with
Balfe conducting. The concerts were particularly successful as
singers got to perform music outside the normal repertoire of the
season. It appealed to the audience and generally the concerts were
very well attended.

As the season came to a close in August 1850 the big news was
not the activity at either of London's Italian opera houses but the
departure of Jenny Lind for America in September 1850. Lind had
signed a contract with the famous America showman P. T. Barnum

to visit America in the autumn of 1850. Barnum agreed to pay Lind one hundred and fifty thousand dollars for 120 concerts in America, along with paying her expenses and the cost of a maid, a secretary and a companion. There is little doubt that Balfe would have been her first option to be her musical director for the American tour. However, it appears that he had to decline for personal reasons which will be discussed later. The highly competent composer and musician Jules Benedict, who had been her accompanist in England when Balfe was abroad, was selected instead. In contrast, Benedict got paid twenty-five thousand dollars by Barnum; while still a reasonable amount for the time, it did show the difference in each one's value as far as the American promoter was concerned.

Lind sailed for America in September 1850, singing 'God Save the Queen' as she departed from Liverpool on the Collins Line ship, *Atlantic*, for New York and into history. Her two years in America made Jenny Lind one of the richest singers of all time and certainly one of the richest women in England on her return to that country. She also got married in America to a pianist friend from Germany, by the name of Otto Goldschmidt, whom she made convert to her Christian religion before the marriage. Lind's visit to America, which was reported all over Europe in the press, resulted in a string of other singers and musicians going to America. One of the first was Catherine Hayes, the Irish prima donna who followed Lind a year later almost to the day on the same steam-ship line as Lind in a comparable cabin and with a send-off concert in Liverpool similar to Lind. Hayes and Lind trailed each other up and down the East Coast of America with great success. Hayes of course did not receive anything like the amount of money Lind earned. However, Barnum was quick to sponsor Hayes on a series of concerts in California, which was something that Lind did not do.

Lind mania amazingly still lives on in our day as Jenny Lind items regularly show up on internet auction sites virtually every month. Lind returned to England, where she settled down to some occasional concerts and oratorios and to have a number of children. She continued her charity work. She died outside London in 1887.[4]

By late 1850, with his season over, Lumley had leased out his theatre to a group for a series of Grand National Concerts which were under the patronage of the Queen and which were to be start in October. Balfe was retained as one of the conductors. The

orchestra was made up of forty members from the Royal Italian
Opera and about the same number from Her Majesty's Theatre.
Composers whose music was featured included Loder, Macfarren
and Glover, together with some of the classic German orchestral
works. The soloists were mostly British singers, and included the
tenor Sims Reeves, while the pianists were Goddard, Thalberg and
Charles Hallé (1819–1895). The principal cello soloist was the
great Piatti. Balfe eventually assumed the role of musical director
for the entire programme. One of the highlights was the planned
performance of the entire chorus from the Berlin Chapel Royal
with permission of the Queen of Prussia.[5]

The concerts continued on into December with considerable
success. For a change, Balfe conducted a number of symphonic
works during this period including Beethoven's Symphony in C,
Mendelssohn's overture to the Isles of Fingal, Beethoven's Egmont
and Eroica Symphonies and others. He also performed Mozart
symphonies and other Mendelssohn works. He took advantage of
the opportunity to compose a new overture for one of the concerts
which received great praise from the critics, although there was
some comment about the orchestra brass instruments being too
loud. However, the Royal Berlin chorus, which consisted of forty
male singers, seemed to be the novelty of the series, along with
Balfe conducting the complete Beethoven's seventh symphony – a
slightly new field for the conductor, which showed his ability to
grow and expand his repertoire.

During this time Lumley had been in Paris finalizing his take-
over of the Théâtre-Italiens, much to the consternation of his former defectors, Giulia Grisi and her partner Mario. Lumley was
quick to start his season there with various members of his operatic troupe from London, including Lablache. With the concert season over in London, Balfe immediately went to Paris to find out if
it was intended for him to have a role in Lumley's new venture.
However, Balfe was due back in London for a benefit concert at
Exeter Hall on 27 January 1851, where 'all available talent in
London' would be performing.

The Balfe Benefit concert was criticized to the extent that it almost
seemed as though he had not put enough thought into the vocal
pieces that were presented. Perhaps his mind was on other things
relating to Lumley's activities. While there was great expectation that

the quality of the evening's presentation at the benefit would be enjoyable given Balfe's involvement, it turned out that a number of the vocal soloists were considered unexceptional. The programme included 'a string of *morceaux*, Italian and English, stale as a nine days' herrings', as one critic put it. Whatever time Balfe put into planning the concert it was obviously not enough, or perhaps his timing for the concert was not the best, something he should have known.

In any event, the instrumental part of the concert, along with the vocal efforts by Sims Reeves, and Frederick Lablache, were praised, but the other vocal soloists did not meet the standard including someone called Mademoiselle Lucciola from Italy, who was billed as a 'female tenor' who attempted a tenor aria from one of Meyerbeer's opera a disastrous outcome. Balfe could not have been satisfied with the event or with himself for permitting such an occurrence to be associated with his name.

The 1851 operatic season at Her Majesty's opened on schedule with *Lucia di Lammermoor* with the young French soprano, Caroline Duprez (1832–1875), in the title role. She was the daughter of the renowned tenor Gilbert Duprez, who came to London along with his wife who was also a singer, to be at their daughter's debut. The soprano had a brilliant debut with great praise for her singing and acting. Balfe was applauded for his conducting, energy, zeal and for the 'manifest improvement in his orchestra'. The season opener was followed by the London premiere of Auber's opera *Gustav III*, which was performed with great success. Balfe was given credit for his 'indomitable zeal' in getting up the opera at very short notices. All of the singers were praised.

As the year progressed, the Great Exhibition in London of 1851 was scheduled for opening in July. It was primarily an industrial exhibition in which the latest technological achievements of the major nations would be exhibited. While some concerts were being performed to celebrate the event, Balfe was not in a position to directly participate, even if he had been asked to be one of the conductors, as he was obligated to his schedule at Her Majesty's. However, in May, he was part of a benefit concert given at Her Majesty's Theatre for his friend Giovanni Puzzi's wife, Giacinta, a well-known singing teacher in London.

For this special benefit event, Balfe composed what must have been one of the most extraordinary cantatas ever written. It was structured for nine female voices and called, presumable in honour of the Great Exhibition, '*Inno Della Nazioni; Onore alla Gran Bretagne*'. Each singer musically represented a country in Europe as well as America. The whole programme went off exceedingly well. The whereabouts of the music for this cantata is unknown. The music for the cantata may possibly reside in the Giovanni Puzzi collection in the library in Parma. Details are given in Appendix IX – 25.

The critics had the following to say about the cantata:

> The task was not easy, to satisfy all of the *prime donne*, but Mr Balfe, who is of course, well acquainted with their respective peculiarities, has managed it with address, and given to each a verse, or a *trait* of vocalization, sufficient to allow them all to shine in their turns, and obtain the applause of the audience, the chief post being allotted to Madame Sontag, in just deference to that distinguished lady's position in the artistic world. In addition to this Mr. Balfe has provided accompaniments for horn, harp, and pianoforte ...[6]

Another interesting fact about this piece is the title. Giuseppe Verdi composed a cantata with the very same title for the Great Exhibition of 1861 in London. The Exhibition committee, however, refused the piece primarily because of his timing.

As the Balfe season at Her Majesty's was drawing to a closed he was permitted a benefit evening for himself. He chose to present one of his own operas. However, since all operas performed at Her Majesty's Theatre had to be in Italian, he requested his friend, the translator and librettist Manfredo Maggione, to complete a translation of his French comic opera *Les quatre fils Aymon* into Italian for his benefit.

One of the sopranos he worked with that season was an influencing factor on his decision. During the season he had performed Beethoven's *Fidelio* and Bellini's *Norma* with the dramatic coloratura soprano Sofia Cruvelli (1824–1907), then only twenty-seven years old. He was amazed by her stunning performances, as indeed were the critics. Because of her skills and vocal technique he decided to augment the operatic score for his Italian version of his opera, which Maggione had now named *I Quattro Fratelli*. The newly reworked score included a major scene with a Cavatina and a rondo finale for Cruvelli. He also wrote a new tenor aria for Italo Gardoni.

The music Balfe wrote for Cruvelli is fascinating. It is a long scene, probably around twenty minutes or more, sung by the soprano Erminia. This is a remarkable piece of vocal writing, highly demanding with its runs, trills and roulades, and indeed it is a challenge that awaits one of today's coloratura sopranos, as the whole scene and finale is intact in the British Library. See Appendix IX-26 for details.

After the performance of *I Quattro Fratelli* the critics had this to say about the opera and Cruvelli in particular:

> The production of Balfe's comic opera, *Les Quatre fils Aymon* on Monday night under its Italian title, *I Quattro Fratelli*, for the benefit of the composer was an event of more than ordinary interest. The plot and the music are well known ... Balfe never wrote music more lively, untiring, and vivacious.

The reviewer continues:

> The music of Erminia is well fitted to Cruvelli; and to make the part of more importance Balfe has written two new *airs de bravoure*. The first is a complete *feu d'artifce* of difficulties, requiring a facility of execution, a power and a range of voice which few singers possess, but which Cruvelli, thanks to nature, has entirely in command. The burden of the song goes to say that Erminia does not care to be a duchess; and Cruvelli sings it as if she did care to be a duchess, or indeed anything but a singer. The second air, a *rondo finale* in the modern style, is even more brilliant and showy than the first. At the same time it is more concise, and consequently more effective. Cruvelli sang it superbly. The trills, and scales, and arpeggios, and roulades and *points d'orgue*, were executed with marvelous skill. In short, we have never listened to a more finished and admirable exhibition of vocal talent. It created a *furore*; and no wonder.[7]

The following is an extract from the *Times* newspaper reports on the opera:

> Mdlle. Cruvelli was entrusted with two bravura airs composed by Mr Balfe for the occasion. The first of these, 'Di Duchess il nome altero' is very long, full of *traits de force*, intricate *fioriture*, *points d'orgue* of the most elaborate nature, scales,

chromatic and diatonic, arpeggios, &c., involving endless mod-
ulations, and taxing the register of a voice throughout a compass
of nearly three octaves – from D in alt to nearly F sharp below
the lines. Nevertheless, although executed with marvelous
adroitness by Mdlle. Cruvelli, it failed to produce a proportion-
ate effect – providing that extraneous intervals, velocitous
roulades, and trills and flights, that are nothing northing more
than trills and flights, have no absolute charm unless accompanied by sentiment, and made subservient to form, in the absence
of which the office of music as a medium of expression is set at
nought, and the astonishment of the few who comprehend the
difficulties surmounted, becomes a very poor compensation for
the indifference of the crowd, untouched and apathetic without
being able to explain the reason. The second air, the rondo
finale of the third act (*Or qui verra*) was quite another thing.
Here the difficulties were even greater and more various; but the
theme was joyous and appropriate to the matter in hand, the
design simple and more interesting. A more brilliant and dexter-
ous piece of vocalization has seldom been heard; and as there
was nothing forced or unnatural in the music, the rich voice of
the young singer, full clear, and telling from the highest note to
the lowest, gave an additional charm to the extreme facility of
her execution, and stirred up the audience to a genial display of
enthusiasm.[8]

Operatic performances at Her Majesty's Theatre continued with an
extended season into October 1851, at reduced ticket prices. There
were also rumoujrs that Balfe was taking retirement as Lumley had
hired the German musician Ferdinand Hiller (1811–1885), to be
his new director for Paris and London. The editor of *The Musical
World* was quick to mention that as far as he was aware that a Balfe
retirement was not planned.[9] However, there was no comment
from Balfe, or for that matter from Lumley or Hiller.

Between the rumours and the need to compose again, Balfe, it
seems, was once again active in writing some new operas. There
was also some good news for him in terms of getting his music
performed, as his old friend Alfred Bunn had again taken over the
management of Drury Lane Theatre.

It was also announced around the same time that Balfe was

working on two new operas and that one would be with a Bunn libretto, while the other would be with a libretto by his Dublin friend, the actor and dramatist Dion Boucicault (1820–1890). He completed the new opera for Bunn, *The Sicilian Bride*, which premiered on 6 March 1852. Later in the year Balfe completed another English opera, *The Devil in It*, which was first performed on 26 July 1852.

The possible association with Boucicault would have been an interesting arrangement and perhaps given Balfe one of his best librettos yet. However, nothing transpired. Many years earlier Balfe had invited his friend Boucicault to work on a libretto for him. They agreed on a subject. In an amusing article written fifty years after the fact Boucicault tells the story of what happened when he presented his libretto to Balfe. Apparently the composer was furious with him, saying:

> It would not do at all. I was ignorant of the musical plan on which an opera is constructed. Balfe was writing at the time for the French opera with Scribe and St Georges, past masters, as librettists, so it is needless to describe the respect with which I listened to the information Balfe gave me, as to their method. [Balfe outlined a diagram of the structure by each act showing the scenes, choruses, arias, duets etc.]. The Dramatist is invited to put flesh on this skeleton? he must subordinate his drama in every respect to the necessities of the musical form! Feeling unable to accomplish the feat, the work was abandoned.[10]

Of course Boucicault later provided the libretto for Jules Benedict's masterful *The Lily of Killarney*, one of the best English operas, which premiered in 1862 in London. What a lost opportunity for Balfe.

During the early 1850s there were continued discussions again in the periodicals about organizing a National Opera Company. Despite the renewed interest in English Opera in the media it would be another five years before Balfe put pen to paper to compose another opera for London. At that time the circumstance would be quite different from his current 1852 environment.

The 1852 season at Her Majesty's started again at the beginning of April with Balfe as the musical director. *The Musical World* made the following announcement:

It is with untold satisfaction we announce that Mr. Balfe is again at the head of the musical department. Many and various were the rumours about a new successor to Balfe as conductor of Her Majesty's Theatre; but we, who knew the difficulty of providing a competent person to fill Balfe's place, [with] no trust in the rumour, [we] held to the belief that Balfe would return to his old post.[11]

The repertoire of Her Majesty's was expanded, with more opera performances to compete with the cross-town Royal Italian Opera, which had also greatly expanded its season. Lumley continued to add new singers. The soprano Johann Wagner (1826–1894), the niece of the composer Richard Wagner (1813–1883), was signed by Lumley only to find that she had also signed with his competition. Lumley got an injunction; however, Johann Wagner never sang with either opera company during that period, deciding instead to return to Germany.

In May Balfe's close friend and fellow musician Julius Benedict lost his wife. Balfe and his wife had been particularly close friends with the Benedicts. A mass was said for her at the French Chapel in central London. Balfe conducted a performance of Mozart's *Requiem Mass No. 18* in her honour at the chapel. The singers included Lablache and his son, the soprano Castellan and the tenor Gardoni. It was the first time that Balfe was associated with an event of this nature in a church.

After the opera season was over the management of Her Majesty's Theatre was reorganized into what appeared to be a limited liability company. Lumley was mentioned as being associated with the theatre; however, as time would tell that was not to be the case. Apparently there was difficulty getting a charter for the new theatre management group and as a result, the theatre was not able to open it doors for the years 1854 through March 1856. For the present, Lumley was out of theatre management, as his contract in Paris had not been renewed.

With the close of the season, Balfe and his family travelled to Danzig to be with their daughter Louisa and her husband and to see their first grandchild, Theodore William Behrens, who was born earlier in the year and called after his two grandfathers. Balfe wrote a letter from Danzig on 2 October 1852 to his lawyer Harry Surman in London about arranging a new letter of credit and other business-related items, saying as he closes, we are all well and start for St

Petersburg tomorrow. However, as a P.S. to the letter he adds the following very personal comment: "'My grandson is charming.'[12]

The Balfe children were now growing up – Michael junior was now sixteen and Victoire fifteen. After spending Christmas and the New Year in Danzig they departed for St Petersburg in Russia, where Balfe had been invited to join Lablache and others at the Italian Opera season for some concerts.[13]

On 1 February 1853, an afternoon concert was given in St Petersburg devoted to the works of Balfe. Lablache and members of his family and others participated. The tenor Mario translated a duet from Balfe's opera *Keolanthe* into Italian and performed it probably with Lina Balfe, since his partner Grisi was not in St. Petersburg during this period. See Appendix IX-39.

While in St Petersburg he wrote a letter to his attorney, Harry Surman, on 12 March 1853 detailing some of his musical compositions, marches, songs etc., and estimating what they may be worth in terms of income if Beale or Chappel the London music publishers wanted to purchase them. However, the final paragraph of the letter is the most interesting. It reads as follows:

> You asked me to tell you confidentially what I would take to come to H.M.T. [Her Majesty's Theatre], London, nothing less than Eight hundred pounds secured, and the money Lumley owes me paid before I should quit this country. I must also tell you, that I did not care one bit for London this past year for it will be no go, and [anyway] I want to return to London with something like éclat. Why does not Gye [manager at Covent Garden] engage me *to compose an opera for his theatre.*

Obviously Balfe and Lumley had a falling out at the end of the 1852 season and Lumley apparently did not pay Balfe everything he was supposed to. This may be one of the reasons why Lumley did not rehire Balfe when he reopened the theatre some years later in 1856.

Balfe participated in a series of other concerts in St Petersburg but did not conduct any operas, nor were any of his operas performed despite their popularity in Berlin, Vienna and other cities. Artists participating in the concerts included Pauline Viardot Garcia, Mario, Emilie deMeric, Achille de Bassini (1819–1881) and Madame Caradori (1800–1865). After St Petersburg he went to Moscow for more concerts. While in Moscow it's possible he may have visited the grave of his fellow Dubliner, the great pianist John Field, who had died there a number of years previously.

His visit to Russia was not very satisfactory professionally. Apart from the concerts he spent most of the time giving singing and music lessons to the daughters of society. He got paid well for it but it could hardly have been satisfying professionally. He felt that he had made enough contacts in Russia for a return visit the following year. However, the Crimean War broke out between Russia and France and Britain, which precluded him from going.

They left Russia in May 1853, travelling back to the Behrends at Danzig on the Baltic Sea, where apparently they spent a few weeks before departing for Vienna, where he had a contract to produce one of his operas.

By now there was direct rail services to Vienna and beyond from various points in Europe, so the journey would have been reasonable, particularly during the summer months of 1853 when he was travelling. Most probably Lina and the children made the journey with him. She would have wanted the children to visit her father's native city.

The opera he chose to give in Vienna was *Keolanthe*. However, he reworked the score to augment the opera significantly and had it translated into German. They arrived in Vienna some time in July 1853. The opera had its first performance on 27 August at the Court Theatre (Kärntnertor).[14] It was still being played several months later, right into January 1854. Given the success of his earlier operas, *Die vier Haimonskinder* and *Die Zigeunerin*, and the frequency with which they had been performed in Vienna, his new opera was basically assured of success.

He left Vienna some time after the opera premiere to travel to Trieste, where he had a commitment to produce an Italian version of his ever popular *Bohemian Girl*. Since Trieste was under Austrian rule and a sea port, and the Austrians had built a railway from Vienna to Trieste, which gave them access to the Mediterranean for trade. Trieste had been made a free city and it was now populated by all sorts of nationalities involved in trade.

The next year of Balfe's life was spent in Italy. Initially he worked on a translation of his *Bohemian Girl* score into Italian, for Trieste. The translator was Riccardo Paderni. Because of the politics (Austrian rule of Trieste), the story location had to be changed from Pressburg in Bohemia to Scotland. Name changes for the characters also resulted. The opera premiered at the Teatro Grande on 12 February 1854 as *La Zingara*, and as always for *The Bohemian Girl*, regardless of the language it had resounding success. The production moved on later to Brescia, Verona, Bologna where Balfe also conducted it. The music publisher Ricordi released the vocal score of the opera. It was the first opera Balfe had published by Italy's most prestigious music publishing house.

La Zingara would later be performed in London, Dublin, New York, San Francisco and other places in America as his 'girl' as he called it, got renewed vigour with the Italian translation. It still continued to be performed in Germany and Vienna in its German-language version, for many years.

Its success in Trieste resulted in another contract, this time for a completely new opera. He had the opportunity to work with one of Italy's great librettists, Francesco Maria Piave (1810–1876). Piave had already completed several operatic librettos for Giuseppe Verdi, including, *Ernani, Rigoletto* and *La Traviata*. The story chosen by Balfe related to a real life sixteenth century painter called Antonio Moro. It was set in Antwerp and it had high dramatic content. Piave gave the title of *Pittore e Duca* to the opera. Balfe's choice of cast included two leading Verdi protagonists, the soprano Fanny Salviani-Donatelli (1815–1891) then age forty, who had created Verdi's lead role in *La Traviata* in Venice the previous year. The tenor was Raffaele Mirate (1815–1895), who had created the role of the Duke in Rigoletto in Venice in 1851 and various roles for Donizetti and Verdi.

The opera opened at the Teatro Grande in Trieste on 21 November 1854.[15] For whatever reason, the opera was not a success. It had only had a few performances when Balfe withdrew it. The problem in some way appeared to be related to the soprano, Salviani-Donatelli, who was not in good vocal condition, or was not satisfied with her part. In any event it was withdrawn. This was not the first failure that Salviani-Donatelli had experienced. She had had a similar failure in the premiere of Verdi's *La Traviata* the year before in Venice in 1853. It would be almost thirty years before the opera would be heard again in an English version at Her Majesty's Theatre in London in 1882, when it did experience some success and a number of performances.

Balfe travelled on to Milan and Turin, where he had discussions about new operas, but nothing really resulted.

In New York around this time the impresario Max Maretzek, who was managing the Academy of Music, an opera house on 14th Street, wrote to his friend Balfe in Italy to advise him of some news being reported in the New York papers. Maretzek and Balfe had known each other since Maretzek managed the chorus at Her Majesty's Theatre under Balfe's direction. He wrote to Balfe to tell him that there was a report in one of the local newspapers to say, 'M. W. Balfe has been engaged to come to America, for the purpose of taking the place of Max Maretzek during the next opera season.' Obviously, Maretzek was probably somewhat concerned about his job and seemed to be sounding Balfe out to see if there was in truth in the story.[16]

This reference to Balfe going to America is interesting, since it would have been a logical move for him at that time of his life. So many of his associates did go to America, some for short tours, other remaining there. Indeed, during the 1850s there was an enormous amount of traffic across the Atlantic, first to New York and elsewhere on the east coast by musicians from Europe. Many continued on to San Francisco, which had regular opera seasons. Some ultimately continued to Australia and New Zealand, where opera was being performed by travelling troupes on a regular basis by the 1860s.

For many years the question about Balfe not going to America has been raised without any satisfactory answers. His music was as popular in America as in Britain and Ireland. His name was well known and certainly New York would have loved to have had him as a musical director at one of its many venues for opera and concerts. America probably would have changed Balfe's life, certainly financially. In Europe so much of his time was spent chasing new opportunities in order to maintain his income. One visit to America probably would have made him rich for life given his celebrity status similar to what it did for Jenny Lind, Catherine Hayes, Giulia Grisi and Mario and others. There can be little doubt that Balfe must have received numerous offers from people in America interested in him and his talents.

In recent times a copy of a letter written in 1848 by Balfe to his friend the musician John Hatton (1809–1886), prior to Hatton's departure for America came into the possession of the author.[17]

Balfe clearly indicates his long time interest in going to America and his reason for not being able to make the journey, saying:

London June 29th, 1848

My dear Hatton:

I hear that you are going to America and much regret that we shall be deprived [of] the society of such an excellent companion, but your *friends* must not be selfish and therefore, God be with you; you are sure to make your fortune in that enlightened country. They are certain to appreciate your great talents.

Many a time have I wished to visit America but I dread the long sea voyage and therefore fear that I never shall have the pleasure of setting my seat on their hospitable shore [where] several of my off-springs have met with a friendly welcome, *The Bohemian Girl*, *The Siege of Rochelle* which I hear are favourites, but enough of me. You are sure to delight them with your light fantastic pieces, but still do not forget the classical, Bach, Handel, Mendelssohn all of which can really excel – God be with you my dear Hatton. Success is sure to crown your efforts.

Yours most truly,

M.W. Balfe

Sadly, Balfe never did visit America. We know that he suffered from a serious bronchial/ asthmatic condition most of his life and certainly as he grew older he seemed to experience more frequent attacks. Possibly most of this was caused by London's climate and the infamous London fog (smog), as the industrial age progressed. Eventually, Balfe would die from the problem.

However, it is strange that he was not able to overcome his fear of the transatlantic voyage, which only took about ten to fifteen days in his time in the 1840–50s. Yes, some of the sailings did not make it. The London stage actor Tyrone Power, whom Balfe had known (grandfather of the film star of the same name), disappeared on one of the sailings around the 1850s. However, Balfe travelled to Russia in the middle of winter from Danzig, a journey probably of almost two weeks, which required him to travel overland as the Baltic Sea link would have been frozen over. A trip to

Russia with his chronic problem was probably far more hazardous that a transatlantic crossing.

One can only speculate at this point in time what a trip to America would have meant to him and his family and to his musical output. There is no doubt whatsoever that his financial welfare for the remainder of his life would have been vastly changed.

After Trieste, Balfe went to Milan, where he spent several months, perhaps as the guest of Ricordi or some of his other friends. He worked on another opera, *Lo Scudiero,* based on a Piave libretto, but nothing came of it. It seemed to be a time of rest and giving thought to what he wanted to do next. Italy had greatly changed from his early days there. Verdi was now the dominant composer in most cities, Rossini was no longer being performed with the frequency of two decades earlier. While he had made a considerable amount of money during the previous seven years he now needed to get back to work, so early in 1856 Balfe returned to London.[18]

Alfred Bunn was no longer the manager at Drury Lane. His options for composing new operas were slim; as a result he devoted most of his time to composing songs and teaching singing.

It was during this period also that his series of songs with words provided by Longfellow were published. They became immensely popular. The six songs were:

The Reaper and the Flowers	*Good Night! Beloved, Good Night!*
Annie of Tharaw	*The Green Trees Whispered Mild and Low*
The Day is done	*This is the Place – stand still my Steed*

In addition there was a duet, *Trust Her Not*, which is still performed in today's concert halls. Balfe sold them to the music publisher Boosey and Sons for one-hundred guineas. Around the same time there was also a song called *The First Kiss*, published by Boosey; the words were by *The Musical World* sub-editor, Desmond Ryan. With Balfe's return to London a profile of him was done during this period by *The Musical World*. The extensive article spanned several issues of the publication, commencing in March.[19] Its timing almost suggests that the editor of *The Musical World* wanted to help Balfe get back into circulation in London and remind readers of his past achievements after his four-year absence from the country.

In July 1856 a Balfe benefit was mounted at Drury Lane. Balfe, apparently somewhat doubtful that his name would draw the crowds given his long absence from London, planned an evening extravaganza. Ticket prices were doubled for the event with no drop in demand. It started with a performance of *The Bohemian Girl* with the ever popular tenor, Sims Reeves and his wife, Emma Lucombe (1820–1895), and Balfe's former pupil, Willoughby Weiss (1820–1867), with Balfe conducting. As Balfe entered the orchestra pit, the composer was received with 'uproarious and long continued applause'. The whole evening was classified by the critics as an extraordinary affair of wonderful entertainment. After the opera, there was a concert in which many of his songs were sung, also excerpts from *The Maid of Artois*. Pauline Viardot Garcia was one of the many singers performing. His long-time friend George Osborne and Arabella Goddard (1836–1932) performed Osborne's duet for four hands from Meyerbeer's opera *L'etoil du Nord*. The evening closed with the last act of Verdi's *Il Trovatore*. The event concluded after midnight. According to reports hundreds of people were turned away from the event, which was crowded in every nook and corner of the house.[20]

Towards the end of 1856 Balfe went to Paris for discussions on performing his *Falstaff* at the Théâtre-Italiens. However, for some reason it didn't work out and after some months Balfe returned to London in January 1857. He apparently brought his daughter, Victoire to Paris with him and on his return he said that 'the whole Parisian world is telling of the talents of his daughter'. Obviously, he was very proud of Victoire. No doubt that Lina would have accompanied them.[21]

Balfe's daughter Victoire, now nineteen, had been studying music and singing and was preparing herself for an operatic debut sometime in the not too distant future. Balfe and Victoire were very close. She not only studied with her father but also with Manuel Garcia for voice and William Sterndale-Bennett (1811–1876), for piano. Victoire went on to make her debut at the Italian opera at the Lyceum Theatre in Bellini's *La sonnambula* on 28 May 1857.[22] She had a good voice and technique. A few months later she travelled with the London Company to Dublin for her debut there in the same opera as London. She sang in Donizetti's *Lucia di Lammermoor*, and in Bellini's *I Puritani*. She also performed in a benefit concert while in Dublin.

Her father arrived in Dublin to assist at a benefit which was for her. It was given in August 1857. The highlight of her evening was when she sang 'I dreamt that I dwelt in marble halls' from her father's opera *The Bohemian Girl*. Her performances achieved great acclaim in the house and by the critics. Later in the following year she visited Italy with her parents. She performed the role of Zerlina in *Don Giovanni* in Turin with her parents in the audience.

By now Balfe had written eighteen operas for London alone, much less his works that were produced in continental Europe. He was still the most important operatic composer in Britain. No one had emerged to challenge his position in any meaningful way. It was quite natural that when two enterprising singers decided to form a new English Opera Company they should look to Balfe to support their venture, which was to be known as the Pyne-Harrison Opera Company. William Harrison was an old friend of Balfe's from the composer's *Bohemian Girl* days. Louisa Pyne (1832–1904) was a young energetic soprano with an excellent technique and a quality voice. They had joined forces in 1854 and visited America, where they performed in English opera (mostly Balfe and Wallace works) in major cities such as New York, Boston, and Philadelphia along the East Coast for almost three years.

On their return to London they formed their new company and had invited Balfe to write a new work for them. Their company was well structured they had good singers in the company and their administration was efficient and in the hands of the experienced impresario Frederick Gye (1809–1878), who most recently had being managing the Covent Garden, Royal Italian Opera until a fire closed the house down in 1856. It was an ideal situation for Balfe at this stage of his life. He would be provided with librettos and he simply had to compose the operas and the Pyne-Harrison Company would pay him for his work. They would own the right to the opera. Balfe didn't even have to conduct. Balfe's first work was the *Rose of Castille*, which he wrote specifically to suit Louisa Pyne's voice. It premiered on 29 October 1857. The opera was an immediate success. The following is an extract from the long report that appeared in *The Times* the day after the premiere:

> The ancient glories of the Bohemian Girl were revived at this theatre [Lyceum] last night, when a new opera by Mr Balfe,

entitled The Rose of Castille, was produced with a success as great as was probably ever achieved by the composer of the first-named popular work ...

He continues:

> Mr Balfe in composing music for the peculiar talent of Miss Louisa Pyne, has gone far beyond his French predecessor [French composer Adam had composed an opera to a similar libretto]. Whether the Irish musician wrote from a conviction that Miss Pyne could execute even greater difficulties than Madam Cabal [Adam's prima donna] whose gift was to astonish by her facile execution almost as much as to enchant by the graces of style we are unable to guess. At any rate, he [Balfe] has not written in vain; for vocalization more finished and extraordinary than with which, Miss Pyne repeatedly roused the audience to enthusiasm last night, was never listened to.[23]

The opera had over one hundred performances at the Lyceum within a year of its premiere, and most of the critics were of the opinion that the work was one of Balfe's finest. The composer obviously had not lost his touch. He came roaring back. Once again he was in the right place at the right time and had the skills capable of delivering a successful work for London audiences. It was an invigorating moment for Balfe, who had been somewhat adrift over the past few years. Over the next seven years he composed several operas for the Pyne-Harrison troupe. Several were remarkably well received, entering the repertoire of future opera companies. These were Balfe's final years as a major composer. During the period, he composed *The Puritan's Daughter*, *Satanella*, and other less popular ones, with intriguing titles such as *The Armourer of Nantes*, *Bianca*, *The Bravo's Bride* and *Blanche de Nevers*.[24] Each of these operas is fully documented and addressed in Tyldesley's book. After this it remained for Balfe to compose what might be classified an operetta, *The Sleeping Queen*, in August 1864, which had some modest success in Britain and America.

Over the previous decade or so Balfe had a very good regular income from his years as a conductor at Her Majesty's which was supplemented by his earnings in off-season months in places such as Germany, Russia and Italy. However, he had spent excessively during his four years abroad in the mid-1850s, without any real regular income to underwrite his expenses during the period. His income from the Pyne-Harrison arrangement, while significant, was quite limited.

It was strange that at that point in his career that he did not try to seek out a position with one of the many musical organization, that existed in Britain, given his reputation and skills. A position at one of Britain's academies probably was not feasible for him because of his lack of formal academic training. His musical skills were the result of years of on-the-job training and since he had never had any formal training, although one could argue that the year or so he spent with Cherubini in Paris was the equivalent of academic training, since the Italian headed up the Conservatoire in Paris. The other difficult fact to understand is why he never again took up conducting. Apart from his experience as an operatic conductor, which placed him in the top tier across Europe, he also seemed to have significant success based on what the critics said performing the works of the classic masters such as Beethoven, Mendelssohn, Mozart and others, which would have presented his another option. Nothing in any of his correspondence sheds light on this. He did endeavour to get his old conducting job back at Her Majesty's Theatre in 1856 when Lumley reopened the theatre; however, Lumley by that time had made commitments to others.

Apart from his financial needs these years were also difficult times emotionally for the composer. Several of his friends were no longer around. Luigi Lablache, the greatest bass singer of the century, the friend of Beethoven and one who had helped Balfe many times in his career pursuits, died in Naples in January 1858. Alfred Bunn died in December 1860. Balfe attended the funeral and there were others. In 1860 Balfe was now fifty-two years old, and while his daughter Louisa had married well neither his son Michael, now twenty-four, nor his daughter Victoire, twenty-three, had found suitable partners yet so they were living at home, which was now 16 North Audley Street, London.[25]

Balfe's old restless spirit came to the fore once again for travel in 1860. It seems that a combination of motives were to drive him on this occasion. Max and Louisa usually spent the summer in Berlin, returning to Danzig for the winter season. They now also had five children and Lina most probably would have wanted to visit her grandchildren. There was also another factor: the Behrens were interested in moving to England permanently, because of the political climate in Germany. The country's unification under Bismarck and the aftermath of the Crimean War had drastically affected the corn trade. The Danzig Corn Exchange in which the Behrens family business had a large stake was virtually moving towards collapse.[26] Also the industrial growth in Britain with its expanding Empire provided some good business opportunities for Behrens, in timber, corn and other commodities. They had a small office or representative in Liverpool and later would open an office in London.

The Balfes left for Danzig probably in December 1860. How long they spent there is not known. However, while there a decision was made to visit St Petersburg in Russia, probably early in the New Year. The trip to Russia would have been initiated by Max, who was used to doing business in Poland and Russia where he bought timber.[27] They all arrived in St Petersburg in January or February 1860, which was normally the social season with the Italian Opera running from October into February. However, in 1860 there does not appear to have been any Italian opera being performed during this period. This tends to support the fact that the Balfes joined Behrens on business and that was what brought them to St Petersburg, not any artistic or musical endeavor on the part of the composer.

In some respects the trip was fortuitous, at least initially for Victoire, as she met the fifty-three-year-old, wealthy, Sir John Fiennes Crampton (1807–1886), who was then Her Majesty's Minister, to the Court of Russia. Victoire was an attractive twenty-two-year-old sophisticated young woman who spoke French and Italian along with English, and Crampton was immediately infatuated with her, so much so that he proposed and they were married on 31 March 1860.[28] This was a whirlwind marriage, particularly during the Victorian era. Crampton had a distinguished career as a diplomat in America in addition to Russia and so he would certainly have been welcomed by the Balfes into the family, except perhaps for the age difference of more than thirty years.

As time would show, this would create a disaster of major proportions for Victoire and the Balfe family, but that was all in the future, for now in St Petersburg it was a time for celebration with Victoire, her family and the Behrens.

NOTES

1. Documentation in the Rothschild Archives, London shows that Behrend financed some of his timber and corn business through the Rothschild Bank in London.
2. Copy marriage certificate showing that the marriage took place on 15 April 1850.
3. See *Catherine Hayes; The Hibernian Prima Donna* by Basil Walsh.
4. For a full account of Jenny Lind's life, her career and time in America, see *Jenny Lind the Artist* by Holland and Rockstro.
5. *The Musical World*, 9 November 1850, front page.
6. *The Times*, 27 May 1851.
7. *The Musical World* 16 August 1851, pp. 522–523.
8. *The Times*, 13 August 1851.
9. *The Musical World* 4 October 1851, p. 635.
10. *The North American Review*, Vol. 144, issue 365, April 1887.
11. *The Musical World*, 27 March 1852, p. 194.
12. Copy letter to H. Surman dated 2 October 1852 from Danzig provided by the Lilly Library, Indiana University, Bloomington, Indiana.
13. During this period Eric White in his *History of English Opera*, p. 283 says that Balfe first went to Vienna before going to St Petersburg. He probably took this information from Barrett, one of Balfe's early biographers. This is incorrect. After Lumley's extended opera season, which finished in October 1852, Balfe and his family went to Danzig to see his daughter Louisa and her husband and their first grandchild. From there they went on to St Petersburg early in the New Year, where he participated in a series of concerts. After St Petersburg they first went back to Danzig and then later that year (1853) to Vienna.
14. Copy programme of the performance in the possession of the author.
15. The premiere date of 21 November 1854 is the correct date for the opera *Pittore e Duca*. The opera premiere date is misquoted in various works, for example Tyldesley in his Balfe book says that it occurred in September 1854, which is not correct.
16. See *Crochets and Quavers: or Revelations of an Opera Manager in America* by Max Maretzek, pp. 175–215.
17. Balfe letter dated 29 June 1848 to John Hatton held by the National Library of Ireland, Dublin under Balfe's name. The call number possibly ACE 1790 for this item. The number is unclear.
18. Balfe's return to London after a most successful tour in Russia, Germany and Italy by *The Musical World* in it, 12 January 1856 issue, p. 28.
19. *Sketches of English Artists No. V. Michael William Balfe – The Musical World*, issue 8 March 1856 through issue 21 June 1856.
20. *The Musical World* 12 July 1856, p. 439.
21. *The Musical World*, 27 September 1856, p. 615; *The Musical World*, 31 January 1857, p. 72.
22. Tyldesley in his book on Balfe says that Victoire Balfe made her London debut at the Lyceum in La sonnambula in 1855, which is incorrect. The correct date was 28 May 1857.
23. *The Times*, 30 October 1857.
24. For details of the musical structure of these Balfe operas see Tyldesley's book on Balfe; for performance and casts information see Appendix III of this book.
25. Address shown in the 1861 British census.
26. I am indebted to Friederike Hammer of London, a descendant of the Behrens family of Danzig for providing some of this information about the family background.
27. Documentation in the Rothschild Archives in London shows that Behrens made various purchase of commodities in Poland and Russia.
28. *The Times*, report of 5 April 1860, '*Marriage of Mademoiselle Victoire Balfe*'.

CHAPTER TEN

The Final Years
1861–1874

After their visit to St Petersburg, the Balfes returned first to Danzig, and later to London, where the composer was obligated to work on another opera for the Pyne-Harrison Company. Victoire, now Lady Crampton of course, stayed in St Petersburg with her new husband. It was an emotional farewell when Victoire's family left to return to Danzig. She had not been away from her family for any length of time before.

While in Danzig a general agreement within the family was reached in which the Behrens would plan for a move to England in the near future. Louisa also wanted to have her children educated there. The Balfes subsequently returned to London. In a joyous reunion in the autumn of 1860 the Cramptons visited London, where Victoire had the honour of being presented at Court as, Lady Crampton. While in London *The Times* reported that they stayed with the Balfes at their North Audley Street Home.[1]

During this stay, there was obviously nothing to indicate that there were any problems with the marriage at this point in time. However, very shortly the marriage would begin to unravel at a rapid rate to become a very significant scandal in London. It would be extremely traumatic time for the entire Balfe family.

After the departure of the Cramptons, Balfe continued working on his next opera for the Pyne-Harrison company. Generally, during this stage of his career Balfe appeared to be quite content to be somewhat inactive, and to stay at home. He now had two daughters married off to wealthy individuals. Strangely, his son Michael, who was now twenty-five years old, never seemed to have much of a relationship with the family, or for that matter, to accompany the family in their trips abroad.

In early 1861, the Balfes were still living at North Audley Street in London.[2] Michael junior does not appear to have been a member of the household at the time. It's also interesting that Louisa and one of her children, the two-year-old Lina Behrend, were shown as residents. Possibly, Louisa was just a visiting guest in her parents' household at the time the census was taken. There were also five household servants shown as residing in the Balfe domain.

Later in the year, in May, the Cramptons paid another visit to London when they again stayed at the Balfes' home. By now the Balfes were living at 7 Upper Seymour Street. The Cramptons'visit this time was related to Victoire's health, and to consult with Sir Charles Laycock (1799-1875), a famous London specialist. Laycock was obstetrician to the Queen. According to a report the Balfes were not made aware of the results of the examination, which is somewhat hard to believe.[3] In any event, Victoire, considered to be out of danger, returned to St Petersburg with her husband.

Meanwhile, Balfe continued to try to focus on his work. He had recently received a request from his Parisian friend, Vernoy de Saint Georges, to produce a French version of *The Bohemian Girl* in Rouen for which St Georges would write the libretto. Balfe was agreeable to the proposition, but did not know if he could attend the premiere; possibly because of his deteriorating financial situation, although he claimed ill health was his problem. It was agreed that St Georges would supervise the production as soon as Balfe had completed the reworked score to the French libretto.

The new French version of *The Bohemian Girl*, with the title *La Bohémienne*, premiered at the Théâtre Lyric in Rouen in April 1862. The future great singer and creator of the title roles in the French operas *Carmen* and *Mignon*, Celestine Gallie-Marié, sang the role of the Gypsy Queen in the opera. The part as rewritten had a much more dominant role in this version of the opera. Remarkably, the conductor for the premiere was a twenty-year-old, Jules Massenet (1842–1912), just starting out, on what would be a brilliant career as a musician and composer. There were thirteen performances of the opera, which made it quite a successful premiere, particularly for a provincial location.[4]

In 1862, the Crampton family moved to Madrid; presumably another diplomatic assignment brought them there. They stayed there until April 1863, when they moved to Paris. Shortly after their arrival in Paris, Lina Balfe received a telegraph message from her daughter that she was 'dangerously ill'. Lina immediately went to visit Victoire in Paris. The marriage was in a mess, Crampton apparently had been impotent since the beginning and now there was great emotional stress between them. Victoire was emotionally distraught, supposedly to the extent that she was on the verge of a complete nervous breakdown. Once Lina got all of the facts from her daughter, she quickly returned to London to her husband, insisting that he visit Crampton without delay. Balfe, also very upset at the news and the action he had to take, travelled to Paris to speak with his daughter's husband.

It seems that after a lengthy discussion with Crampton, which took place in the open air of the Tuileries Gardens, Crampton was quite amenable and sympathetic to Victoire's situation. Presumably the discussion included the fact that Victoire wanted children. Crampton was agreeable that the best course was divorce. He advised Balfe that he would not contest such an action.

Balfe returned to London with Victoire in tow. When Lina learned about the proposed divorce she was adamant that it was not an option, as her daughter was Catholic. She also wanted to give her daughter the option of remarrying, which divorce would not permit in her eyes. So Balfe consulted with his London solicitor on the best course of action. He eventually directed the lawyer to file papers to have the marriage annulled on the grounds of the impotency of Sir John Crampton. It was an incredible decision and it clearly shows how much Lina influenced the family.

Such a court action in Victorian London meant that all the facts of the case would be made public and that Victoire would have to give oral testimony in open court. It was a very difficult and decision that would cause no end of embarrassment for the Balfes and for Crampton alike. Lina was uncompromising, knowing full well that it would be scandalous as far as Victorian society was concerned. The Balfes moved forward with the court case. They filed their petition in May 1863.

The hearing took place on 20 November 1863. The judge had agreed that Balfe could testify in lieu of his daughter, because of the sensitive nature of the facts of the case. Crampton did not appear, and his lawyer, who did appear as a formality, did not contest the case, nor did he see a need for any cross-examination of the composer. The judge made the statement that he had read all the affidavits and that it was not necessary to read them in court. He ruled in favour of the Balfes and the annulment was granted along with the costs of the case.[5]

During all of the recent month's legal activity and related distractions, the composer continued his basic work of writing new operas. The day after the court decision was made, Balfe's sixth opera for the Pyne-Harrison company, *Blanche de Nevers*, had its premiere at the Covent Garden Theatre.

The newspapers of the time reported on the 'Balfe Falsely Called Crampton vs Crampton' case, which must have created significant "gossip" interest among society throughout London. With the court case behind her, Victoire proceeded to apply to the Pope in Rome to have the marriage formally annulled by the Catholic Church. Victoire was twenty-six years old at the time. Balfe must have blamed himself for all the emotional problems he had created for his family when he allowed Victoire to rush into a marriage with a man more than thirty years her senior.

However, Victoire may not have been quite as naïve as the court documentation might have implied. Despite all of the frenzy she created around her marriage to Crampton, she had met someone her own age, a very attractive and equally rich and titled single man, the twenty-six-year-old, Duc de Frias, while in Madrid with Crampton. Perhaps she met him at an Embassy function or at church.

The de Frias family had a long prestigious heritage in the history of Madrid and the Burgos areas of Spain. Victoire met the Duc de Frias again in London during this period, which was shortly after her annulment from Crampton. How they might have renewed their relationship, or if in fact it was a renewal, is not known. Perhaps he saw some reference to her annulment in the newspapers. A romantic relationship had developed with a commitment to marriage by de Frias, once a Papal dispensation was granted, as de Frias was also Catholic.

The ability of Victoire to be suddenly able to rush into another marriage so quickly after her 'dangerously ill' marriage problem with Crampton has to be questioned. She possibly was obviously looking for a way to get out of her fruitless marriage with Crampton, as she desperately wanted children, and the Crampton relationship had no hope. Obviously, the significantly younger de Frias offered her everything.

During the same period, the Balfes, somewhat weary of their recent experiences, decided early in 1864 to leave London for the countryside. They leased a house called Rowney Abbey in the small village of Ware in Hertfordshire, which had farming potential. The property was quite large and it included a lake.[6] This would be where Lina and Michael Balfe would spend the rest of their days together. Balfe in his more restful country environment started work on a new opera based on a Sir Walter Scott story, *The Talisman*, with a libretto provided by Arthur Matthison. He did not have any special assignment for it initially. It just seemed to be something that he wanted to take his time at so that he could develop it without the normal time pressure associated with composing. He also worked on an operetta called *The Sleeping Queen*, which would have it premiere in August of 1864.

The only real good news that the Balfes had had in recent times was a notification from Rome that Victoire's long-delayed dispensation had eventually been granted by the Pope in August 1864.[7]

Within a period of two weeks after receiving the Papal dispensation Victoire was married to the Duc de Frias, in September 1864, which clearly suggests that there had been a relationship going on between the two for some considerable time. Victoire, now somewhat less naïve and more self-assured, broadcast her Papal annulment around town to various society members along with a formal invitation to her marriage. A letter dated 17 August 1864 from Charlotte Rothschild in London to her son, Leopold, on the situation makes for interesting reading as follows:

Alfy [Alfred, son of Charlotte Rothschild] delivered the lovely ex-Lady Crampton's letter; it was an invitation for Evy, Papa [Lionel Rothschild] and me to witness the solemnization of the lady's nuptials. The long wished-for, long delayed and anxiously expected dispensation from the Pope arrived yesterday morning [16 August 1864], and on the 1st of September Victoire Balfe is to become Duchesse de Frias! I am glad of it for her sake, and glad also because many spiteful people were wishing that His Holiness might not allow the marriage – but no power on earth would take me to the wedding, nor can I allow Evy to appear. I dare say your brother will go, but that is quite a different thing.[8]

The tone of the final section of this letter suggests that Victoire and the Balfe family may have become *personae non gratae* given the manner in which the Crampton affair was handled, since he was a very distinguished member of the aristocracy and for many years one of Her Majesty's representatives in continental Europe, at the Russian Royal Court and also an Ambassador in America.

Victoire after her marriage to de Frias went to live in Madrid. It appears to have been a good marriage, though short in duration due to Victoire's untimely death. The de Frias had two sons, both born in Madrid; Bernard was born in 1866 and William in 1870. Bernard married a Mary Cecil Knowles and William, Caroline Sforza Cesarni.[9] They also had a daughter, 'Pepe'. Victoire died in Madrid in January 1871 from rheumatic fever. She is said to be buried in the Cathedral in Burgos.

Victoire's new direction and the Balfes' move to the countryside did not eliminate all of their family problems. Their son, Michael, who now lived at Carlton Road, St Pancras in London, had been living with a young woman, Norah Maglin, who was now pregnant. Their daughter was born on 7 August 1864. Appropriately, the new baby was christened Maud Lina Balfe. The parents decided to marry a few weeks later now that they had a child, so they had a quick ceremony performed at a register office on 28 September 1864. Neither Balfe nor Lina witnessed the marriage. Lina must have been too upset to consider attending.

Michael Balfe junior appears always to have been something of an enigma to his parents. He tried music and several other jobs to no avail. At one point in time he had signed up to work for the East India Company but elected to opt out at the last moment. He eventually did what his father never did: he went to America early in 1865. There he had another daughter, Victoria Balfe, who was born in New York in 1870. They also had two sons, Michael W. Balfe, who was born in Manhattan in May 1873, and William Balfe, born in Brooklyn in September 1867. His wife died and he remarried someone whose first name was Jane. The 1880 US census shows that she was born in England.

The two daughters, Maud Lina and Victoria, married in New York on the same day, 29 November 1888 – Maud to a George Terry who was English-born; Victoria married Anthony Peruise, who was Italian-born. What happened to them is not known.

Michael Balfe junior seemed to continue to do odd jobs, sometimes as a 'fitter', other times as a 'peddler', and then as a life insurance salesman. He lived at various addresses in downtown Manhattan and in Brooklyn, never staying too long in any one place. He eventually did return to London when his father died and again when his mother died. Whatever was left of his father's estate he sold it off after his mother's death including some of his father's memorabilia and decorations. He returned to America for a number of years before eventually going back to London, where he died at an infirmary in London 5 August, 1915, penniless at the age of seventy-nine, of bronchitis and cardiac failure. What happened to his family is unknown.

Meanwhile, in 1865 at Rowney Abby, Lina Balfe organized things to the point that she managed to develop the farmland enough for them to be self-sufficient. She prepared for the arrival of the Behrends. They came in 1865 with all seven children, whose ages ranged from thirteen down to a one-year-old and they all stayed for a time at the Balfe home in Ware. They eventually resettled closer to London. Shortly after their arrival in England they had a daughter named Josephine, who was generally know as 'Pepita' as she grew up.

Balfe was not feeling particularly well at the end of the summer of 1865. He decided to spend some time in Eastbourne by the sea for the better air and to provide an environment that would allow him to continue working on his new opera. Perhaps he was finding it exhausting to work and also deal with all of the young Behrend children around the house.

He went to Eastbourne with Victoire (she must have been visiting) and apparently someone called 'Pepe'; who she may have been is unknown. If it was a daughter the child would have been very young. The Behrend child of that name would also have been too young, so the "Pepe" referred to in the letter shown below has not been clearly identified. While there, Balfe wrote this very personal letter to Lina, which in the second half shows his deep affection for his family and Lina in particular:

East Bourne
9th August 1865

Dearest Wife,

The air in this place does me a great deal of good. I have
entirely finished composing the first act of 'King Lion Heart'
[The Knight of the Leopard] libretto which I brought away
with me and Vic and Pepe think that I have never created anything more charming than a melody to be sung by the tenor
which terminates the Act, the first Act [The Rose
Song/Candido fiore].

I have completely finished the P.F. [Pianoforte] accomp., of
the said act. What do you think of that? Besides which I have
instrumented all the vocal pieces of 'Sleeping Queen' ten in
number which I brought with me from London. If the second
Act of the 'Lion Heart' comes as well as the first I will immediately write to Mapleson telling him, that I cannot compose
anything else for the present. But you must not speak of this
to *anybody* before I tell you to do so.

Farnie must be ménage! [Farnie was the librettist for the
Sleeping Queen].

The friendship & affection of both of our dear children (I
mean of course that of Vic & Pepe) is shown in every word in
[their] every act. They cannot bear to be without me one
instant, indeed I am very happy and comfortable. I feel for
you my darling, having to work so hard and be put to such
inconvenience, ma che vuoi – tu ti sei sempre sacrificata per
marito e sei figli (Spl?)

It is a consolation to you to know that you are fully appre-
ciated & adored by us all. Hug my Gigia for me – trusting that
you received a long letter from Vic yesterday & that my darling first born [Louisa/Gigia] is getting better, I remain as ever,

Your loving old hub.

The success of the Rouen performances of *The Bohemian Girl*
made de St Georges interested in putting on the opera in Paris,
which was by now one of the few major cities in Europe that had
not heard it. He invited Balfe to come to Paris to discuss the
proposition. Balfe arrived in Paris some time in the middle of

1868. After lengthy discussions he and de St Georges agreed that they would rework the score further to augment the production for Paris versus the Rouen copy of the score. Balfe returned to England. The Théâtre Lyrique management, Léon Carvalho (1825–1897) had in the meantime agreed to put on the opera in 1869. Then suddenly there were financial problems with Carvalho and he was forced to resign later in 1868. He was replaced by Jules Pasdeloup (1819–1892?), who also agreed to perform the opera.

It was also during this time-frame in 1868 that Balfe's early mentor, the Italian composer Gioachino Rossini, died in Paris. Balfe was not able to travel to the funeral because of ill health, or perhaps it may have been Lina's decision because they could not afford the expense. He had shortly before returned from a visit to Paris anyway.

Balfe eventually returned to Paris in 1869. He and de St Georges worked on the opera during the summer months. However, Balfe was not in the best of health as he seemed to be suffering from recurring bronchial attacks. To add to his difficulties, in June he receive an urgent telegram from Lina to say their daughter Louisa was seriously ill and that he should come home quickly. He returned immediately to London only to find that Louisa, aged thirty-seven, was close to death, with an acute bladder problem and a kidney infection. Louisa died on 14 June 1869. It was an enormous shock for all of the family. She was their first born.

A short time after the funeral, Balfe returned to Paris to complete his work on *La Bohémienne* for the Théâtre Lyric. There is some evidence to suggest that Lina most probably accompanied him, or possibly joined him a little later. Obviously, she would have emotionally needed support after the tragedy she had just experienced and probably visiting Paris would have helped her, particularly with a new opera about to be completed.

The *La Bohémienne* premiere was eventually scheduled for 30 December 1869. A party was held the day after the first night in which members of the original Rouen cast (Gallie-Marie and Rozé) who were in attendance came and champagne was enjoyed by all, since it was New Year's Eve.

The opera had a total of twenty-nine performances, which meant it ran on well into February, which made it very successful. Balfe stayed in town, apparently not feeling well enough to travel as he was still suffering from a bad case of bronchitis. He wrote to his friend Bill Davison, the brother of the *Times* critic Jim Davison, from an address at 154 Avenue des Champs Elysées on 23 February 1870 as follows:

> My dear Bill,
>
> In consequences, and in consideration, of the genuine success of 'La Bohémienne' the Emperor has been pleased to confer upon me the decoration of the Légion d'Honneur, I w a n t you, like a good fellow, to announce this to my friends in England in your prettyist (*sic*) style. I have knocked at Death's door, and the fellow would not let me in this time, for which I feel very grateful. You know, I suppose, that I have been for four months confined to the house with an attack of bronchitis which would have killed many a finer fellow than M.W.B. *Heureusément, ni la mort, ni la Diable*, would have anything to do with me. I hope soon to get back to London. I am longing for the English air and British roast beef. My wife sends love. Tell this to Jim – I mean about the Légion d'Honneur – but he cares no more for his old chum.
>
> Yours for ever and a day.
> M.W. Balfe
>
> P.S. – The old 'Bohemian Girl' has saved the Théâtre Lyrique from shutting its doors, and really the French public love Balfe's music. This is a fact! Undeniable.[10]

Based on the statement in this letter 'My wife sends love'. it would imply that Lina was with him in Pairs on this occasion.

Shortly afterwards he also received a similar award and honour from Carlos III of Spain, no doubt through the influence of Victoire and the de Frias family.

In any event, Balfe arrived back in Rowney Abbey in May 1870. While he continued to work on his new opera, *The Knight of the Leopard*, based on the Scott story *The Talisman*, his health continued to deteriorate. On 20 October 1870 he died from 'Bronchitis and congestion of the lungs.' He was sixty-two years old. He was buried in the prestigious Kensal Green Cemetery, just a short distance from his fellow composer, William Vincent Wallace, who

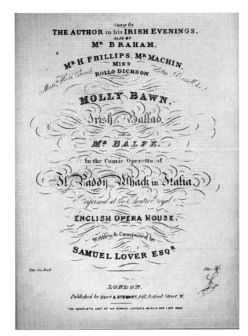

24. The song *Molly Bawn*, from Glover's *Il Paddy Whack in Italia*, made popular by Balfe in 1841.

25. The playbill for Balfe's *Keolanthe*, in which Lina Balfe made her London debut.

.26. The interior of the Theatre Royal, Drury Lane, London, where Balfe had so much success.

27. Portrait of the great soprano Jenny Lind, who made her London debut with Balfe conducting.

28. Giuseppe Verdi around the time he first visited London, where Balfe worked with him.

29. Verdi premiered his opera *I Masnadieri* in 1847; Balfe conducted two performances.

30. The soprano Christine Nilsson, who sang in Balfe's *Il Talismano* in 1874.

31. The lyric tenor Italo Gardoni, who premiered one of Balfe's operas in Paris.

32. The American soprano Z. De Lussan, who made her operatic debut in a Balfe opera.

33. The great British tenor Sims Reeves.

34. Benjamin Lumley, manager of Her Majesty's Theatre.

35. Balfe's opera *Keolanthe*, Vienna, 1853.

36. The first performance of Verdi's *Nabucco* in London conducted by Balfe.

37. American poet H.W. Longfellow.

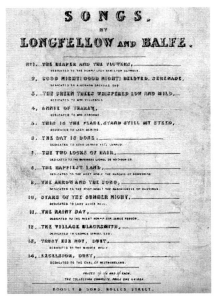

38. Longfellow songs composed by Balfe.

39. The French opera *La Bohémienne* (*The Bohemian Girl*), premiered in Rouen,

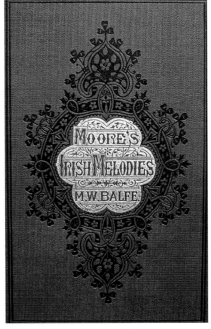

40. Balfe's arrangements of Moore's Irish Melodies.

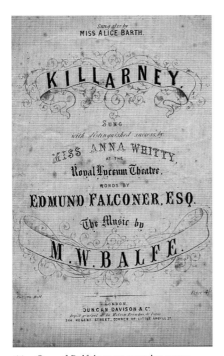

41. One of Balfe's most popular songs, *Killarney*

42. The song *The First Kiss* by Balfe's friend Desmond Ryan.

43. Balfe's gravesite at Kensal Green, London.

44. Portrait of Balfe's at the age sixty.

45. Rowney Abbey, Balfe's house where he died in 1870.

46. Balfe portrait *circa* 1860, by London photographer Henry Watkins.

died in 1865, and also not too far from the great Irish soprano, Catherine Hayes, who died in 1861.

Balfe's funeral was a quiet one, attended by Max Behrend and two of his sons, Lina, and his friends for many years, Jim Davison of *The Times* and his brother William, Dion Boucicault, George Osborne, Jules Benedict and the tenor Italo Gardoni. It is not known if Victoire attended; she may have been too ill to do so, as she died from rheumatic fever just a few months later in January 1871. For Lina probably it had to be the most difficult of times, losing her husband and only daughter within a few months of each other.

Lina lived on for many years. With the help of her son-in-law Max, she arranged for her husband's final unfinished work to be finished by his friend Michael Costa and produced at Her Majesty's Theatre with an Italian libretto and the title of *Il Talismano* on 11 June 1874.

The Prince of Wales attended the dress rehearsal and all London turned out for the premiere. The cast could not have been better, The Swedish soprano Christine Nilsson (1843–1921), who had known Balfe in recent years in Paris and in fact claimed that he had written the opera for her, sang the lead soprano role. The Italian tenor, Italo Campanini (1845–1896) partnered her. The opera was very successful. These two singers went on to open the inaugural season of the new Metropolitan Opera in New York in *Faust* in 1883. The following is a brief extract from a lengthy review of the opera premiere by the *Times*.

> The house was crowded with a brilliant audience, and rarely have we seen an audience more eager to be pleased, or more anxious to single out every point that might be worthy [of] attention and applause. It appeared strange to see the name of Balfe once more connected with a 'first night' but to all who cherish a regard for that name? and there can hardly be a lover of English opera who does not? it was a revival of old times. The Balfe, now passed away, who in 1835 and 1836 first courted notices with his Siege of Rochelle and Maid of Artois, and who afterwards, for a quarter of a century, was the constant purveyor of works which the public took speedily into favour, comes again before us unexpectedly, and, perhaps, for

that reason is all the more welcome. There could hardly be a single person in the house last night who was not pleased to recognize another touch of the old Balfeian melody – that melody which has not only charmed every homestead in Britain but has penetrated to the furthest limits of the civilized world.[11]

He went on to say:

Il Talismano is one of the composer's most carefully considered and best balanced works; that it abounds in melody from the first scene to the last; and that it has that   p u r e ring about it at once proclaiming it Balfe's, and thus making it all the more   acceptable to so many admirers of Balfe's music.[12]

Balfe's final opera has some remarkable music, reminiscent of early Verdi. Balfe felt it was his greatest work, as did some of the critics. It was also performed in other places in Britain and in New York in 1875. The last known performance was in Monte Carlo with the new title of *King Richard in Palestine* in March 1918.

Some time after her husband's death Lina left Rowney Abbey and moved to 126 Belgrave Road in the Victoria area of London. She seemed to live a reasonably good life with friends and visitors. Max, her son-in-law, supported her as indeed he apparently did while they were all in Rowney Abbey. In 1873 Lina did an amazing thing: she donated all of her husband's original autograph (in the composer's handwriting) scores to the British Library, or, as it was called then, The British Museum. This was an enormous collection as can be witnessed today by going online to see the collection. Her intention was to preserve his scores so that future generations could study his work and perform his music. It's also possible that part of Lina's motivation was to protect Balfe's scores from their wayward son Michael junior, who apparently sold anything he could get his hands on.

The Balfe collection in the British Library is one of the most important collections of autograph scores of any nineteenth century operatic composer anywhere. The scores are beautifully bound and maintained under the best of conditions. All are available to the public or those interested in the study of this unique and important

Victorian composer. It is a credit to Lina's intellect and respect for her husband of thirty-nine years that she had the foresight to do what she did.

The last major production of an opera by Balfe during his century was in 1882, when an English version of his 1854 Trieste opera, *Pittore e Duca* was mounted in London with the title *Moro the Painter of Antwerp*. Balfe of course never saw the libretto so in effect it was not really an opera approved by him. However, the opera was later performed elsewhere in Britain. Somehow it did not achieve the great success of other Balfe works including *Il Talismano*. Some of the critics felt its style and the music was outdated, having been written almost thirty years previously.

Lina died in June 1888 and is buried in Kensal Green with her husband. Max Behrend lived on to 1890 when he too died. His descendants, and there are many, mostly live in Britain today.

By any standard Michael Balfe's career was amazing. His driving energy stayed with him to the very end. He believed in his talents and his work and he never really wavered from that course. He never worked at anything but music and the theatre. His discipline from an early age was commendable. He was bright, street-smart and gregarious. People liked his style right from the start. Physically he was a small man, probably around five feet four. Generally, males in the nineteenth century were somewhere in the five feet four to five feet eight height range. There were obviously exceptions. Balfe was quite handsome and very articulate in English, French, and Italian. He also had some knowledge of German. He had an outgoing gregarious personality. All his life he was highly energetic, despite his bronchial problems.

When he first went to Italy in 1825 at the age of seventeen he must have wondered what fate had in store for him. There were so many singers and composers in Italy at that time that the odds must have seemed insurmountable, yet he never flinched at the challenge. He learned Italian so that he could live and work like an Italian. That was why the British called him an "Irish Italian" when he made his first professional entry as a composer in London in 1835.

Certainly many nineteenth-century operatic composers, particularly in Italy, who were his contemporaries came from poor circumstances and were driven economically for most of their life.

Balfe was no exception except that he was Irish-born. Composers such as Bellini and Donizetti had to fight time and time again to receive better pay from impresarios at opera houses in Italy and France. Most nineteenth-century impresarios by their nature were devious and some were outright thieves.

There were no copyright laws in effect until later in the century, even in Britain. For example Balfe's music circulated freely all over the eastern part of America without him getting paid anything for it. He understood the system. He didn't agree with it but there was nothing he could do. He had been involved in it in Italy, where he became a copyist in order to survive. Copyists rewrote the orchestral parts from the composers' original score or a copy of it and then those parts were sold to impresarios and theatres for performance purposes. There was a whole underground trade in this in Italy with little or no controls in the first half of the nineteenth century and beyond. Verdi complained about it during his time.

When Balfe arrived in London in 1835 and his career was launched with *The Siege of Rochelle.* He basically enhanced Barnett's model of the previous year and added his melodies to produce a work that had great appeal to the public. Balfe's primary predecessors apart from Barnett in the quasi-opera business in London included Henry Bishop and Michael Rophino Lacy. Their works were the equivalent of plays with music or bastardized reworked operas by Rossini and Mozart and others which never had much appeal for the aristocracy, who were more interested in Italian opera.

Balfe's new approach, starting in 1835 with *The Siege of Rochelle,* gave the music equal prominence to the drama on stage and in a cohesive way. It was a major cultural change that brought the aristocracy and the common people to English opera – and on frequent occasions, the Queen and her party too. In the process, he democratized English opera. He had perfected a fresh new approach. The music was memorable and sparkling; the stories were for the most part, classical Victorian 'love triumphs over evil' and on some occasions with of 'oriental or Mediterranean mystique' and the public loved it. The important London periodical *The Musical World*, which reported on musical active in Britain and from around Europe for almost half a century, said the following about Balfe's unique audience: 'Balfe's admirers include, aristocrats and underbred, artists and artisans, amateurs and connoisseurs, rich and poor, simple and wise – a true compound of the good and the brilliant, the solid and the taking.'[13]

In some ways it was not unlike how the great musicals hit New York and London a century later in the late 1940s. Balfe gave people melodious popular tunes, with a good wholesome story. He tried on some occasions to raise the bar and use the Italian model, by adding recitatives and eliminating the spoken dialogue between the music numbers – but the public rejected is vehemently and he immediately switched back to his basic format.

His own frustrations in London must have been many. Every time he seemed to get on a roll something changed outside his control, such as the theatre manager going bankrupt. The theatre business during the first half of the nineteenth century in London and elsewhere was very unstable. Fires, bankruptcies and management changes happened with great frequency. When the opportunity arose and he had a contract to compose an opera generally he was successful and in some cases very successful.

Like Donizetti he had the amazing facility to write complete operas in as little as six weeks. On occasions he borrowed from himself. He was known to say that he sometimes he went to the fountainhead – Beethoven! He was criticized sometimes in Britain for seeming to be a clone of France's Auber or Italy's Rossini. Yet when his operas were produced in France he was seen as something new, different and fresh, not Auber plagiarized. So much so that he was the only British composer in the nineteenth century to be given an assignment to compose a work for the Paris Opéra, the most prestigious musical environment in France.

In the background for him there was always Lina Balfe. Her early life was spent mostly in Vienna and later in Berlin and Milan. While she was born in Pest (Budapest), an Austrian city at the time, it is almost certain that her mother died in childbirth. She was taken in by friends of her father, the Vogels, who became her foster parents and who reared her. So her early life would possibly have been insecure, as she never knew her mother and rarely if ever saw her father once she was in foster parent care. When her father died in Pest in 1830 she was already in Italy singing. So her family and her husband would have given her the stability and the personal emotional experience that was not present in her childhood, even though her foster parents seemed to take good care of her. Tragically, her two daughters and her husband died before her. Her wayward son outlived her by many years.

Initially in London, Lina's English was not good, and indeed her early letters with her almost 'gothic' style handwriting were very difficult to read. Throughout her life in London she was very much in the background. However there's no doubt that she controlled the purse-strings. She was also known to manage all of his scores over the years and indeed one wonders how much space they took up in their apartments in London before they moved to Rowney Abbey where there was adequate storage room. She was also known to keep track of sheet music song sales and the sale of sheet music from his operas. She also handled the farming they did at Rowney Abbey. Generally she travelled with him most times when he went to Paris, Russia, Dublin, Berlin, Vienna or Italy. Sometimes she took the children along.

Since Balfe was a gregarious character it is almost certain that Lina would have been the stabilizing factor. He probably could not have managed without her. That she was a staunch Catholic there is little doubt. Her religion meant a lot to her. Balfe himself seemed to be ambivalent to religion. He never composed any religious works and never seemed to be involved in any way with the church except through Lina or when his daughters got married.

Lina in later years did emerge socially in London and indeed her writing and her English seemed to be greatly improved as time went on, which says something about her ability to learn and grow. The letter from Balfe to his wife quoted in this chapter clearly shows the affection that still existed between them in 1865 and with their family. It gives a rare glimpse at how they communicated with each other.

A few remnants of part pages from his diaries exist. He seemsonly to have kept track of important events, such as the award from the Emperor of France, the success of the Paris version of *The Bohemian Girl* and similar things. Unfortunately no complete diary is known to be extant.

As a composer Balfe was in the right place at the right time, when he came to London from Italy in 1835. However, in later years, time seemed, in some ways, to pass him by. The fact that he spent seven years working as a conductor and musical director at

Her Majesty's Theatre probably gave his family great stability in terms of income and it also had many benefits creatively; however, it virtually dried up his creative talents as a composer at least in London.

Lumley, the theatre manager for whom Balfe worked for seven years, was a control fanatic by his own account, so Balfe was always going to be an "employee" for him. When Lumley gave credit to Balfe for something he seemed to do so begrudgingly. Balfe's ability to put the orchestra back together at a time when Lumley's austere and arrogant policies had driven most of London's best musical talent out of Her Majesty's Theatre to a start-up competitor was basically 'glossed over' by Lumley in his autobiography. The London musical critics of the time saw Balfe as the 'bedrock' that put the whole orchestra back together into a quality ensemble comparable to anything in Europe. Without a top -quality orchestra Lumley would not have had an Italian Opera House, or a business for that matter.

Perhaps the biggest mistake Balfe made, at least financially, was not going to America. While he never would have made the type of money Jenny Lind made, he certainly would have made much more than he could have earned in Europe, over a longer period. In the late 1840s, his friends Mr and Mrs Wood, the singers, had invited him to accompany them to America, but he turned them down saying that he wanted to stay in England.

Later, his friend Giulia Grisi made the trip in 1854, with her partner Giovanni Mario, and granted she only made it once, although she was even scared crossing the Irish Sea from Wales (Holyhead) to Dublin which she did many time to sing in that city. She may have influenced Balfe's decision not to go to America because of the 'long' voyage across the Atlantic, and the sickness she experienced. Balfe went to Russia in the middle of winter on two occasions; at least one of those trips (before railways were in operation) was something far more hazardous that a transatlantic voyage during the same period, particularly for someone with a chronic bronchial condition.

There is no question that if Balfe had gone to America for a 'tour' assuming he had the right management agent (which was somewhat questionable in New York in those days) he would have been financially stable for the rest of his and Lina's life. It was a major mistake for him on all accounts. What he continually pursued in Europe – new commissions and the like – would have been offered to him in so many places in America in the 1850s that he would have been able to write his own contract.

Balfe as a conductor was in the forefront of what was to become the 'classic mould' for conductors later in the century. He was so good at his business that he would have been very demanding as a task master, possibly quite 'imperious' on the podium. In his early days in Italy, he did on at least one occasion humiliate an instrumentalist by demonstrating how to execute a particular passage for the violin. It was a an action he regretted deeply afterwards, since the elderly violinist died some days later. By all accounts Balfe was probably one of the best conductors in Europe in his day. Yet he suddenly gave it all up, at his peak, which seems strange.

The time that he elected to get out of conducting was a time of great expansion in choral societies, musical festivals, and oratorios as well as touring opera groups in Britain and America. Balfe would have made a great musical director at any one or more of these musical organizations. Yet he never decided to take that route. Perhaps he was bored with the business at that stage, and yet he really hadn't made enough money to be able to retire, so he kept on doing what he always did – composing operas and songs. It's possible that his restless spirit may have stopped him from taking a 'regular' job as a conductor. While he was with Lumley as a musical director he was operating in an Italian operatic environment with quality Italian artists in a prestigious position, so that would have satisfied most of his needs in some way.

Financially, Balfe was successful, certainly during the 1840s. He was not a good money manager, and got himself into trouble on a number of occasions. He was on a personal friendship basis with Charlotte and Lionel Rothschild, the London banking arm of the Rothschild family, yet he did not use that connection to manage his finances. However, the Rothschilds did help his son get a job on one occasion, no doubt at the father's request. They also contributed to the large memorial statue of Balfe that stands in the lobby of the Drury Lane Theatre today.

While we know about some of his earnings and what he was been paid for his efforts it is very difficult to convert that for a comparison with earnings in the twenty-first century. There was so much inflation, changes in currencies, the aftermath of wars and currency adjustments by banks that there is no true formula to be able to measure how well someone of Balfe's calibre did financially in the nineteenth century, compared to someone today.

Balfe mixed freely with people at all levels of society. He was well liked and indeed unlike many theatrical personalities, what you saw was what you got. He was always very open and helpful to people when he could. He had a lot of friends. There is some documentary evidence to suggest that he may have given lessons to Queen Victoria at some point in time, as she was a good musician and enjoyed his operas. She had the famous Luigi Lablache as her voice teacher for about twenty years. The Queen did make state visits to a number of Balfe's operas, but as far as it is known Balfe never officiated in a musical capacity at any of the Queen's concert functions in Buckingham Palace, which does seem strange. His friend and competitor Michael Costa appeared there many times.

Balfe had a limited number of pupils, the most noted being Willoughby Weiss, the bass-baritone. Both of Balfe's daughters studied with him and both sang. Victoire sang professionally for a few years, Louisa only sang at family concerts, but usually chose operatic arias, and not always her father's music.

In the final analysis Balfe's legacy is his music. The librettos to his English operas – many with impossible word-settings and archaic language have tended to create a performance barrier by their halo effect.

In 1951, Sir Thomas Beecham mounted a completely new arrangement of *The Bohemian Girl* for the Festival of Britain at the Royal Opera House, Covent Garden in London. His arrangement included a libretto re-write by the experienced Dennis Arundel. In addition, Beecham added recitatives in place of the traditional dialogue (Balfe would have been proud of him). He also incorporated selected music from Balfe's French and Italian versions of the opera to augment the work. The opera ran for nineteen performances, to sold-out houses. It was also broadcast by the BBC. And yes, some of the cognoscenti were critical of Beecham for tampering with such a traditional "period piece' of British music. The fact is that the audiences enjoyed it, and it worked. Listening to Beecham's performance today one can readily understand why the audience reacted so positively about his arrangement of *The Bohemian Girl*.

Balfe's Italian-language *Falstaff* and his French-language *Les quatre fils Aymon* certainly deserve hearings or recordings as does probably his last opera, which he felt was his best, *Il Talismano*. The full orchestral scores are available from the British Library for the first two and most of the latter appear to be intact. A listening to excerpts from *Falstaff* clearly shows it to be an interesting, somewhat vocally difficult work, but sparkling in the classical Italian buffa tradition. It was of course written for four of the greatest Italian singers of the nineteenth century. His other comic opera, *Les quatre fils Aymon*, by all accounts from reviews of the time is a quality work. It had an amazing life, as it was performed in French, English, German and Italian versions. It was incredibly successful in Germany and in Vienna during the nineteenth century. There is also an orchestral score of the German version in the Austrian National Library in Vienna.

Whatever one might say about Balfe's practice of providing tuneful ballads and duets within an English operatic framework but not placing much emphasis on the dramatic aspects it is important to remember that it was a long time ago when these operas were composed and tastes differed greatly in those day from our century. With the exception of the Loder and Barnett works there was really nothing to compare Balfe operas to, as very little existed in terms of so called English opera before he arrived in London. He did dominate the scene for thirty years and very few composers of the period, with perhaps the exception of Wallace, provided anything like the same level of composition as Balfe's during the middle period of the nineteenth -century.

Given Balfe's prominence in London and abroad, it has always been a mystery why he was never knighted. The first musician in London to be knighted in the mid-nineteenth century was Henry Bishop, in 1842. Some time after Balfe died, in 1870, Michael Costa and Jules Benedict were knighted, as was Sterndale Bennett. In retrospect, even at this point in time it seems extraordinary that Balfe would have been overlooked, even posthumously. The fact that the Prince of Wales showed up for the dress rehearsals of *Il Talismano*, and that he agreed to have the score dedicated to him by Lina, has to mean that the royal family still thought something of Balfe. The Queen since the death of Prince Albert in 1861 became reclusive as far as the theatre was concerned, so she did not attend the premiere.

The only conclusion that one can arrive at regarding Balfe not receiving a knighthood is that the Crampton affair and its related scandal must have precluded Balfe from any official recognition, particularly where the Church of England was involved in the decision. The fact that the Balfe Memorial Commission was initially refused a memorial in Westminster Abby by the then Dean of Westminster, Dean Stanley, tends to support this theory. The Church certainly would have been involved in some way in a knighthood appointment or recommendation, as would the Prime Minster's Office. However, the Church could have had a strong influence in such a situation. It seems almost certain that the Crampton affair, which was publicly reported in *The Times* for all to read, was perhaps the true cause for Balfe not receiving a knighthood. There is no other apparent reason.

Balfe is best remembered today by a very large statue which stands in the vestibule to the Theatre Royal at Drury Lane in London. It is the very same theatre where Balfe had so many successes during his long career. Balfe is flanked by three other British immortals of the theatre, David Garrick, Charles Keane and William Shakespeare. The statue was erected in 1874 as a result of a number of Balfe's friends starting a fund for its erection. The contributors to the fund came from a wide range of admirers. One of the largest contributors was the Duc de Frias. Max Behrend was also a large contributor. There were many others, such as Christine Nilsson, Sir Julius Benedict, George Osborne, the Duke of Leinster, the Marquess of Downshire, S & P Erard, Sims Reeves, Charles Santley, J. W. Davison and his brother, W. D. Davison, Manuel Garcia, Dion Boucicault, Baron J. M. de Rothschild, Baron Charles de Rothschild, A. de Rothschild, Augustus Harris, Chappel & Company, Boosey & Co., and Giovanni Puzzi.

In 1876 a Balfe Memorial Festival was held at Alexander Palace in London. The concept of the event was to create a Balfe Scholarship at the Royal Academy of Music (Balfe never attended the Academy). It was a very successful event, with many old and new singers participating including tenor Edward Lloyd, Sims Reeves, Christine Nilsson, Marie Rozé, the young Irish bass Signor Foli (A.J. Foley), and the Irish soprano with Italian experience, Elena Conrani (Ellen Conran). The initial funding was achieved; however the funds did not last too long so the Balfe Scholarship eventually lapsed.

A number of years after his death a new bishop gave approval for a plaque to be erected to Balfe' memory in Westminster Abbey, London. Later in Dublin a stained glass window was installed in St Patrick's Cathedral and there were also a number of busts of the composer executed that are now held in various museums. It is surprising that a statue of the composer has not been erected in Dublin's St Stephen's Green just a short walk from where Balfe was born. The beautiful park in central Dublin would be an ideal place to honour the composer in the city of his birth. The park contains statues and busts of a number of distinguished Irish people. Balfe certainly should also be one of them.

Balfe's music lives on today. A search on various internet auction and book sites will find a significant amount of Balfe's music being offered every week. Without doubt, he was Victorian Britain's most unique composer: all in all quite an extraordinary person.

The fact that Balfe's music still sells today over the internet superhighway and from catalogues to a whole different generation is perhaps the greatest validation of all of the immense appeal of this unique Victorian composer.

NOTES

1. *The Times*, 21 November 1863.
2. The British Census of 1861. The Balfe family is shown as residing at 15 Audley Street, London.
3. *The Times*, 21 November 1863.
4. See *Second Empire Opera: The Théâtre Lyrique Paris 1851–1870* by T. J. Walsh, p. 264. Also for more information on the possibility that Balfe and St. Georges may have worked together on *The Bohemian Girl* libretto and score, before Bull worked on the libretto, see this reference also.
5. *The Times*, 21 November 1863.
6. Rowney Abby (Priory) is frequently referred to as a 'small property' by Balfe's biographers and reference books. Having visited the property in 2003, I feel it certainly could not be considered 'small' even by today's standards. The house is an extremely large house which is now set up into multi flats/apartments.
7. Letter from Charlotte Rothschild to her son Alfred written 17 August 1864. The Rothschild Archives London ref# RAL000/841.
8. Ibid.
9. I'm indebted to Mary Quinton of Ware, Herts, for providing this information and other information about the Balfe family members.
10. Letter from Michael Balfe to Bill Davison dated 23 February 1870, in the collection of the Pierpont Morgan Library New York ref No. MFC B1765.D265.
11. *The Times*, 12 June 1874.
12. Ibid.
13. *The Musical World*, 3 February 1849.

Appendices

APPENDIX I – FRANCE AND ITALY – BALFE CHRONOLOGY; OPERAS SUNG

By the mid-1820s Balfe found himself the possessor of a good quality baritone voice, with a range of two octaves and excellent flexibility. As a result, he began to pursue a singing career in France and Italy. Additionally, by then he was also a competent musician. During this period he also became fluent in French and Italian. While working in Italy as a singer and composer he used the name 'Guglielmo' Balfe. The listing below is in chronological sequence based on when Balfe first sang the featured opera and role. In many instances he sang several performances of these operas, at each listed location.

Operas and Roles	Composer	Year	Location
Il barbiere di Siviglia (Figaro)	Rossini	1828	Paris – Théâtre-Italien
		1831	Pavia – Teatro Condomini
		1835	Venice – Teatro La Fenice
La Cenerentola (Dandini)	Rossini	1828	Paris – Théâtre-Italien
		1835	Venice - Teatro La Fenice
La gazza ladra (Podesta/ Fernando)	Rossini	1828	Paris – Théâtre-Italien
		1830	Piacenza –Teatro Comunale
L'inganno felice (Batone)	Rossini	1828	Paris – Théâtre-Italiens
		1833	Milan – Teatro Carcano
Don Giovanni (Masetto/ Don Giovanni)	Mozart	1828	Paris – Théâtre-Italien
Mosè (Farone)	Rossini	1829	Bologna – Sala Marchese Sampieri
Bianca e Falliero (Capiello)	Rossini	1829	Palermo – Teatro Carolino
Bianca e Gernando (Filippo)	Bellini	1829	Palermo –Teatro Carolino
		1834	Mantua – Teatro Regio

Operas and Roles	Composer	Year	Location
I rivale di se stessi (Dumont?)	Balfe	1829	Palermo –Teatro Carolino
L'Ajo nell'imbarazzo (Don Giulio)	Donizetti	1829	Palermo – Teatro Carolino
La pastorella feudataria (role?)	Vaccaj	1829	Palermo – Teatro Carolino
Amazilia (Cabana)	Pacini	1829	Palermo – Teatro Carolino
La straniera (Valdeburgo)	Bellini	1830	Palermo - Teatro Carolino
Matilde di Shabran (Aliprando)	Rossini	1830	Piacenza -Teatro Comunale
Gli Arabi nelle Gallie (Gondair)	Pacini	1830 1831 1833	Piacenza –Teatro Comunale Bergamo –Teatro Riccardi Milan – Teatro Carcano
Semiramide (Assur)	Rossini	1830	Piacenza – Teatro Comunale
Demetrio e Poilibio (Polybius)	Rossini	1830	Piacenza-Teatro Comunale
La seccia rapita (Il Conte di Culagna)	Celli	1830	Varese – Teatro Sociale
Il barone di Dolsheim (Federico)	Pacini	1830	Varese –Teatro Sociale
Un avvertimento ai gelosi (Berto)	Balfe	1831	Pavia – Teatro Condomini
I Capuleti e i Montecchi (Tebaldo) (Capellio)	Bellini	1831 1831	Varese – Teatro Sociale Novara – Teatro Nuovo
Il falgename di Livonia (Carlo)	Pacini	1831 1832 1833	Novara – Teatro Nuovo Bergamo – Teatro Riccardi Bergamo – Teatro Riccardi
Il Nuova Figaro (Leporello)	Ricci, L.	1832	Bergamo (?) – Teatro Riccardi
Enrico IV al passo della Marna (Constantino)	Balfe	1833	Milan – Teatro Carcano
L'elisir d'amore (Belcore)	Donizetti	1833	Milan – Teatro Carcano
Elisa di Montaltieri (Roberto)	Granara	1833	Milan – Teatro Carcano

Chiara di Rosembergh (role?)	Ricci, L.	1834	Mantua – Teatro Regio
Zampa (Daniele)	Hérold	1834	Turin – Teatro Carignano
Otello (Jago)	Rossini	1834	Milan – La Scala
(Elmiro)		1835	Venice – La Fenice
La sonnambula (Rodolfo)	Bellini	1835	Venice – Teatro Malibran/ Emeronittio

APPENDIX II – ITALIAN STAGE – OPERA PREMIERES, DATES AND CASTS; LIBRETTOS AND SCORES.

Soprano (s);   Mezzo-soprano (ms); Contralto: (ct)   Tenor (t);   Baritone (br); Bass (bs);   Buffo-bass (bfb).

Opera	Premiere Date	Location
1. *I rivali di se stessi*	29 June 1829	Palermo, Teatro Carolino

Publisher: *Societa Tipographica*,
   Palermo 1829.
Libretto: A. Alcozer

Cast for Premiere
Madama Derville: C. Lipparini (s)
Lisa: G. Suster (ms)
Durmont: G. Balfe? (br)
Derval: F. Boccaccini (bs)
Ferville: R. Scalese (bfb)
Un Cameriere: M. Sansone (t)
(No Chorus)
Director of Music: Francesco La Manna

Brief Description
The premiere date for the opera as it appears on the front of the libretto is shown as, 29 June, 1829. Most reference books show the date for the premiere as February 1830, which is incorrect. Additionally the opera was also performed in September 1829 and again in February 1830.

   This is a two-act comic opera comprising eight scenes in the first act and nine in the second act. The libretto was based on the French work *Les rivaux d'eux-mêmes* by C.A. Pigualt-Lebrun. Balfe composed the opera at the request of the Conte di Sommatino, who was director and administrator of the Teatro Carolino in Palermo. Apparently with his chorus 'on strike' for more money or more likely back-pay, Sommatino asked Balfe to create a work minus a chorus. Balfe complied.

> Aria – Madama Derval: Amar senza conosere
> Aria – Ferville: Ma vè, ma vè, che giovane! Vorrebbe
> Aria – Derval: E ancor son qui! Dal campo
> Aria – Madama Derval: Misero cor… speravi

Location of Libretto, Score and Sheet Music
The opera libretto is available from the Instituto per la Musica, Fondazione Giorgio Cini, Venice; code identifier: IT\ICCU\DE\98103003494.

The location of the autograph score and/or sheet music from the opera, if they exist, is not known.

2. *Un avvertimento ai gelosi*   11 May 1831   Pavia, Teatro Condomini

Publisher: *Bizzoni,* Pavia 1831
Publisher: Milan, *Luigi Bertuzzi* 1831
Libretto: G. Foppa

Cast for Premiere
Sandrina: A. Parlamagni (s)
Ernesta: G. Corini (ms).
Il Conte di Ripaverda: L. Valencia (t)
Berto: S. Milani (br), role later taken over by G. Balfe (br)
Don Fabbio: C. Cambiaggio (bfb)
Menico: C. Crosa (bs)
Chorus
Director of Music: G. Balfe (?)

Brief Description
One act comic opera (Farsa) with sixteen scenes.

> Cavatina – Berto: *È una cosa da scioccone*
> Cavatina – Il Conte: *Nel vagheggiar quel viso*
> Duet – Sandrina and Berto: *Sono qua di su che vuoi*
> Trio – Don Fabbio, Berto and Menico: *Che comanda siam per lei nella farsa*

Other production: Teatro Re, Milan, July 1831 with cast changes that included, S. Rubini-Desanctis (s), A. Taddei (ms), T. Alexander (t) G. Ronconi (br). C. Cambiaggio (bfb) and F. Biscottini (bs).

Location of Libretto, Score and Sheet Music
The opera libretto is available from, Biblioteca della Fondazione Giorgio Cini, Venice; code identifier: IT\ICCU\DE\98103003486. It is also available from the Österreichische Nationalbibliothek, Vienna. The code identifier is 107252-A Mus. The Biblioteca nationale di Firenze also has a libretto; the identifier is Mus 1924.287 inv. CF000729046 1v.

Selected vocal sheet music from the opera is held by Biblioteca del Conservatorio di musica Giuseppe Verdi, Milan. Code identifier: IT\ICCU\DE\89020600681.

There are also other selected pieces (see above) from the opera available at Biblioteca National Marciana, Venice. Code identifier: IT\ICCU\DE\98101609403; IT\ICCU\DE\981092105413. The whereabouts of the autograph score is not known.

3. *Enrico IV al passo della Marna* 19 February 1833   Milan, Teatro Carcano

Publisher: Lucca, Milan 1832
Teatro Carcano
Libretto: Unknown

Cast for Premiere
Cristina: L. Roser-Balfe (s)
Enrico IV: L. Bonfigli (t)
Costantino: G. Balfe (br)
Gervasio: C. Cambiaggio (bfb)
Du-Champ: C. Crosa (t)
Chorus
Director of Music: Antonio Daville

Brief Description
It seems there was also earlier performance of this opera in Milan, (1831?) with what was probably the first version of the libretto. It was structured for two acts with the performance given at the *Oratory of San Carlo* in Milan; possibly it was sung by the novitiates since there was no female role in the earlier libretto, instead there was a part for a youth called 'Carlino.'

The main aria for Carlino, 'Un ragazzo più felice', was changed to 'Una donna più felice' for the soprano in the Carcano performance. Also the words, 'Figlio mio,' in the earlier text were changed to 'Moglie mia'.There were also some cuts in a trio that involved Cristina's music. Balfe of course had written the soprano role of Cristina for his wife for the Carcano performance in 1833.

It is difficult to understand when this might have been performed at the Oratory. The libretto says that the music was specially written for the *Oratory*. While Balfe's name is not actually printed on the libretto his name is written on it in handwriting that's definitely of the period. Chances are that the performance that occurred in the Oratory was sometime before the commercial premiere at the Carcano.

The Carcano libretto is essentially the same as the Oratory *San Carlo* libretto. The part of Carlino the youth changes to the soprano role of Cristina. What caused the work to be performed the Oratory or if Balfe was in some way involved with the monastery is not known, unless possibly it was where he and Lina were married in 1831? Since Lina was a Catholic she may have had some influence on the event. (I'm indebted to Alexander Weatherson of the Donizetti Society in London for bringing this to my attention and for a copy of the earlier libretto.)

The opera premiere as performed at the Teatro Carcano in February 1833 was a one-act melodrama with thirteen scenes. The librettist is unknown.

> Aria – Enrico IV: *Non sperate o miei nemici*
> Duet – Constantino and Gervasio: *Alle corte quet soldato*
> Cavatina – Cristina: *Una donna piu felice**

Duet – Constantino and Enrico IV: *Se il labbro tuo è verdico*
Cavatina – Constantino: *Io credea che sconquassarsi*
Cavatina – Gervasio: *Stavano tutti nel mio mulino*

*Balfe later used this piece in the autograph score of his opera *Falstaff* in London in July 1838.

There were also other productions of the work, 1834 to 1836 in Genoa (Teatro Carlo Felice); in Lecco and in the Turin area, at Bra and possibly also in Florence.

Location of Libretto, Score and Sheet Music
The libretto for the Teatro Re performance is available from the Österreichische Nationalbibliothek, Vienna. The code identifier is 180567-A Mus. There is also a copy of the libretto in the Library of Congress, Washington, DC. The call number is: ML50.B188 E6 1833. There is another copy of the libretto from the Teatro Carcano premiere which is held by Harvard University in its Theatre Hollis Catalog collection: Call numbers TS 8200.70 1833.

Sheet music from the opera including arias and duets (see above) is available from Biblioteca National Marciana, Venice. Code identifier: – IT\ICCU\DE\98102105396; IT\ICCU\DE\981092105413. and from Biblioteca del Conservatorio di Musica Giuseppe Verdi, Milan. The code identifier is, IT\ICCU\DE\89020602953, 60, 61, 62, 63, 64, 65, 66, 67 and 68. This latter collection probably represents most of the music from the opera. The location of the original manuscript score is unknown.

There also appears to be at least two original manuscripts documents, ('*Non Sperate o miei nemici*' – IT\ICCU\DM\000602953 and '*Io credea che sconquassarsi*' IT\ICCU\DM\00060602984) held in the collection at the Biblioteca Musicale Opera Pia Greggiati, Ostiglia, Mantua, Italy.

4. *La Zingara*   12 February 1854*   Trieste

Publisher: Ricordi, Milan 1853
Teatro Grande
Libretto: R. Paderni

Cast for Premiere
Arlina: A. Valesi (s)
Gualtiero: F. Mazzoleni (t)
Il Conte Albano: C. della Costa (br)
Federico: D. Aliprandi (bs)
Yelva: F. Leon (ct)
Falco: P. D' Ettore (bs)
Un Uffiziale: G. Panizza (t)
Chorus
Conductor: M.W. Balfe

*Loewenberg shows a performance (Italian libretto by Paderni) of the opera as having taken place in Madrid on 9 April 1845. This is obviously an error. The year should have been 1854.

Description

This is an opera in three acts. It was the first Italian translation of Balfe's most popular opera, *The Bohemian Girl* (1843). The libretto for this performance of *La Zingara* was created by Riccardo Paderni, a Padua-based lawyer and composer. The spoken dialogue of the original production was replaced by sung recitatives.

> Aria – Il Conte: *E lieto un cor belligero*
> Romanza – Arlina: *In una reggia splendida*
> Aria – Il Conte: *D' Arlina mi rammentati*
> Romanza – Gualtiero: *Tu M'ami ah si bell' anima*

The original English *Bohemian Girl* libretto placed the story in the Presburg (Bratislava today) area of the Austro-Hungarian Empire which ruled from Vienna. For political reasons, since Trieste at the time was part of the Empire the drama was changed to a location in Scotland. The names of the principal characters were also changed, except for Arline.

Following the Trieste premiere, performances of *La Zingara* were given in Brescia, Bergamo, Verona and Bologna with some cast changes. Balfe apparently also conducted at least the Bologna performances.

This Italian version of the opera with the cast names and story reverting back to the original English libretto was given in1858 in London and Dublin. In1859 it had its local premiere in New York. Performances were later given in Boston and San Francisco and possibly other American cities.

Some confusion appears to have been caused by the fact that another Italian translator, Giuseppe Zaffira, was associated with Balfe's French librettist, M.H. de Saint-Georges, in Paris in 1869. It is difficult to understand what Zaffira's role might have been in the process.

De Saint-Georges worked on creating a significantly augmented French-language version of the opera which was finalized as a four-act opera with a prologue and published by E. Gerard et c ie. It was produced in Paris, December 1869.

Possibly the French librettist had a desire to better understand the structure of the Italian (Paderni's) version which contained some different music when compared to the original English score. So perhaps Zaffira's services were used for that purpose. However, Balfe was present during most of this period, though quite ill at the time. A performance of the Italian-language *La Zingara* does not appear to have taken place in Paris during this period.

To further confuse the issue, a piano vocal score (344 pages) of *La Zingara*, in a translation by Giuseppe Zaffira, is listed as having been printed in Paris (1869) by E. Gérard et cie around the same time as the French score.

By way of comparison the Paderni *La Zingara* piano vocal score has only 265 pages. Perhaps the Zaffira score was an Italian translation of the final French version of the opera which was considerably longer than the two earlier editions of the opera? The French piano vocal score has 361 pages versus the Zaffira Italian score of 344 pages, which puts these two scores much closer in length and significantly larger than the Paderni Italian score, or for that matter, the original English version of the opera.

The Zaffira score is currently held by the Biblioteca del Conservatorio statale di musica A. Pedrollo in Vicenza. The code identifier is: IT\ICCU\DE\03011000002. This score needs to be inspected to try to better understand what transpired.

Giuseppe Zaffira also became the librettist for Balfe's last opera, *Il Talismano*, which premiered in London in 1874.

Location of Libretto, Score and Sheet Music
Libretto by Riccardo Paderni is held by the Biblioteca della Fondazione Giorgio Cini, Venice. Code identifier: IT\ICCU\DE\98103003489. There is also a copy at Biblioteca dell'archivio del teatro municipal Romolo Valli in Reggio Emilla. The identifier is 17\ICCU\REA\0209181.

The Paderni piano vocal score is held by Biblioteca del Conservatorio di musica Giuseppe Verdi, Milan: code identifier: IT\ICCU\DE\89013000046. In addition to the Zaffira vocal piano score mentioned above, selected sheet music is held at the Biblioteca della Fondazione Giorgio Cini, Venice. The code identifier is: IT\ICCU\DE\98103003488.

5. *Pittore e Duca*	21 November 1854	Trieste

Publisher: Ricordi, Milan 1854
Teatro Grande
Libretto: F.M. Piave

Cast for Premiere
Olivia: F. Salvini Donatelli (s)
Antonio Moro: R. Mirate (t)
Duca D'Alba: G. Ferri (br)
Donna Ines: T. Gridelli (s)
Vargas: A.Belli (bs)
Orsino: A. Della Costa (t)
Chorus
Conductor: G.A. Scaramelli

Brief Description
The opera has a prologue with three scenes. The first act has eleven scenes; the second act has six scenes and the last act has seven scenes. The librettist Francesco Maria Piave was a close friend of Verdi's. Earlier Piave completed librettos for two Verdi operas, *Il corsaro* and *Stiffelio*, both of which premiered at Trieste in the same theatre as Balfe's opera. *Pittore e Duca* was not a success, despite the experienced librettist and an important cast. The opera only had a few performances.

Aria – Antonio: Oh Dio! ... grand Dio! ... era dessa
Aria – Duca: Sì ben dicesré; il mio signore e vostro
Aria – Olivia: Ebben la storia ascolta del mio core
Aria – Antonio: Merta pur lacrime il mio dolore
Aria – Olivia: E Antonio doe andrà? ... veder vuol forse

The story is a historical drama set in Antwerp (Low Countries) in the 1570s with its main characters playing historical figures. The drama circulates around the Dutch-born painter Antonio Moro. An English-language version of the opera, *Moro, the Painter of Antwerp*, was performed in London in 1882, at Her Majesty's Theatre.

Location of Libretto Score and Sheet Music
The Italian libretto is held by the Biblioteca del Conservatorio di musica Giuseppe Verdi, Milan. The code identifier is: IT\ICCU\DE\03042401047. Location of the original autographed score is not known. A complete orchestral score of the English version *(Morro, the Painter of Antwerp)* of the opera is held by the Carl Rosa Archives in Liverpool, England.

The piano vocal score of *Morro, the Painter of Antwerp* is held by the Library of Congress in Washington, DC. The call number is: M1503.B185 P52 (258 pages). There is also a copy of the piano vocal score held by Harvard University in its Loeb music collection: call numbers 627.7.611. The National Library of Ireland also has a piano vocal score, call number: N6023 P.6672 and an English libretto (36 pages), call number: Ir 780P.43

APPENDIX III – LONDON STAGE – OPERA PREMIERES, DATES AND CASTS; LIBRETTOS AND SCORES

Balfe's output for the London stage totalled twenty-five operas and one operetta, as detailed below. These works were composed over a span of around forty years. This listing includes English translations of operas that were written for Paris and Trieste. The listing also includes three works that were produced in London with Italian librettos. The last opera (*Morro*), on the list in its English format was not a conception of Balfe's. The music was taken from one of Balfe's Italian operas (*Pittore e Duca*), and an English libretto was added many years after Balfe's death, so technically it is not a work that had the composer's approval.

As far as the opera premiere cast details are concerned a listing of the principal roles is given here. The full cast is identified by name in Appendix VII of this work. All of these operas premiered in London on the dates indicated and at various theatres. The majority were performed at the Theatre Royal, Drury Lane. The Italian-language operas were performed as indicated, at Her Majesty's Theatre, or at the Theatre Royal Drury Lane.

Because of the great success of many of these operas there was a strong demand, particularly during the nineteenth century, and early twentieth century, for sheet music of arias and other numbers from most of these operas. As a result, a listing of the incipits or first line of the principal arias, duets and other numbers has been provided. Sheet music for many of the pieces is available from the British Library or from other internet sources today.

The original manuscript scores listed below are located at the British Library in London. These primarily consist of the many scores donated by the composer's widow, Lina Balfe in 1873. There are also a number of vocal scores and librettos available from the online catalogue at the Library of Congress in Washington, DC.

Operas written to Italian librettos that premiered in London are discussed more fully in the text of this work, since they have not been covered in any detail by other authors.

Opera/Original Cast	Premiere Date	Score/Manuscript Location
1. *The Siege of Rochelle*	29 October 1835	BL 29,325, 29, 326 vol. i, ii

Clara: J. Shirreff (s)
Valmour: J. Wilson (t)
Michel: H. Phillips (br)
Montalban: T. Giubilei (bs)
Rosemberg: E. Seguin (bs)

A grand opera in two acts; Libretto by E. Fitzball, based on a story *Le siège de la Rochelle* by Comtesse de Genlis. The opera was performed at the Theatre Royal, Drury Lane, London.

Selected numbers:

> Aria – Michel: *Trav'llers all of every station*
> Aria – Clara: *'Mid the early scenes of youth*
> Aria – Michel: *When I beheld the anchor weighed*
> Aria – Clara: *'Twas in that garden*

Comment: The opera was exceptionally well received by the critics. In London, it ran for seventy nights initially. It was also performed in Dublin in 1836; New York in 1838, Vienna in 1846 and in Sydney in 1848.

2. *The Maid of Artois*	27 May 1836	BL 29, 329, 29328, vol. iii, iv

Isoline: M. Malibran (ms)
Jules: J. Templeton (t)
Marquis: H. Phillips (br)
Sans Regret: T. Giubilei (bs)

A grand opera in three acts; Libretto by A. Bunn, based on the Manon Lescaut story by A. Prévost. The opera was performed at the Theatre Royal, Drury Lane, London. It was revived in London in 1839 and in 1846. It was also performed in Dublin in 1840 and in Philadelphia in 1847. A recent CD set of the opera was released in England. See discography section for details.

Selected numbers:

> Aria – Isoline: *The heart that once hath fondly teemed*
> Aria – Isoline: *Yon moon o'er the mountains*
> Duet – Isoline and Jules: *I have strength to bear*
> Aria – Marquis: *The light of other days has faded*
> Aria – Isoline: *The rapture swelling through my breast*

Comment: The presence of Malibran ensured a great success for the opera. It was very well received by the critics. It was also a great financial success for both Balfe and Bunn.

3. *Catherine Gray*	27 May 1837	BL 29,329, 29330. vols. v, vi

Lady Catherine: M. Paton-Wood (s)
Queen Elizabeth: E. Romer (s)
Cecil: Mr. Henry (t)
Earl of Hertford: M. W. Balfe (br)
Lord Grey: E. Seguin (bs)

A grand opera in three acts; libretto by G. Linley. The opera was performed at the Theatre Royal, Drury Lane, London. The opera was never performed outside London.

Selected numbers:

(Unknown)

Comments: Balfe changed his format for this opera. He used recitatives instead of spoken dialogue between the main music a numbers. The opera was a failure. It had only four performances. No sheet music of any of the main pieces was ever published. The opera was performed at the Theatre Royal, Drury Lane, London.

4. *Joan of Arc*   30 November, 1837   BL 29, 331,
                                                            29, 332, vol. viii

Joan: E. Romer (s)
Count Dunois: J. Templeton (t)
Theodore: M. W. Balfe (br)
Beauvais: J. Anderson (t)

A grand opera in three acts; Libretto by E. Fitzball. The score was dedicated to Queen Victoria with permission. The opera was performed at the Theatre Royal, Drury Lane, London, not Covent Garden as mentioned in some works.

Selected numbers:

Aria – Joan: *Peace in the valley*
Duet – Joan and Theodore: *O'er shepherd pipe*

Comments: Balfe reverted to dialogue in the opera. The critics appeared to enjoy the music but the opera was a modest success, as it did have twenty-two performances. The opera was not revived. A number of pieces from the opera were published in sheet music format, and later performed at concerts in Dublin and London.

5. *Diadeste/The Veiled Lady*   17 May 1838   BL 29, 333,
                                                         vol. ix

Celina: E. Romer (s)
Manfredi: J. Templeton (t)
Count Steno: H. Phillips (br)
Zambo: T. Giubilei (bs)
Countess of Amalfi: F. Healey

This is an opera buffa in two acts; libretto by E. Fitzball. The opera was performed at the Theatre Royal, Drury Lane, London.

Selected numbers:

> Aria – Celina: *Diadeste, charming play*
> Duet – Manfredi and Steno: *Life is but a summer day*
> Aria – Steno: *In the winter of one's age*
> Quartette: *Come listen all*

6. *Falstaff***   19 July 1838   BL 29, 334, vol. x

Falstaff: L. Lablache (bfb)
Mrs Ford: G. Grisi (s)
Carlo Fenton: G.B. Rubini (t)
Mr Ford: A. Tamburini (br)

Mrs Page: Mlle. Caremoli (s)
Annetta Page: Mme. Albertazzi (ct)
Mr Page: Sig. Morelli (bs)
Mrs Quickly: Mme. Castelli (ms)
George: Sig. Galli (br)

This is an opera buffa in two acts; Italian libretto by S.F. Maggione. Maggione was a London based translator of Italian and French opera librettos. This libretto was based on Shakespeare's *The Merry Wives of Windsor* play, with some modifications. The opera was performed at the Italian Opera, His Majesty's Theatre, London. Attempts were made to revive the opera later in London and Paris but a revival did not happen.

Selected numbers:

> Aria – Falstaff: *Ho bisogno dei danari*
> Aria – Mrs. Ford: *Ah, vecchiaccio scostumato*
> Trio – Mrs. Ford, Mrs. Page & Miss Page: *Vorrei parlar, ma l'ira*
> Duet –Ford & Fenton: *Non credete poi chio sia*
> Duet – Ford & Falstaff: *Voi siete un uom di spirito*
> Aria – Fenton: *Ah! la mia mente estatica*
> Duet – Mrs. Ford & Falstaff: *Siete qui, caro amico*
> Aria – Ford: *Che mai vedo?*
> Aria – Annetta: *Una donna più felice*
> Duet – Fenton & Annetta: *Ah! sì, tu m'ami, o cara*
> Aria – Falstaff: *È l' ora stabilita, ardente nume*

Comments: This was a very successful opera which Balfe composed for leading Italian singers of the time. Several of the principal pieces from the opera were published in sheet music format in London, Paris and Milan.

7. *Keolanthe* 9 March 1841 The Österreichische

Keolanthe: L. Balfe (s)
Nationalbibliothek in
Andrea: J. Wilson (t)
Vienna holds a score;
Ombrastro: H. Phillips (br)
Pavina: M. Gould (s)
Filippo: Mr. Stretton (bs)
No.: 987124 & 25

A grand opera in two acts; libretto by E. Fitzball. Balfe conducted all perform-
ances. This opera was written for the start of Balfe's management of the English
Opera House. It was also the opera in which Lina Balfe made her London debut.
The opera was performed at the Theatre Royal, English Opera House, Strand,
London. The opera was later performed in Vienna in 1853 in a three-act version
and in Melbourne in 1855 in its original format.

Selected numbers:

> Aria – Pavina: *Vows are too often broken*
> Aria – Andrea: *Why should I gaze on those dear eyes*
> Aria – Keolanthe: *Let me hear*

Comments: The opera received good reviews from the critics. It was quite successful. Balfe later created a German version which was performed in Vienna. A
duet from the opera was later translated into Italian. See Appendix Ix-32 for
details.

8. *Geraldine/The Lover's Well* 14 August 1843 (not known)

Geraldine: E. Garcia (s)
Edward the Third: H. R. Allen (t)
Lord Nottingham: Mr. Walton (br)
Lord Salisbury: G. Barker (t)
Quance: P. Bedford (bs)

This is a three-act opera which was based on Balfe's first French opera *Le puits
d'amour*, which premiered in Paris early in 1843. It was performed at the
Princess Theatre in London.

Selected numbers:

(Unknown)

Comments: The opera in its English translation appeared to do well with several performances. No sheet music appears to have been published from it. The whereabouts of the original score is not known.

9. *The Bohemian Girl*   27 November 1843   BL 29,335

(imperfect)
Arline: E. Rainforth (s)
Thaddeus: W. Harrison (t)
Count Arnheim: C.G. Borrani (br)
Devilshoof: Mr. Stretton (bs)

A grand opera in three acts; libretto by A. Bunn. This became Balfe's most famous opera. During the first year the opera ran for over one hundred nights. The opera was performed at the Theatre Royal, Drury Lane, London. Performances followed immediately in 1844 in Dublin, New York and Philadelphia. In 1846 it reached Sydney. It was revived many times throughout the nineteenth century and in the twentieth century. A CD recording of the opera was made in England in 1991. See discography section for details.

Select

> Aria – Arnheim: *A soldier's life*
> Aria – Arline: *I dreamt I dwelt in marble halls*
> Aria – Arnheim: *The heart bow'd down*
> Aria – Thaddeus: When other lips and other hearts

Comments: The critics really liked this opera with its memorable ballads. The opera was later performed all over Europe in different language versions. It also had great appeal in America Canada, Australia and New Zealand and places as far away as South Africa.

10. *The Castle of Aymon*   20 November 1844   (not known)

Hermine: H. Condell (s)
Oliver: H. R. Allen (t)
Baron Beaumanoir: Mr Walton (bs/br)
Allurd: C. Horn (t)
Richard: Mr. Hime
Ivon: A.Leffler (bs)
Renaud: Mr. Mattacks (br)

This is a comic opera in three acts. It was a translation of Balfe's second French opera *Les quatre fils Aymon*. The English translation was done by G.A. Beckett. The opera was performed at the Princess Theatre, London.
Selected numbers:

Duet – Beaumanoir and Ivon: *The boundless riches of the Duc d'Aymon*
Aria – Oliver: *In the chapel all is ready*

Comments: While the opera received good reviews it did not receive many performances in London. It was also performed in a German version in Vienna and other German-speaking cities such as Berlin, Prague, Frankfurt, Leipzig, Basle, Munich and Hamburg with great success during the nineteenth century. There was also an Italian-language version performed in London in 1851 which got excellent reviews.

11. *The Daughter of St. Mark* 27 November 1844 BL 29, 341–29, 343, vol. xvii–xix

Caterina: E. Rainforth (s)
Adolphe: W. Harrison (t)
Moncenigo: W. H. Weiss (br)

This is a grand opera in three acts; libretto by A. Bunn after V. de Saint Georges' story *La reine de Chypre*. Balfe reverted to recitatives for this score. The opera was performed at the Theatre Royal, Drury Lane, London.

Selected numbers:

Aria – Adolphe: *We may be happy yet*

Comments: The opera had only a short run. Generally it got good reviews; however, it did not have the impact or the staying power of *The Bohemian Girl*. However, the opera was later performed in Sydney in 1852 and in New York in 1855.

12. *The Enchantress* 14 May 1845 BL 29, 344, 29, 343, vols. xx, xxi

Stella: A. Thillon (s)
Silvio: W. Harrison (t)
Regent: W.H. Weiss (bs/br)
Ramir, the Hermit: Mr. Borrani (bs/br)
Dr Mathanasian: Mr. Harley (t?)

This is an opera in three acts with a prologue. The first act action takes place fifteen years after the prologue. The libretto was by V. de Saint Georges. The opera was performed at the Theatre Royal, Drury Lane, London.

Selected numbers:

> Aria – Stella: *A youthful knight*
> Aria – Stella: *Who has not heard*

Comments: The soprano Anna Thillon was the star of the show. There appears to be some melodious music and duets and trios in the opera, which many of the critics liked. The opera was never revived. It was performed in Philadelphia in 1846, in New York in 1849, in Sydney in 1851 and in San Francisco in 1854, probably with Anna Thillon in the title role in California.

13. *The Bondman*   11 December 1846   BL 29, 346, 29, 347, vols. xxii, xxiii

Corinne: E. Romer (s)
Ardenford: W. Harrison (t)
Floville: Mr. Rafter (t)
Vernon: W.H. Weiss (br)
Jaloux: S. Jones (bs)

This is a grand opera in three acts; Libretto by A. Bunn. The opera was performed at the Theatre Royal, Drury Lane, London.

Selected numbers:

> Aria – Corinne: *Is it not form, is it not face*
> Aria – Ardenford: *They say there is some distant land*
> Aria – Vernon: *There is nothing so perplexing*
> Aria – Ardenford: *Child of the Sun*

Comments: This was a successful work and it had a good run. Balfe later composed a German-language version of it which was performed in Berlin in 1850 with the composer conducting.

14. *The Maid of Honour*   20 December 1847   BL 29, 348, 29, 349, vols. xxiv, xxv

Lady Henriette: C. Birch (s)
Alison: M. Miran (ct)
Lyonnel: S. Reeves (t)
Tristram: W. H. Weiss (bs/br)
Walter: J. Whitworth (br)

This is a grand opera in three acts; libretto by E. Fitzball. It was performed at the Theatre Royal Drury Lane, London. The opera was conducted by the French composer Hector Berlioz.

Selected numbers:

> Aria – Tristram: *Stay, bright enchantress of my fate*
> Duet – Lyonnel and Walter: *Country Lasses*
> Aria – Henriette: *Sweet rose*
> Aria – Lyonnel: *Behold the happy home*
> Duet – Lyonnel and Henriette: *I know not by what spell*
> Aria – Walter: *Prime the cup*
> Aria – Lyonnel: *In this old chair*

Comments: Most of the critics were favourable to the opera. The story is similar to that of the opera *Martha*, by von Flotow. The opera was not an overall success, as it never appears to have been revived, even though Balfe personally liked it.

15. *I Quattro Fratelli***   11 August 1851   (see *Les quatre fils Aymon* in the follow ing section on French operas)

Erminia: S. Cruvelli (s)
Olivero: I. Gardoni (t)
Iolanda: Mme. Feller
Clara: Mde. Giuliani
Ricciard: Sig. Pardini
Allardo: Sig. Mercuriali
Rinaldo: Sig. Balanchi
Uberto: Sig. Dai Fiori
Baron di Beaumanoir: J. A. Massol (bs)
Ivon: F. Coletti (br)

This is a three-act opera buffa with an Italian translation by S.F. Maggione of the original French libretto. Balfe augmented this version of the opera with new music for the tenor, soprano and contralto. The opera was mounted at Her Majesty's Theatre as a benefit for Balfe; as a result there were only a few performances.

Selected numbers:

> Aria – Erminia: *Di Duchessa il nome altero*
> Rondo finale – Erminia: *Or qui verra*
> Aria – Olivero: *Gia tarda e nera*
> Aria – Erminia: *Giovin Bella*
> Duet – Erminia and Olivero: *Quando tornar ridente*
> Aria – Clara: *Tutto ben riusci*

Comments: The opera was received with great éclat. Most of the leading critics thought it was one of Balfe's best works apart from the fact that it had outstanding singers performing it.

16. *The Sicilian Bride*   6 March 852   BL 29, 350, 29, 351,
                                                          vols. xxvi, xxvii

Bianca: Miss Crichton (s)
Rodolfo: S. Reeves (t)
Marquis Montluc: J. Whitworth (bs)
Duke de Sangenaro: S. Jones (bs)
Count Andreozzi: E.O. Toulmin (t)
Sirena: R. Isaacs (ct)
Pietro: P. Horton (ct)

This is a grand opera in four-acts; libretto by V. de Saint Georges, translated by A. Bunn. It was performed at the Theatre Royal, Drury Lane, London.

Selected numbers:

> Aria – Rodolfo: *When we recall the happy scenes*
> Aria – Montluc: *The sorrow of the heart*
> Aria – Bianca: *'Tis mine to weep*

Comments: This opera was written after a long absence from English opera. It was also unusual for Balfe to write a four-act opera. There was a feeling he was trying to copy Meyerbeer and his French grand operas. In any event, it was nor particularly successful and it did not have a revival.

17. *The Devil in It*   26 July 1852   (not known)

Letty: E. Romer (s)
Bridget; H. Coveney (ms)
Count Wallenberg: Mr. Travers (t)
Countess Wallenberg: E. Poole (ms)
Lucastro: C.G. Borrani (br)
Hermann: H. Corri (bs/br)
Albert; C. Romer (t)

This is a comic opera in three acts; libretto by A. Bunn. It was performed at the Surrey Theatre, London, which was under the management of the soprano Emma Romer.

> Aria – Wallenberg: *Oh1 did we know or could we learn*
> Aria – Lucastro: *If in the future's mystic book*
> Duet – Letty and Hermann: *'Tis your duty*
> Aria – Letty: *With dance and song*

Comments: This was another successful work by Balfe. The premiere was well attended and Balfe was loudly applauded at the end of the evening. The opera was later revived as *Letty the Basket Maker*.

18. *The Rose of Castille*   29 October 1857   BL 29, 352, 29, 353,
                                                                 vols. xxvii, xxix

Elvira: L. Pyne (s)
Manuel: W. Harrison (t)
Don Pedro: W.H. Weiss (br)
Don Florio: G. Honey (bs)
Don Sallust:

This is an opera in three acts; libretto by A. Harris and E. Falconer. It was performed at the Lyceum Theatre, Strand, London. Balfe composed it under contract for the Pyne Harrison Company.

Selected numbers:

> Aria – Manuel: *I am a simple Muleteer*
> Duet – Manuel and Elvira: *Dost thou fear me?*
> Rondo – Elvira: *Oh! Were I the Queen of Spain*
> Aria – Elvira: *Ah, far more than my crown*
> Aria – Elvira: *The Convent cell*
> Aria – Manuel: *'Twas rank and fame*

Comments: The opera represented a remarkable come back for Balfe since it was
highly successful and had a long run. It was also performed in Vienna in 1859
and in New York in 1864. It was revived in London in 1871.

19. *Satanella/The Power of Love* 20 December, 1858   BL 29, 354, 29, 355,
                                                            vols. xxx, xxxi

Princess Satanella: L. Pine (s)
Count Rupert: W. Harrison (t)
Arimanes: W.H. Weiss (br)
Hortensius: G. Honey (bs)
Karl: A. St. Albyn (t)
Lelia; R. Isaacs (ct)
Stella: S. Pyne (ct)
Bracaccio: H. Corri (br)

This is a romantic opera in four acts; libretto by A. Harris and E. Falconer. It was
performed at the Royal English Opera, Covent Garden, London. Balfe composed
it under contract for the Pyne Harrison Company.

Selected numbers:

> Aria – Lelia: *Our hearts are not our own to give*
> Aria – Rupert: *The glorious vintage of champagne*
> Aria – Satanella: *The power of love*
> Aria – Rupert: *An angel form in dreams beheld*

        Aria – Bracaccio: *My brave companions*
        Aria – Satanella: *Let not the world distaining*

Comments: The critics saw the libretto as complex with its subject matter mystical in nature. It was felt that it was not a suitable story for Balfe. However, there was also the reference to the fact that Balfe was known to be generally indifferent to the merits of librettos. A number of the duets were cut after the first performance, also some other music. Despite the libretto and the adjustments to the score after the first night the opera was well received. It ran for over fifty performances. It was later performed in Sydney in 1862 in New York in 1863 and in Philadelphia in 1871. It did have revivals in London in the nineteenth century.

20. *Bianca, the Bravo's Bride*　　　6 December 1860　　　BL29, 356, 29, 357,
                                                  vols. xxxii, xxxiii

Bianca: L. Pyne (s)
Fontespada (Bravo): W. Harrison (t)
Duke of Milan: A. Lawrence (bs)
Memmino: H. Corri (br)
Beppo: A. St. Albyn (t)
Count Malespina: H. Wharton (br)
Montalto: T. A. Wallworth (br)

This is a melodramatic opera in four acts; libretto by P. Simpson based on M. Lewis' story the 'Bravo of Venice.' It was performed at the Royal English Opera, Covent Garden, London. Balfe composed it under contract for the Pyne Harrison Company.

Selected numbers:

        Aria – Fontespada: *I know your secrets*
        Aria – Malespina: *Yes, proud Bianca*
        Duet – Bianca and Malespina: *Although with cold disdain*
        Aria – Fontespada: *Thou art the Bravo's bride*
        Aria – Bianca: *In vain I strove to teach my heart*
        Aria – Duke: *If treachery base*
        Aria – Bianca: *Yes, I shall see him once again*
        Aria – Fontespada: *Once more upon the path of life*

Comments: The critics really liked this opera when it was first produced. There were references to some of the musical scenes being somewhat like Verdi's music, and the overall spectacle similar to a Meyerbeer work. It had a good initial run of more than thirty performances but did not have any revivals. As far as it is known it was not performed outside London.

21. *The Puritan's Daughter*   30 November, 1861   BL 29, 358–29, 360,
                                                          vols. xxxiv–xxxvi

Mary Wolf: L. Pine(s)
Rochester: W. Harrison (t)
Clifford: C. Santley (br)
Wolf: H. Corri (br)
Seymour: A. St. Albyn (t)
Drake: T. A. Wallworth (br)
Ralph: G. Honey (bs)
Jessie: S. Pyne (ct)

This is an opera in three acts; libretto by J. V. Bridgeman. It was performed at the Royal English Opera, Covent Garden, London. Balfe composed it under contract for the Pyne Harrison Company.

Selected numbers:

> Duet – Ralph and Jessie: *I would ask a question?*
> Aria – Mary: *I swear by all I love*
> Aria – Mary: *Pretty, lovely modest flower*
> Duet – Clifford and Mary: *Yes, thou must cease to love me*
> Aria – Clifford: *Oh1 would that I had died ere now*
> Aria – Clifford: *How peal on peal of thunder rolls*
> Aria – Rochester: *Though we fond men all beauties woo*
> Aria – Rochester: *Let others sing the praise of wine*
> Aria – Clifford: *Bliss forever past*

Comments: Some of the critics continued to note that, once again, Balfe's orchestration showed signs of Verdi's influence. This was the first opera where Balfe gave the lead role to the baritone, something that Verdi did also. Charles Santley the baritone in the premiere was Italian trained and he became one of the outstanding singers of the second half of the nineteenth century. One of the pieces, the baritone song 'Bliss forever past', was later interpolated by touring companies into the score of *The Bohemian Girl* and sung by the Gypsy Queen in that opera. The opera did receive revivals in London, Birmingham and Leeds. It was also performed in New York in 1869 and Dublin in 1920.

22. *The Armourer of Nantes*   12 February 1863   BL 29, 363, 29, 364,
                                                          vols. xxxix, xxxxi

Marie: L. Pine (s)
Raoul: W. Harrison (t)
Fabio Fabiani: C. Santley (br)
de Villefranche: W.H. Weiss (bs)
Dame Bertha: H. A. Cook (ms)
Anne, Duchess of Brittany: A. Hiles (ct)

This is a grand romantic opera in three acts; Libretto by J. V. Bridgeman. It was performed at the Royal English Opera, Covent Garden, London. Balfe composed it under contract for the Pyne Harrison Company. There have been some discrepancies about the dates of the premiere. The correct date is that shown above.

Selected numbers:

> Aria – *Marie: Oh would that my heart*
> Aria – Raoul: *In the desert waste of life*
> Duet – Marie and Raoul: *Where all the earth's dark treasure*
> Aria – Fabio: *The Flower is beauty*
> Aria – de Villefranche: *Truth and beauty*
> Aria – Marie: *There's one who fear'd me*
> Aria – Raoul: *Oh, love is like a reed*

Comments: The critics were favourable to the opera. It had an extended run of more than twenty-five nights. It did not have a revival, nor was it performed elsewhere. While some of the main numbers were published in sheet music, none became 'hits' like the *Bohemian Girl* pieces.

23. *Blanche de Nevers*   21 November 1863   BL 29, 361, 29,362,
Blanche: L. Pine (s)

                                    vols. xxxvii, xxxviii

Lagardére: W. Harrison (t)
Prince of Gonzagues: W.H. Weiss (br)
Princess of Gonzagues: E. Heywood (ct)
Zillah: A. Hiles (ct)
Philip of Orleans: A. St. Albyn (t)
Cocardasse: H. Corri (bs)

This is a romantic opera in three acts; libretto by J. Brougham. It was performed at the Royal English Opera, Covent Garden, London. Balfe composed it under contract for the Pyne Harrison Company. There were also some discrepancies about the dates of the premiere of this opera. The correct date is that shown above. It was also Balfe's last English opera. The Pyne Harrison Opera Company, which had contracted Balfe for this series of operas, disbanded in 1864.

Selected numbers:

> Aria – Lagardére: *When I think of the days that are gone*
> Aria – Blanche: *There is a void within my heart*
> Duet – Blanche and Lagardére: *Must we part, and part for ever?*
> Aria – Blanche: *As the mountain streams*
> Aria – Gonzagues: *The old vine tree*
> Aria – Lagardére: *Wilt thou think of me*

Comments: There were favourable reviews by most of the critics. The opera ran for almost a month. No one saw this as being Balfe's last English opera. The music was considered to be 'sparkling'. Additionally, according to some of the critics, Balfe seemed to move away from his traditional 'ballad of the old form'- to a more integrated opera. On the night of the premiere virtually every solo was encored. The opera was not performed outside London.

24. *The Sleeping Queen*+   31 August 1864   (not known)

Maria Queen of Leon: D. Finlayson (s)
Philippe: T. Whiffin (t)
The Regent: R. Wilkinson (bs)

This was an operetta in one act. It had its premiere at the Royal Gallery of Illustrations, London. The libretto was by H.B. Farne. Balfe reworked this at a later date and made it into a two-act opera. In addition to its London performances it was also performed in Boston in 1876.

25. *Il talismano***   11 June 1874   BL 37, 265

Edith Plantagenet: C. Nilsson (s)
Sir Kenneth: I. Campanini (t)
Richard Coeur de Lion: Sig. Rota (b)
Queen Berengaria: M. Rosé

This was an opera that Balfe was in the final stages of completing when he died in 1870. He had written it to an English libretto with spoken dialogue. Balfe's widow Lina afterwards worked with the conductor and composer Michael Costa and the manager of Her Majesty's Theatre, James H. Mapleson (operating on a temporary basis from the Theatre Royal Drury Lane, while his other theatre was being rebuilt), to have the opera finalized and performed. At Mapleson's suggestion the opera was translated into Italian by Giuseppe Zaffira and produced at the Theatre Royal Drury Lane on 11 June 1874. The opera was subsequently produced in Liverpool, Glasgow, Edinburgh and Dublin. It was also performed in New York in 1875 and in Monte Carlo in 1918.

Selected numbers:

>   Aria – Edith: *Placida Notte*
>   Aria – Sir Kenneth: *Candido fiore*
>   Aria – Edith: *Nella dolce trepidanza*
>   Duet – Sir Kenneth and Edith: *Quest' annel*
>   Aria – Richard: *Oh! chi d'amor fuo mai*
>   Aria – Sir Kenneth: *A te coll'aure a sera*

Aria – Queen Berengaria: *La guerra appena*

Comments: Balfe received full honours from the major critics for his final work. It was considered one of his best. The structure and style is Italianate and indeed brings to mind the work of Verdi's middle period.

26. *Moro, the Painter of Antwerp**28 January, 1882   Carl Rosa Archives,
                                                                  Liverpool Library

Olivia: A.Valleria (s)
Antonio: B. McGuckin (t)
Duke of Alba: L. Crotty (br)

This is a grand opera in three acts. It was originally written for Trieste with the title of *Pittore e Duca*. The opera was not a success in the Italian city. This version of the opera was put together by one of Balfe's early biographers, W. A. Barrett, who wrote the libretto. This English version of the opera was first performed at Her Majesty's Theatre, 28 January 1882, by the Carl Rosa Opera Company. In this form, it was not an opera that was approved by the composer as he had died several years earlier.

Selected numbers:

Aria – Antonio: *Farewell, ye thoughts of joy and gladness*
Aria – Olivia: *As by the rivers straying*
Aria – Antonio: *On my gondola so lonely*
Aria – Duke: *Bold knight his armour waiting*

Comments: The opera was not a great success. It was performed by the Carl Rosa Opera Company, who revived it later.

NOTES

*Translations – *Geraldine, or the Lover's Well* was an English version of the French opera, *Le puits d'amour,* first performed in Paris in 1843. *I Quattro Fratelli* was an Italian version (with some new music added) of the French opera *Les quatre fils de Aymon,* which was first performed in Paris in 1844. *Moro, the Painter of Antwerp* was an English translation of the Italian opera *Pittore e Duca,* which first premiered in Trieste in 1854.

** Italian-language librettos. +Operetta

APPENDIX IV - FRENCH STAGE – OPERA PREMIERES, DATES AND CASTS; LIBRETTOS AND SCORES

During the nineteenth century in Paris it was generally the practice to print full orchestral scores of operas that were performed. As a result, it's possible some of these printed orchestral scores of Balfe operas may be held in the extensive library collections of the Paris Opera, or the National Library of France in Paris. However, the whereabouts of the original autographed scores for Balfe's French operas is not known.

Opera	Premiere Date	Location
1. *Le puits d'amour*	20 April, 1843	Paris, Opéra Comique

Publisher: Bernard Latté, Paris 1841
Libretto: E. Scribe and A. de Leuven

Cast for Premiere
Edouard III Roi d'Angleterre: J.B. Chollet (t)
Le Comte Arthur de Salisbury: M.P. Audran (t)
Fulby, page du Roi: Mlle Darcier (ms)
Bolbury: M. Henri (bs)
Lord Nottingham: E. Daudé (bs)
La Princesse Philippine de Hainaut: Mlle Melotte (s)
Géraldine: A. Thillon (s)
Chorus
Conductor: (?)

Brief Description
This is a three-act opera with a story that is set in London. The opera was so successful in Paris (twenty-eight performances including the premiere) that Balfe was offered an extension of his contract to compose another opera for the Opéra Comique. In August of the same year Balfe had an English language version of this opera performed in London under the title *Geraldine, or The Lover's Well*.

Duet – Bolbury and Geraldine: *Compter sur la constance d'un matrlot*
Recitative and Aria – Edouard: *C'est bien ici qu'hier j'apperçu cette belle*
Duet – Edouard and Geraldine: *Voici l'heure de la vengeance*
Aria – Geraldine: *Il s'éloigne et pourtant je reste*

Location of Libretto, Score and Sheet Music
The libretto is available from Österreichische Nationalbibliothek in Vienna. The identifier is: 641440-C. 30,21 Mus. The full orchestral operatic score is held at the British Library, London: mss. 29,337 and 29,338, vols xiii, xiv. The author has a complete piano vocal score (191 pages). It's also possible that copies of the

score and libretto may be held in the Paris Opera library. Check identifier number: A-548 I-III.

A German language version (*Der Liebesbrunnen*) of the score is held at Österreichische Nationalbibliothek in Vienna. The identifier is: 757461-A. Alt Mag. There is also a French-language version there; the identifier is: 130813-C. Mus. There is also a piano vocal score (191 pages) in the Library of Congress, Washington, DC: call number: M1503.B185 P8.

2. *Les quatre fils Aymon*	15 July 1844	Paris, Opéra Comique

Publisher:Bernard Latté, Paris 1844
Libretto: A. de Leuven and L. L. Brunswick

Cast for Premiere
Baron de Beaumanoir: M. Thermann (br/bfb)
Hermine: Mlle Darcier (s)
Gertrude: Mme M.A. Potier (ms)
Oliver: J.B. Chollet (t)
Allard: C.L. Sainte Foy (t)
Richard: M. Mocker (t)
Rinald: M. Emon? (bs)
Clara: Mlle. Melotte (ms/s)
Jolantha: Mlle Duvernoy? (s)
Eglantine: ? (ct)
Ivon: H. Léon (bs/br)
Chorus
Conductor: M.W. Balfe (?)

Brief Description
This is a comic opera in three acts, based very loosely on the medieval legend and fable about Charlemagne and the four sons of the Duc d'Aymon. The story was very popular in both France and Germany during the nineteenth century. Following the premiere there were sixteen performances of the opera, which made it quite successful.

There are six scenes in the first act, six in the second act and five in the final act. In addition to several arias including a romanza for the tenor, and several duets, the opera contains four quintets, a quartet and a trio. There is a baritone and buffo bass duet in the second act that was highly praised by the critics.

> Aria – Oliver: *L'eure du soir était venue*
> Aria – Hermine: *Une jeune et noble fille*
> Aria – Rinald (?): *Honneur et gloire aux quatre fils Aymon*
> Trio – Baron, Oliver and Hermine: *A la douce espérance*

Given its success in Paris, Balfe later created an English-anguage version called

The Castle of Aymon, which premiered in London in November 1844.

The opera was also performed in Vienna in a German-language version, *Die vier Haimonskinder*, in December 1844. It quickly became very successful in the German speaking cities throughout Europe. (See next section for details.)

Balfe also produced an Italian-language version, *I Quattro Fratelli*, of the opera for London in 1851. He added new arias to the opera. The music for the soprano Sophie Cruvelli in the Italian version was considered exceptionally challenging and exciting by the critics. Since the Italian version was initially produced as a benefit performance for Balfe it had a short run. A number of the critics considered it the composer's best work to date. The Cruvelli music is available. See below.

Location of Libretto, Score and Sheet Music

A copy of the libretto for the Italian-language version of the opera is held by Harvard University in its Theatre Hollis Catalog collection; call numbers: TS 8551.70 1851. A copy of the French printed orchestral operatic score is held by the British Library: mss 29,339, 29,340 vol. xv. and xvi. There is a piano vocal score (200 pages), of the French version of the opera at the Library of Congress: call number: M1503.B185 Q2. The author also has a copy of the German-language piano vocal score (245 pages) of the opera.

The British Library holds sheet music from the Italian version of the opera. These pieces include some of the arias specially written for Cruvelli and others, for the London performance. Call number H.193.q and H.194.

3. *L'Étoile de Séville*   17 December 1845   Paris

Published: Michel Frères, Paris
    Also Lelong, Bruxelles, 1846.
Libretto: H. Lucas

Le Théatre de
l'Académie
Royale de Musique
(Paris Opéra)

Cast for Premiere
Dona Estrelle: R. Stoltz (ms)
Zaida: M. Nau (s)
Don Sanche: I. Gardoni (t)
Don Bustos: H. Brémont (t?)
Le Roi: P. Baroilhet (br)
Don Arias: M. Menghis (bs)
Gomez: F. Prévost (br)
Pedro: M. Paulin (t)
Chorus
Conductor: (?)

Brief Description

A grand opera, in four acts, with a ballet. The opera was given fifteen performances. The composers Chopin, Meyerbeer, Auber and others were in the audience for the premiere.

> Duet – Don Sanche and Le Roi: *Je sais qu'au rivage du Maure*
> Aria – Don Sanche: *Depuis deux ans auprès d'Estrelle*
> Aria – Dona Estrelle: *Sais-tu bien quel tourment*
> Barcarolle – Oliver: *O nuit, de ton silence*

Location of Libretto, Score and Sheet Music

The Libretto by H. Lucas is based on a work by Lope de Vega, *La Estrella de
Sevilla,* a subject matter that was used by other composers. The French libretto
is held by Österreichische Nationalbibliothek, Vienna. The code identifier is,
641440-C.30,21 Mus. There is also a copy of the libretto at the Harvard Hollis
Catalog collection: call number 002676027. A copy of the French piano vocal
score (527 pages) is held by the British Library, call number: H.193.z.

It's quite possible the original manuscript operatic score could be at the Paris
Opéra Library. It does not appear to be in the National Library at rue Richelieu
in Paris.

4. *La Bohémienne*   23 April 1862   Rouen, Théâtre des Arts

Publisher: E. Gérard et cie
Librettist: J.H. Vernoy de Saint Georges

Cast for Premiere

Sarah: I. Lambert (s)
La reine Mabb: C. Galli-Marié (ms)
Stenio de Stoltberg: H. Warnots (t)
Le comte D'Arnheim: M. Bonnesseur (br)
Trousse-Diable: M. Dubosc (bs)
Narcisse de Krakentorp: M. Paris (t)
Un Officer: P. Edmond (t)
Martha: L. Bourgeois
Ballet
Chorus
Conductor: J. Massenet

Brief Description

The first French version of Balfe's very successful English opera *The Bohemian
Girl* was produced in Rouen by Balfe's close friend, Jules-Henri Vernoy de Saint-
Georges. Balfe did not attend the premiere in April 1862. There were thirteen
performances including the premiere, which made it quite successful.

This version of the opera has four acts, with a ballet. Sung recitatives were added to replace the spoken dialogue of the English version of the opera. As part of the augmentation, additional arias were added for Sarah (Arline) and the role of the Queen of the Gypsies was expanded. This version was later also performed at Liége in Belgium in February 1863.

> Aria – D'Arnheim: *Vivant au sein des armes*
> Aria – Sarah: *A mes pied, dans un doux servage*
> Aria – Stenio: *Quand une voix bien tendre*

Location of Libretto, Score and Sheet Music
The location, of the libretto used for the Rouen production and the original manuscript scores are not known. It's possible they may be with the papers of J.H. Vernoy de Saint-Georges or in the Paris Opéra library. The Harvard Library has copy of the Rouen piano vocal score (339 pages) from 1862. The call number is Mus 627.7.629. There is also a copy held by the Bibliothèque nationale de France (Richelieu). Identifier: FRBNF 38755206.

5. *La Bohémienne (Revised)*   30 December 1869 Paris

Publisher: E. Gérard et cie
Libretto: J.H. Vernoy de Saint-Georges   Théâtre Lyrique

Cast for Premiere
Sarah: H. Brunet-Lafleur (s)
La reine Mabb: P. Wertheimber (ct)
Stenio de Stoltberg: J.S. Monjauze (t); M. Coppel (t)
    (replaced Monjauze who became ill)
Le Comte D'Arnheim: F. Lutz (br)
Trousse-Diable: M. Bacquié (bs)
Narcisse de Krakentorp: M. Jalama (t)
Un Officer: M. Brisson (t)
Martha: M. Andrieux (s)
Ballet
Chorus
Conductor: J.E. Pasdeloup

Brief Description
The second French version of Balfe's *The Bohemian Girl* was produced in Paris by Balfe and his friend J.H. Vernoy de Saint Georges.

This French version of the opera has a prologue, four acts and a ballet. Sarah (Arline) retained her arias in the third and fourth acts in addition to her more famous music, 'romance du rêve' (I dreamt I dwelt in marble halls) in the second Act.

> Aria – D'Arnheim: *Vivant au sein des armes*
> Aria – Sarah: *A mes pied, dans un doux servage*

Aria – Stenio: *Quand une voix bien tendre*
Aria – La reine Mabb: *L'amour qu'il m'inspire*

The role of the Queen of the Gypsies was reduced somewhat from Rouen and some of her music was deleted. The recitatives were rewritten. Musical changes included the addition of a quartette and a duet along with some other changes that can't now be fully identified. The story location was switched from Scotland back to Austria which was the setting for the original English version. The opera became significantly longer than the original English version.

Location of Libretto, Score and Sheet Music
A copy of the operatic orchestral score is located at the British Library. Call numbers: 29,336. vol. xii. A piano vocal score (361 pages) is held by the author. The location of the French libretto is unknown.

APPENDIX V – GERMAN-LANGUAGE OPERA PREMIERES AND DATES; LIBRETTOS AND SCORES

Balfe never composed a specific opera for Vienna or any other German speaking city. All of his operas that were performed in Vienna and Berlin and other German cities were adaptations from operas that had been originally produced sometimes in a shorter or different format in London or Paris.

The interesting fact is that a number of these adaptations became even more popular that the original version of the scores.

Opera	Date	Location
1. *Die vier Haimonskinder*	14 December 1844	Vienna, Josefstadt Theater

Publisher: A. Diabelli & Comp., Vienna
Libretto: German Translation: J. Kupelwieser

Brief Description:
This is a translation of the Balfe's French opera, *Les quatre fils Aymon.*
The opera had great appeal in German-speaking cities in Europe. It quickly became very successful. By early 1845 it was being performed in places such as Frankfurt, Leipzig, Prague, Budapest, Linz, Braunschweig, Stuttgart and Hamburg. In 1846 Basle in Switzerland heard it. It was also repeated in Vienna, this time at the Theater an der Wien in October 1845, and again in 1846 and 1847. It was later performed in Amsterdam and in Berlin. It success in Germany continued well into the 1880s. It was revived several times in Vienna at different theatres.

Location of Libretto, Score and Sheet Music
A German-language libretto (95 pages) of the opera is held by the National Library of Ireland. Call number: P2472. The orchestral operatic score of the German-anguage version is held by the Österreichische Nationalbibliothek in Vienna. The identifier is: 299209-A Mus. A piano vocal score (245 pages) of the German version of the opera published by Diabelli in Vienna circa 1844 is in the possession of the author. There is also a similar copy of the piano vocal score at the Library of Congress; call number: M1503.B185 Q4. The Harvard Library in its Loeb Music collection also has a piano vocal score. Call number: Mus 627.7.605

2. *Der Liebesbrunnen*	4 November1845	Vienna, Theater an der Wien

Publisher: A. Diabelli & Comp., Vienna (?)
Libretto: German Translation: J. Kupelwieser

Michael W. Balfe

Brief Description:
This is a translation of Balfe's French opera *Le puits d'amour*. This German version of the opera was later also performed in Linz, Austria.

Location of Libretto, Score and Sheet Music
A German language orchestral version of the score is held at, Österreichische Nationalbibliothek in Vienna. The identifier is: 757461-A. Alt Mag. There is also a French language version there; the identifier is: 130813-C. Mus.

3. *Die Zigeunerin*   24 July 1846   Vienna, Theater an der Wien

Publisher: J. B. Wallishausser, Vienna
Libretto: German translation, J. Kupelwieser*

Brief Description
This is a three-act German-language translation of *The Bohemian Girl*. Similar to the Italian version the story is placed in Scotland. However, there are some character name changes for the German version. The opera was performed in most of the German-speaking cities throughout Europe from the middle to the late nineteenth century. Balfe conducted performances at the Theater an der Wien (Vienna) in September and October 1846, with immense success. It was particularly popular in Vienna, where it was performed for many years. Balfe also conducted the opera in Berlin in 1851.

Interestingly, in 1848, it was performed in Pressburg (now Bratislava), which was the location of the story setting for the original English version of the opera.

* Loewenberg shows a translation being done by a J.P. Lyser; however, advertisements of the period, the German libretto and available scores show J. Kupelwieser as the translator.

Location of Libretto, Score and Sheet Music
The libretto is held by the Österreichische Nationalbibliothek in Vienna. The identifier is: 685271-B Mus. The orchestral score is also at the Österreichische Nationalbibliothek in Vienna. The identifier is: 813455-B and 685270-A. Mus., 685271-B. Mus., and 179257-B. Mus. A piano vocal score (244 pages) is in the Library of Congress: call number: M1503.B185 B62

4. *Die Belagerung von Rochelle* 24 October, 1846   Vienna, Theater an der Wien

Publisher: A. Diabelli & Comp, Vienna
Libretto: German translation by Dr. A. J. Becher

Brief Description
This is a German translation of Balfe's English opera *The Siège of Rochelle*.

As far as is known the German version of the opera was not performed outside Vienna.

Location of Libretto, Score and Sheet Music
There is no known German-language version of the libretto or score available.
The full English manuscript score is held by the British Library in London. Call
number: mss. Add.29.325/29 326. A piano vocal score of the English version is
held by the author.

5. *Der Mulatte* 25 January1850 Berlin, Royal Grand Opera

Publisher: Pietro Mechetti, Vienna
Libretto: German translation by J.C. Grübaum

Brief Description
This is a German translation of Balfe's three-act English opera, *The Bondman*,
which premiered in London in 1846. Although the opera was very well received
with packed houses in Berlin it does not appear to have been performed outside
that city or in Austria.

Location of Libretto, Scores/Sheet Music
No copy of the German-language orchestral score could be traced in the
libraries in Berlin, Vienna, Washington or London. A piano vocal score (233
pages) of the German version is held by the Library of Congress: call number:
M1503.B185 M84.

The British Library has the Balfe manuscript of the English (*The Bondman*) ver-
sion of the opera: call number: mss. 29, 346, 29,347. vols, xxii and xxiii.
There is also a German language piano vocal score (233 pages) at the
Biblioteca at the Academy of Santa Cecilia in Rome: code identifier:
IT\ICCU\RMR\0049355.

6. *Keolanthe or, Das Traumbild* 3 December 1853 Vienna, Kartorntheater

Publisher: A. Diabelli & Comp., Vienna
Libretto: German translation by Karl Gollmick

Brief Description
This three act German version of the opera had additional music and arias added
to the original English score, for Vienna. The opera was quite successful. It was
still being performed there later in the 1850s.

Location of Libretto, Scores/Sheet Music.
The Österreichische Nationalbibliothek in Vienna holds a score of the German
version of the opera: Identifier is: 987124-A. Mus. and 987125-A. Mus. There
is also another score; identifier: 32255-B. Mus.

The British Library does hold some of the music from the opera but the original manuscript score is apparently lost. The call number for the music held at the British Library is: 33,799.

Harvard Library in its Hollis Catalog holds music (23 pages) from the opera; call number: 006929279. The Library of Congress holds what appears to be either sheet music or a piano vocal score of the opera. The call number is: ML50B188K3 1841.

APPENDIX VI– INTEGRATED CHRONOLOGY OF ALL BALFE OPERA PREMIERES (ITALIAN, ENGLISH, FRENCH AND GERMAN)

This listing provides an overview of all of Balfe's published operas over a period of forty years and when they were first performed. Frequently when an English opera was translated into another language, Balfe added new scenes and/or arias, duets etc., or changed the structure of the work. He can be credited with a total of forty-three operas.

Year Opera Premiered	Opera – Title at Premiere/ other Language Versions	Premiere Location	Language of Libretto
1829	1. *I rivale di se stessi*	Palermo	Italian
1831	2. *Un avvertimento di gelosi*	Pavia	Italian
1833	3. *Enrico IV al passo della Marna*	Milan	Italian
1835	4. *Siege of Rochelle*	London	English
	Die Belagerung von Rochelle (1846)	Vienna	German
1836	5. *The Maid of Artois*	London	English
1837	6. *Catherine Grey*	London	English
1837	7. *Joan of Arc*	London	English
1838	8. *Diadeste, or The Veiled Lady*	London	English
1838	9. *Falstaff*	London	Italian
1841	10. *Keolanthe, or The Unearthly Bride*	London	English
	Keolanthe or Das Traumbilde (1853)	Vienna	German
1843	11. *Le Puits d'Amour*	Paris	French
	Geraldine (1843)	London	English
	Der Liebesbrunnen (1845)	Vienna	German
1843	12. *The Bohemian Girl*	London	English
	Die Zigeunerin (1846)	Vienna	German
	La Zingara (1854)	Trieste	Italian
	La Bohémienne (1862)	Rouen	French
	La Bohémienne (1869)	Paris	French
1844	13. *Le Quatre Fils Aymon*	Paris	French
	The Castle of Aymon (1844)	London	English
	Die vier Haimons-kinder (1845)	Vienna	German
	I Quattro Fratelli (1851)	London	Italian
1844	14. *The Daughter of St. Mark*	London	English
1845	15. *The Enchantress*	London	English
1845	16. *L'etoile de Séville*	Paris	French
1847	17. *The Bondman*	London	English

	Die Mulatte (1850)	Berlin	German
1847	18. *The Maid of Honour*	London	English
1852	19. *The Devil's in it*	London	English
	Letty the Basket Maker (1871)	London	English
1852	20. *The Sicilian Bride*	London	English
1854	21. *Pittore e Duca*	Trieste	Italian
	*Moro the Painter of Antwerp** (1882)	London	English
1857	22. *The Rose of Castille*	London	English
	Die Rose von Castilien (1859)	Vienna	German
1858	23. *Satanella, or The Power of Love*	London	English
1860	24. *Bianca, or The Bravo's Bride*	London	English
1861	25. *The Puritan's Daughter*	London	English
1863	26. *The Armourer of Nantes*	London	English
1863	27. *Blanche de Nevers*	London	English
1874	28. *Il talismano**	London	Italian

* Performed posthumously, as Balfe died in October 1870.

APPENDIX VII – SELECTED SINGERS AND MUSICIAMNS WHO PERFORMED IN BALFE OPERAS

Many major international singers sang in Balfe operas and cantatas. He was very well respected as a musician, composer and conductor. This listing endeavours to provide a better understanding of who sang what and where. There will be many surprises.

For example, four of the greatest singers of the nineteenth century who created operas for Bellini, Donizetti, Rossini and others, Giulia Grisi, Luigi Lablache, Antonio Tamburini and Giovanni Battista Rubini, created Balfe's *Falstaff* in London in 1838. Giorgio Ronconi, the renowned Verdi and Donizetti baritone who created several roles for these two Italian composers including Verdi's first big success, *Nabucco*, sang in an early Balfe opera in Milan in 1831.

Celestine Galli-Marie, the mezzo-soprano who later created Bizet's *Carmen* and Thomas' *Mignon*, sang in the first French version of Balfe's *La Bohémienne* (*The Bohemian Girl*), in Rouen in 1862. The great mezzo-soprano Rosine Stoltz, who created Donizetti's *La favorite* in Paris in 1840, also created the part of Estrella in Balfe's *L'étoile de Seville* at the Paris Opéra in 1845. The renowned French tenor Gilbert Duprez sang in a Balfe cantata in Paris in 1842.

The future great tenor Jean de Reszke sang (as a baritone) in Balfe's *Il Talismano* in Britain and Ireland at the beginning of his career in 1874. The tenor Italo Campanini and soprano Christine Nilsson, who created *Il Talismano* in London in 1874, went on to open the first Metropolitan Opera season in New York in 1883 in Gounod's *Faust*.

The Italian tenor Rafael Mirate, who created the part of the Duke of Mantua in Verdi's Rigoletto in 1851, created the tenor role in a new Balfe opera in Trieste in 1854. There are many more, as the list will show.

There are also some of best singers of the period from Britain, Ireland and America to be found on the list.

Albertazzi, Emma, contralto
 Falstaff (London 1838); Anne Page
Alboni, Marietta, mezzo-soprano
 La Zingara (London 1858); Queen of the Gypsies
Allen, Henry R., tenor;
Geraldine/The Lover's Well (London-1843); Edward the Third
 The Castle of Aymon (London 1844; Oliver
Alexander, T., tenor;
 Un Avvertimento di Gelosi (Milan-1831); Il Conte
Aliprandi, Domenico, bass;
 La Zingara (Trieste 1854); Federico
Anderson, James R., tenor
 Joan of Arc (London 1837); Beauvais
Anderson, Josephine, mezzo-soprano;
 Joan of Arc (London 1837); Agnes Sorel

Audran, M.P., tenor
   Le puits d'amour (Paris 1843); Le Comte Arthur de Salisbury
Bacquié, M., bass
   La Bohémienne (Paris 1869); Trousse-Diable
Balanchi, Signor, bass;
   I Quattro Fratelli (London 1851); Rinaldo
Balfe, Lina Roser (Mrs), soprano
   Enrico IV al passo della Marna (Milan 1833)
   Keolanthe/The Unearthly Bride (London 1841); Keolanthe
Balfe, Michael W., baritone;
   Enrico IV, al passo della Marna (Milan 1833); Constantino
   Siege of Rochelle (London 1835), selected performances
   Catherine Grey (London 1837); Earl of Hertford
   Joan of Arc (London 1837); Theodore
Balfe, Michael W., conductor
   Un avvertimento ai gelosi (Pavia 1831)
   The Siege of Rochelle (London 1835)
   The Maid of Artois (London 1836)
   Joan of Arc (London 1837) selected performances
   Diadeste/The Veiled Lady (London 1838)
   Falstaff (London 1838)
   Keolanthe/The Unearthly Bride (London 1841)
   The Bohemian Girl (London 1843) First seven nights only
   The Daughter of St Mark (London 1844)
   L'etoile de Seville (Paris 1845)?
   Die Zigeunerin (Vienna 1846; Berlin 1851)
   The Bondman (London1846) First night only
   The Maid of Honour (London 1847) First three nights only
   Der Mulatte (Berlin 1850)
   La Zingara (London 1858)
Balfe, Victoire, soprano
   La Zingara (London1859); Arline
Barker, George, tenor
   Geraldine/The Lover's Well (London 1843); Lord Salisbury
Barroilhet, Paul B., baritone
   L'étoile de Séville (Paris 1845), The King
Bedford, Paul, bass
   The Siège of Rochelle (London 1835); Azino
   Geraldine/The Lover's Well (London 1843); Quance
Belletti, Giovanni, baritone;
   La Zingara (London 1858); Count Arnheim
Belli, A., bass
   Pittore e Duca (Trieste1854); Vargas
Benedict, Julius, conductor
   The Bohemian Girl (London 1943) from eigth night on.

Berlioz, Hector, conductor;
  The Maid of Honour from fourth night (London1847)
Betts, Miss. contralto
  The Bohemian Girl (London 1843); Queen of the Gypsies
Birch, Charlotte, soprano;
  The Maid of Honour (London 1847); Lady Henrietta
Bisconttini, F. bass
  Un Avvertimento di Gelosi (Milan 1831); Menico
Boccaccini, Francesco, bass
  I rivale di se stessi (Palermo 1829); Derval
Bonfigli, Lorenzo, tenor;
  Enrico IV, al passo della Marna (Milan 1833); Enrico IV
Bonnesseur, M., baritone
  La Bohémienne (Rouen 1862); Le comte D'Arheim
Borrani, C. G., baritone (aka Mr Boisragon)
  The Bohemian Girl (London 1843; Dublin 1845); Count Arnheim
  The Daughter of St. Mark (London 1844); Andrea
  The Enchantress (London 1845); Ramir
  The Devil in It (London 1852); Lucastro
Bremond, H. tenor;
  L'etoile de Seville (Paris 1845), Don Bustos
Brunet-Lafleur, H., soprano
  La Bohémienne (Paris 1869); Sarah
Burdini, Mr., baritone/bass
  The Daughter of St Mark (London 1844);The King
Cambiaggio, G., buffo-bass
  Un avvertimento ai gelosi (Pavia 1831, Milan 1831); Don Fabio
  Enrico IV, al passo della Marna (Milan 1833); Gervasio
Campanini, Italo, tenor
  Il Talismano (London 1874; Dublin 1874); Sir Kenneth
Campobello, Enrico, (aka Henry Campbell) baritone;
  Il Talismano (London 1874); L'Emiro
Caremoli, Mdlle., soprano
  Falstaff (London-1838); Mrs. Page
Casaboni, Signor, bass;
  Il Talismano (London-1874); Il Duca D'Austria
Castelli, Mme., mezzo-soprano
  Falstaff (London 1838); Mrs. Quickly
Catalani, Signor, baritone;
  Il Talismano (London-1874); Nectananus
Chollet, J.H., tenor
  Le puits d'amour(Paris-1843); Edouard III, Roi d'Angleterre
  Les quatre fils Aymon (Paris 1844);Oliver
Coletti, Fillipo, baritone;
  I Quattro Fratelli (London 1851); Ivon

Condell, Helen, soprano
   The Castle of Aymon (London 1844); Hermanie
Cook, Thomas Aynsley, bass;
   Blanche de Nevers (London 1863); Aesop
   The Armourer of Nantes (London 1863); Pascal, Governor of the Castle
Cook, Harriet Aynsley, mezzo-soprano;
   The Armourer of Nantes (London 1863); Dame Bertha
Coppel, M., tenor
   La Bohémienne (Paris-1869); Stenio de Stoltberg 9
Corini, G., mezzo-soprano;
   Un avvertimento ai gelosi (Pavia 1831); Ernesta
Corri, Henri, bass;
   The Devil in it (London 1852); Hermann
   Satanella (London-1858); Bracaccio
   The Puritan's Daughter (London 1861); Colonel Wolfe
   The Armourer of Nantes (London 1863); a Jew
   Blanche de Nevers (London 1863); Cocardasse
Costa, Michael, conductor;
   Il Talismano (London 1874)
Costa, Signor, bass;
   Il Talismano (London 1874); Il Re di Francia
Crichton, Miss, soprano;
   The Sicilian Bride (London 1852); Bianca
Crosa, Carlo, bass;
   Un avvertimento ai gelosi (Pavia 1831); Menico
   Enrico IV al passo della Marna (Milan 1833); Du-Champ
Crotty, Leslie, baritone;
   Moro, Painter of Antwerp (London 1882); Duke of Alba
Cruvelli, Sophie, soprano;
   I Quattro Fratelli (London 1851); Erminia
Dai Fiore, Signor, tenor
   I Quattro Fratelli (London 1851); Uberto
Darcier, Mlle., mezzo-soprano
   Le puits d'amour (Paris 1843); Fulby
   Les quatre fils Aymon (Paris 1844); Hermine
Daudé, E., bass
   Le puits d'amour(Paris 1843); Lord Nottingham
Dalle Aste, F., bass
   Die vier Haimonskinder (Vienna 1845); Rinald
   Die Zigeunerin (Vienna 1846); Devilshof
D'Egville, Hervet, tenor
   Moro, Painter of Antwerp (London 1882); Orsini
Della Costa, C., baritone
   La Zingara (Trieste 1854); Il Conte Albano
   Pittore e Duca (Trieste 1854); Orsino

De Reszke, Jean, baritone
Il Talismano (Dublin 1874); Richard Coeur de Lion
D'Ettore, P., bass
La Zingara (Trieste 1854); Falco
Drayton, Henri, bass
The Sicilian Bride (London-1852); Satanico
Dubosc, M., bass
La Bohémienne (Rouen-1862); Trousse-Diable
Duprez, Gilbert, tenor
Cantata (Paris 1842)
Duvernoy, Mlle, soprano
Les quatre fils Aymon (Paris 1844); Jolantha
Emon, M., bass
Les quatre fils Aymon (Paris 1844); Rinald
Feller, Mme, soprano
I Quattro Fratelli (London 1851); Iolanda
Ferri, G., baritone
Pittore e Duca (Trieste 1854); Duca D'Alba
Finlayson, D'Este., soprano;
Sleeping Queen (London 1864); Maria
Forde, Miss, soprano
Joan of Arc (London 1837); St Catherine
Galli-Marie, Celestine, mezzo-soprano;
La Bohemienne (Rouen 1862); La reine Mabb
Galli, Signor, baritone
Falstaff (London 1838); George
Garcia, Eugenia, soprano
Geraldine/The Lover's Well (London 1843); Geraldine
Gardoni, Italo, tenor;
L'étoile de Seville (1845 Paris); Cid of Andalusia
I Quattro Fratelli (London 1851); Oliviero
Gerster, Etelka, soprano
Il Talismano (London 1878); Edit Plantagenet
Giuglini, Antonio, tenor
La Zingara (London 1858; Dublin1858); Gualtiero
Giuliani, C.. soprano
I Quattro Fratelli (London 1851); Clara
Gould, Miss, soprano;
Keolanthe/The Unearthly Bride (London 1841); Pavina
Grattan, Mrs., contralto
Geraldine/The Lover's Well (London 1843); Tresilias
Gridelli, T., soprano
Pittore e Duca (Trieste 1854); Donna Ines
Grisi, Giulia, soprano
Falstaff (London 1838); Mrs Ford

Giubilei, Theodore bass
  The Siège of Rochelle (London 1835); Montalban
  The Maid of Artois (London 1836); Sans Regret
  Diadeste/The Veiled Lady (London 1837); Zambo
  Joan of Arc (London 1837); Old soldier
Harley, Mr., tenor?
  The Enchantress (London 1845); Dr Mathanasian
Harrison, William, tenor;
  The Bohemian Girl (London 1843; Dublin 1844,); Thaddeus
  The Daughter of St. Mark (London 1844); Adolph
  The Enchantress (London 1845); Silvio
  The Bondman (London 1846); Ardenford
  The Rose of Castile (London 1857); Manuel
  Satanella/The Power of Love (London 1858); Count Rupert
  Bianca, the Bravo Bride (London 1860); Prince of Ferrara/Fontespada
  The Puritan's Daughter (London 1861); Rochester
  Blanche de Nevers (London 1863); Lagardere
  The Armourer of Nantes (London 1863); Raoul the Armourer
Hayes, Catherine, soprano
  The Bohemian Girl (Melbourne 1855)
Healey, Fanny, soprano;
  The Siege of Rochelle (London 1835); Marcella
  The Maid of Artois (London 1836); Coralie
  Diadeste/The Veiled Lady (London 1837); Countess Amalfi
Henri, M., bass
  Le puits d'amour (Paris 1843); Bolby
Henry, Mr., tenor;
  Catherine Grey (London 1837); Sir W. Cecil
Heywood, Emma, contralto
  Blanche de Nevers (London 1863); Princess of Gonzagues
Hiles, Anna, contralto;
  The Armourer of Nantes (London 1863); Anne, Duchess of Brittany
  Blanche de Nevers (London 1863); Zillah
Honey, George, bass
  The Rose of Castile (London 1857); Don Florio
  Satanella or the Power of Lover (London 1858); Hortensius
Horton, Priscilla, contralto
Hudson, Mr., tenor
  The Bohemian Girl (London 1843); Florestein
Isaacs, Rebecca, contralto
  The Sicilian Bride (London 1852); Sirena
  Satanella/The Power of Love (London-1858); Lelia
Jalama, M., tenor
  La Bohémienne (Paris 1869); Narcisse de Krakentorp
Jones, S., bass

The Bondman (London 1846), Jalox
The Sicilian Bride (London 1852); Duke de Sangenaro
Lablache, Luigi, bass
Falstaff (London 1838); Falstaff
Lambert, I., soprano
La Bohémienne (Rouen 1862); Sarah
La Manna, Francesco, conductor;
I rivale di se stessi (Palermo 1829)
Lanza, Rosalia mezzo-soprano;
I Quattro Fratelli (London 1851); Eglantina
Lawrence, Alberto, bass
Bianca, the Bravo's Bride (London 1860); Duke of Milan
Leffler, A., bass
The Castle of Aymon (London 1844); Ivon
Léon, F., contralto;
La Zingara (Trieste 1854); Yelva
Léon, H., bass/baritone
Les quatre fils Aymon (Paris 1844); Ivon
Lipparini, C., soprano
I rivale di se stessi (Palermo 1829); Mde. Derville
Lutz, F., baritone
La Bohémienne (Paris 1869); Le Comte d'Arheim
McGuckin, Barton, tenor
Moro, Painter of Antwerp; (London 1882); Antonio Moro, the Painter
Malibran, Maria, mezzo-soprano;
The Maid of Artois (London 1836); Isoline
Manvers, Henry, bass;
The Sicilian Bride (London 1852)
Massenet, Jules, conductor
La Bohemienne (Rouen 1862)
Massol, J.A., baritone
I Quattro Fratelli (London 1851); Barone di Beaumanoir
Mattacks, Mr, baritone;
The Castle of Aymon (London 1844); Renaud
Mazzoleni, Francesco, tenor;
La Zingara (London 1854); Thaddeus
Mecuriali, Signor, tenor
I Quattro Fratelli (London 1851); Allardo
La Zingara (London 1858); Florestein
Mellon, Alfred conductor
The Rose of Castile (London 1857)
Satanella/The Power of Love (London 1858)
Bianca, the Bravo's Bride (London 1860)
The Puritan's Daughter (London 1861)
Blanche de Nevers (London 1863)

The Armourer of Nantes (London 1863)
Melotte, Mlle, mezzo-soprano
   Les quatre fils Aymon (Paris 1844); Clara
Menghis, M., baritone
   L'étoile de Seville (Paris 1846); Arias
Milani, S., baritone;
   Un avvertimento ai gelosi (Pavia 1831); Berto
Miran, Miranda, contralto
   The Maid of Honour (London 1847); Lady Alison
Mirate, R., tenor
   Pittore e Duca (Trieste 1854); Antonio
Mocker, M., tenor
   Les quatre fils Aymon (Paris 1844); Richard
Monjauze, J.S., tenor
   La Bohémienne (Paris 1869); Stenio de Stoltberg (Act I only)
Morelli, Signor, tenor
   Falstaff (London 1838); Mr Page
Nau, Maria, mezzo-soprano
   L'étoile de Seville (Paris 1845); Zaida
Nissen, Henriette, mezzo-soprano
   Cantata, (Paris 1842)
Nilsson, Christine, soprano
   Il Talismano (London 1874); Edith Plantagenet
Panizza, G., tenor;
   La Zingara (Trieste 1854); Uffiziale
Pardini, Signor, tenor
   I Quattro Fratelli (London 1851); Ricciardo
Parlamagni, A., soprano
   Un avvertimento ai gelosi (Pavia 1831); Sandrina
Paris, M., tenor
   La Bohémienne (Rouen 1862); Narcisse de Krakentorp
Patey, John G., baritone:
   The Puritan's Daughter (London 1861); King Charles II
Paton (Wood) Mary A., soprano
   Catherine Grey (London 1837); Lady Catherine Grey
Paulin, M., tenor
   L'étoile de Seville (Paris 1845); Pedro
Phillips, Henry, baritone
   The Siege of Rochelle (London 1835); Michel
   The Maid of Artois (London 1836); Marquis, de Chateau Vieux
   Diadeste/The Veiled Lady (London 1837); Count Steno
   Keolanthe/The Unearthly Bride (London 1841); Ombrastro
Piccolomini, Marietta, soprano
   La Zingara (London 1858; Dublin 1858); Arline
Potier, M.A., mezzo-soprano

Les quatre fils Aymon (Paris 1844); Gertrude
Poole, Elizabeth, mezzo-soprano
    The Maid of Artois (London 1836); Ninka –child part
    Catherine Grey (London 1837); Queen's Maid
    Diadeste/The Veiled Lady (London 1837); Ursula
    Sleeping Queen (London 1864); Donna Agnes
Prévost, Ferdinand, tenor
    L'étoile de Seville (Paris 1845); Gomez
Pyne, Louisa, soprano
    The Rose of Castile (London 1857); Elvira
    Satanella/The Power of Love (London 1858); Satanella
    Bianca, the Bravo's Bride (London 1860); Bianca
    The Puritan's Daughter (London 1861); Mary, Wolfe's daughter
    Blanche de Nevers (London 1863); Blanche
    The Armourer of Nantes (London 1863); Marie, an orphan
Pyne, Susan, contralto
    The Rose of Castile (London 1857); Donna Carmen
    Satanella (London 1858); Stella
    The Puritan's Daughter (London 1861); Jessie
Rafter, Mr, tenor
    The Bondman (London 1846); Count Floreville
Rainforth, Elizabeth, soprano:
    The Bohemian Girl (London 1843; Dublin 1844); Arline
    The Daughter of St Mark (London 1844); Caterina
Reeves, J. Sims, tenor
    The Maid of Honour (London 1847); Lyonnel
    The Sicilian Bride (London 1852); Rodolfo
Rinaldini, Signor, tenor:
    Il Talismano (London 1874); Il Barone de Vaux
Romer, Charles, tenor
    The Devil in it (London 1852); Albert
Romer, Emma, soprano
    Catherine Grey (London 1837); Queen Elizabeth
    Joan of Arc (London 1837); Joan of Arc
    Diadeste/The Veiled Lady (London 1837); Celina
    The Bohemian Girl (Dublin 1845); Arline
    The Bondman (London 1846); Corinne
    The Devil in It (London 1852); Letty
Ronconi, Giorgio, baritone:
    Un Avvertimento di Gelosi (Milan 1831); Berto
Roser-Balfe, Lina, soprano
    Enrico IV, al passo della Marna (Milan 1833); Cristina
    Keolanthe (London 1841); Keolanthe
Rosa, Carl, conductor
    Moro, Painter of Antwerp (London 1882)

Rota, Signor, baritone
   Il Talismano (London 1874); Richard Coeur de Leon
Rozé, Marie, soprano:
   La Bohemienne (Rouen 1862); Sarah
   Il Talismano (London 1874); Queen Berengaria
Rubini-Desanctis, S., soprano
   Un Avvertimento di Gelosi (Milan 1831); Sandrina
Rubini, Giovanni-Battista, tenor
   Falstaff (London-1838); Fenton
   St Albyn, Alfred, tenor
   Satanella/The Power of Love (London 1858); Karl
   The Puritan's Daughter (London 1861); Seymour
   Blanche de Nevers (London 1863); Phillip of Orleans
Sainte Foy, C.L., tenor
   Les quatre fils Aymon (Paris 1844); Allard
Salvini-Donatelli, F., soprano
   Pittore e Duca (Trieste 1854); Olivia
Sannier, Mdlle. mezzo-soprano:
   La Zingara (London 1858); Queen of the Gypsies
Sansone, M., tenor
   I rivale di se stessi (Palermo 1829); Cameriere
Santley, Charles, baritone
   The Puritan's Daughter (London 1861); Clifford
   The Armourer of Nantes (London 1863); Fabio Fabini, alias de Coutras
Scalese, R., buffo-bass
   I rivale di se stessi (Palermo 1829); Ferville
Scaramelli, G. A., conductor
   Pittore e Duca (Trieste 1854)
Schira, Signor, conductor
   The Bondman (1846), second night only
Seguin, Anne, soprano
   The Bohemian Girl (New York 1844; Arline
Seguin, Edward, bass
   The Siege of Rochelle (London 1835); Count of Rosemberg
   The Maid of Artois (London 1836); Synnelet
   Catherine Grey (London 1837); Lord Grey
   Joan of Arc (London 1837); Radet
   The Bohemian Girl (New York 1844); *Count Arnheim*
Shirreff, Jane, soprano:
   The Siège of Rochelle (London 1835); Clara/Olympia
Staudigl, Joseph, bass
   Die vier Haimonskinder (Vienna 1845); Ivo
   Zigeunerin (Vienna 1846); Graf. Alban
Stretton, Mr, bass:
   Keolanthe/The Unearthly Bride (London 1841); Filippo

The Bohemian Girl (London 1843); Devilshoof
Stoltz, Rosine, mezzo-soprano:
  L'étoile de Seville (Paris 1845); Estrella
Suster, G., mezzo-soprano
  I rivale di se stessi (Palermo 1829); Lisa
Taddei, A. mezzo-soprano
  Un Avvertimento di Gelosi (Milan 1831); Ernesta
Tamburini, Antonio, baritone:
  Falstaff (London 1838); Mr Ford
Templeton, John, tenor:
  The Maid of Artois (London 1836); Jules de Montangon
  Joan of Arc (London-1837); Count Dunois
  Diadeste/The Veiled Lady (London 1838); Manfredi
Thermann, M., buffo-bass
  Les quatre fils Aymon (Paris 1844); Baron de Beaumanoir
Thillon, Anna, soprano
  Le puits d'amour (Paris 1843); Geraldine
  The Enchantress (London 1845); Stella
Thomas, Dudley, tenor
  Moro, Painter of Antwerp (London 1882); Vargas
Tietjens, Therese, soprano
  Il Talismano (Dublin 1874); Edit Plantagenet
Toulmin, E.O., tenor
  The Sicilian Bride (London 1852); Count Andreozzi
Travers, Mr., Tenor
  The Devil in It (London1852); *Wallenberg.*
Treffz, Jenny, soprano
  Die vier Haimonskinder (Vienna 1845); Hermine
  Zigeunerin (Vienna 1846); Arline
Turpin, Miss.,
  Geraldine/The Lover's Well (London 1843); Philippina
Valencia, L., tenor
  Un avvertimento ai gelosi (Pavia 1831); Il Conte
Valesi, Signora, soprano
  La Zingara (Trieste 1854); Arline
Valleria, Alwina, soprano:
  Moro, Painter of Antwerp (London 1882); Olivia, Countess of Aramberga
Viardot-Garcia, Pauline, mezzo-soprano:
  Cantata, (Paris 1842)
  La Zingara (Dublin 1858); Yelva/Queen of the Gypsies
Vialetti, Signor, bass:
  La Zingara (London 1858); Devilshoof
Wallworth, Thomas A., baritone:
  The Puritan's Daughter (London 1861); Lt. Drake
  Bianca, the Bravo's Bride (London 1860); Montalto

Walton, Mr
    Geraldine/The Lover's Well (London 1843); Lord Nottingham
Warnots, H., tenor
    La Bohémienne (Rouen 1862); Stenio de Stoltberg
Warwick, Giulia, mezzo soprano:
    Moro, Painter of Antwerp (London 1882); Donna Ines
Weiss, Georgina Mrs., soprano:
    The Maid of Honour (London 1847); Queen Elizabeth
Weiss, Willoughby. H., bass
    The Daughter of St Mark (London 1844); Moncenigo
    The Enchantress (London 1845); Regent
    The Bondman (London 1846); Marquis de Vernon
    The Maid of Honour (London 1847); Sir Tristram
    The Rose of Castile (1857); Don Pedro
    Satanella/The Power of Love (1858); Arimanes
    Blanche de Nevers (1863); Prince Gonzagues
    The Armourer of Nantes (1863); M. de Villefranche
Wertheimber, P., contralto
    La Bohémienne (Paris 1869); La reine Mabb
Wharton, Henry, baritone:
    Bianca, the Bravo Bride (1860); Count Malespina
Whiffin, Thomas, tenor
    Sleeping Queen (1864); Philippe d' Aguilar
Whitworth, Jones, baritone:
    The Maid of Honour (London 1847); Walter
    The Sicilian Bride (London 1852); Marquis Montluc,
Wildauer, M., soprano
    Die vier Haimonskinder (Vienna 1845); Hermine
Wilkinson, R., bass:
    Sleeping Queen (London 1864); The Regent
Wilson, John, tenor:
    The Siege of Rochelle (London 1835); Marquis de Valmour
    Keolanthe/The Unearthly Bride (London 1841); Andrea
Wood (Paton), Mary A., soprano
    Catherine Grey (London 1837); Lady Catherine Grey

APPENDIX VIII – BALFE AS MUSICAL DIRECTOR AT THE *ITALIAN OPERA*, HER MAJESTY'S THEATRE, LONDON – OPERAS CONDUCTED, DATES AND CASTS (1846–1852)

Balfe conducted all of the operatic works listed below except for the premiere of Giuseppe Verdi's new opera, *I Masnadieri*, in July 1847. Verdi conducted the premiere and the second performance, after which Balfe took over as conductor. During this period Balfe conducted the English premiere of several Verdi operas in London.

The opera seasons at *Her Majesty's Theatre* usually commenced between mid-February and early March. There was a break during Easter week, after which it continued through August. Frequently after that the company travelled to Dublin to perform for two weeks at the Theatre Royal. In London, operatic performances were usually given Tuesday night through Saturday night. Thursdays nights were called 'Long Thursdays' as frequently the evening's entertainment did not finish until after midnight.

A ballet was often performed between the acts of the opera or after the opera. Internationally famous ballerinas, such as Maria Taglione, Fanny Essler, Carlotta Grisi, Lucile Grahn and Fanny Cerito, were the stars of the ballets.

Note: Only the first performance of each opera is shown during a season along with the cast, unless there was an important change to the cast, then the repeat performance is also listed. Operas were performed multiple times, sometimes with different or substituted cast members. Additionally, only complete operas performed are included in the listing as there were situations where one or two acts of an opera may have been performed for various reasons.

Date	Opera Directed	Principal Singers

Soprano (s): Mezzo-soprano (ms): Contralto: (ct): Tenor (t): Baritone (br): Bass (bs): Buffo-bass (bfb).

1846

Date	Opera Directed	Principal Singers
3 March	*Nabucco/Nino* (Verdi) (English premiere)	Nabucco/Ninus (br) L. Fornasari Abigaille (s) G. Sanchioli Fenena (ms) A. Corbari Ismaele/Idaspe (t) L. Corelli Zaccaria/Ortaspes (bs) Sig. Rotelli
17 March	Ernani (Verdi)	Ernani (t) Sig. Castaglione Elvira(s) Mde Pasini Carlo (br) Sig. Bencich Don Silva (bs) L. Fornasari
28 March	*Linda di Chamounix* (Donizetti)	Linda (s) A. Castellan Carlo (t) L. Corelli

		Antonio (br) L. Fornasari
		Marchese (bfb) F. Lablache
		Pierotto (ms) G. Brambilla

2 April	*Belisario* (Donizetti)	Antonietta (s) A. Castellan
		Belisario (br) L. Fornasari
		Alamiro (t) Sig. Corelli
		Irene (s) A. Sanchioli
		Eudora (ms) A. Corbari

14 April	*I Puritani* (Bellini)	Elvira (s) G. Grisi
		Arturo (t) G. Mario
		Riccardo (br) L. Fornasari
		Giorgio (bs) L. Lablache

16 April	*Don Giovanni* (Mozart)	Don Giovanni (br) L. Fornasari
		Donna Anna (s) G. Grisi
		Zerlina (s) A. Castellan
		Donna Elvira (s) A. Sanchioli
		Don Ottavio (t) G. Mario
		Masetto (br) F. Lablache
		Leporello (bfb) L. Lablache

21 April	*La sonnambula* (Bellini)	Amina (s) A. Castellan
		Elvino (t) G. Mario
		Rodolfo (bs) F. Lablache
		Lisa (ms) A. Corbari

23 April	*Il barbiere di Siviglia* (Rossini)	Rosina (s) G. Grisi
		Almaviva (t) G. Mario
		Figaro (br) L. Fornasari
		Bartolo (bfb) L. Lablache
		Basilio (bs) F. Lablache

28 April	*Norma* (Bellini)	Norma (s) G. Grisi
		Pollione (t) L. Corelli
		Oroveso (bs) L. Lablache
		Adalgisa (ms) A. Corbari

30 April	*Don Pasquale* (Donizetti)	Don Pasquale (bfb) L. Lablache
		Malatesta (br) F. Lablache
		Ernesto (t) G. Mario

		Norina (s) G. Grisi

7 May	*La Gazza Ladra* (Rossini)	Ninetta (s) G. Grisi Giannetto (t) G. Mario Il Podesta (bs) L. Lablache Pippo (ms) G. Brambilla Fernando (bs) L. Fornasari
12 May	*I Lombardi* (Verdi) (English premiere)	Giselda (s) G. Grisi Arvino (t) L. Corelli Oronte (t) G. Mario Pagano (bs) L. Fornasari Viclinda (ms/s) A. Corbari
28 May	*Il Matrimonio Segreto* (Cimarosa)	Fidelma (ct) A. Sanchioli Carolina (s) G. Grisi Elisetta (ms/s) A. Castellan Paolina (t) G. Mario Count Robinson (bs) F. Lablache Geronimo (bfb) L. Lablache
9 July	*Anna Bolena* (Donizetti)	Anna Bolena (s) G. Grisi G. Seymour (ms) A. Corbari Percy (t) G. Mario Enrico VIII (br) L. Lablache
30 July	*Don Gregorio* (Donizetti) LP (English premiere)	Don Gregorio (bfb) L. Lablache Don Giulio (br) L. Fornasari Gilda (s) G. Grisi Leonarda (s) A. Castellan Enrico (t) G. Mario Simone (bs) F. Lablache

1847

16 February	*La Favorita* (Donizetti)	Leonora (ms/s) A. Sanchioli Fernando (t) I. Gardoni Balthasar (bs) L. Bouché Alfonso (br) Sig. Superchi Ines (ms) D. Nascio
27 February	*Nabucco/Nino* (Verdi)	Nabucco/Nino (br) F. Coletti Abigaille (s) A. Sanchioli Fenena (ms) Mlle Fagiani Ismaele/Idaspe (t) L. Corelli Zaccaria/Ortaspes (bs) L. Bouché

9 March	*Lucia di Lammermoor* (Donizetti)	Lucia (s) A. Castellan Edgardo (t) G. Fraschini Enrico (br) F. Coletti Raimondo (bs) Sig. Solari
18 March	*La sonnambula* (Bellini)	Amina (s) A. Castellan Elvino (t) I. Gardoni Rodolfo (bs) F. Lablache Lisa (ms) Mde. Solari
27 March	*Ernani* (Verdi)	Ernani (t) G. Fraschini Elvira (s) A. Castellan Da Silva (bs) L. Bouché
10 April	*I due Foscari* (Verdi) (English premiere)	Doge (br) F. Coletti Jacopo (t) G. Fraschini Lucrezia (s) C. Montenegro Loredano (bs) L. Bouché
15 April	*I Puritani* (Bellini)	Elvira (s) A. Castellan Arturo (t) I. Gardoni Riccardo (br) F. Coletti Giorgio (bs) L. Lablache
22 April	*L'elisir d'amore* (Donizetti)	Adina (s) A. Castellan Nemorino (t) I. Gardoni Belcore (br) F. Lablache Dulcamara (bs) L. Lablache
4 May	*Roberto il Diavolo* (Meyerbeer)	Alice (s) J. Lind Isabella (s) A. Castellan Roberto (t) G. Fraschini Rambaldo (t) I. Gardoni Bertram (bs) J. Staudigl Sacredote (bs) L. Bouché
13 May	*La sonnambula* (Bellini)	Amina (s) J. Lind Elvino (t) I. Gardoni Rodolfo (bs) F. Lablache Lisa (ms) Mde. Solari
27 May	*La Figlia del Reggimento* (Donizetti)	Maria (s) J. Lind Tonio (t) I. Gardoni Sulpice (bfb) F. Lablache

La Marchese (ms/ct) Mme. Solari

15 June	*Norma* (Bellini)	Norma (s) J. Lind Pollione (t) G. Franchini Adalgisa (ms/s) Mme. Barroni Oroveso (bs) L. Lablache
6 July	*I Lombardi* (Verdi)	Giselda (s) A. Castellan Oronte (t) I. Gardoni Pagano (bs) F. Coletti Arvino (t) L. Corelli
22 July	*I Masnadieri* (Verdi) (Opera premiere conducted by G. Verdi 22 July & 24 July; Conducted by M.W. Balfe 29 July & 10 August)	Amalia (s) J. Lind Carlo (t) I. Gardoni Francesco (br) F. Coletti Massimiliano (bs) L. Lablache Arminio (t) L. Corelli Moser (bs) L. Bouché Rolla (br) Sig. Dai Fiore
17 August	*Le Nozze de Figaro* (Mozart)	Figaro (br) F. Coletti Susanna (s) J. Lind Il Conte (br) J. Staudigl La Contessa (s) A. Castellan Cherubino (ms/s) Mme. Solari Bartolo (bfb) L. Lablache

1848

19 February	*Ernani* (Verdi)	Ernani (t) Sig. Cuzzani Leonora (s) S. Cruvelli Carlo (br) I. Gardoni (tenor!) Da Silva (bs) G. Belletti
27 February	*Il barbiere di Siviglia* (Rossini)	Rosina (s) S. Cruvelli Almaviva (t) I. Gardoni Figaro (br) G. Belletti Bartolo (bfb) F. Lablache Basilio (bs) L. Bouché
6 March	*Attila* (Verdi) LP (English premiere)	Attila (bs) G. Belletti Ezio (t) L. Cuzzani Odabella (s) S. Cruvelli Foresto (t) I. Gardoni
21 March	*I due Foscari* (Verdi)	Doge (br) F. Coletti

		Jacopo (t) Sig. Cuzzani
		Lucrezia (s) S. Cruvelli
		Loredano (bs) L. Bouché
25 March	*Nabucco/Nino* (Verdi)	Nabucco/Ninus (br) F. Coletti
		Abigaille (s) Mlle Abbadia
		Fenena (ms) MlleVera
		Ismaele/Idaspe (t) Sig. Cuzzani
		Zaccaria/Ortaspe (bs) G. Belletti
15 April	*Lucrezia Borgia* (Donizetti)	Lucrezia Borgia (s) S Cruvelli
		Maffio Orsini (ms) Mlle Schwarz
		Gennaro (t) I. Gardoni
		Alfonso (bs) L. Lablache
20 May	*Linda di Chamounix* (Donizetti)	Linda (s) E. Tadolini
		Carlo (t) S. Reeves
		Antonio (br) F. Coletti
		Marchese (bfb) F. Lablache
		Pierotto (ms) Mlle Schwarz
25 May	*Lucia di Lammermoor* (Donizetti)	Lucia (s) J. Lind
		Edgardo (t) I. Gardoni
		Enrico (br) F. Coletti
		Raimondo (bs) L. Bouché
8 June	*L'elisir d'amore* (Donizetti)	Adina (s) J. Lind
		Nemorino (t) I. Gardoni
		Belcore (br) G. Belletti
		Dulcamara (bs) L. Lablache
20 June	*Don Pasquale* (Donizetti)	Norina (s) E. Tadolini
		Ernesto (t) Sig. Labucetta
		Don Pasquale (bfb) L. Lablache
		Malatesta (br) G. Belletti
27 July	*I Puritani* (Bellini)	Elvira (s) J. Lind
		Arturo (t) I. Gardoni
		Riccardo (br) F. Coletti
		Giorgio (bs) L. Lablache

1849

| 15 March | *La Cenerentola* (Rossini) | Cenerentola (ms/ct) M. Alboni |
| | | Clorinda (s) Mme Grimaldi |

		Tisbe (ms) Mme Anglois Don Ramiro (br) I. Gardoni Don Magnifico (bfb) F. Lablache Dandini (br) G. Belletti Alindoro (bs) Sig. Arnoldi
24 March	*Ernani* (Verdi)	Ernani (t) Sig. Bordas Leonora (s) C. Giuliani Carlo (br) I. Gardoni (tenor!) Da Silva (bs) G. Belletti
31 March	*I due Foscari* (Verdi)	Doge (br) F. Coletti Jacopo (t) Sig. Bordas Lucrezia (s) C. Giuliani Loredano (bs) ?
10 April	*Norma* (Bellini)	Norma (s) T. Parodi Pollione (t) Sig. Bordas Oroveso (bs) L. Lablache Adalgisa (ms) C. Giuliani
12 April	*Il Flauto Magico* (Mozart) (Concert version)	Sarastro (bs) F. Coletti Pamina (s) J. Lind Papageno (br) Belletti/Lablache Tamino (t) Bordas/Bartolini
17 April	*La Favorita* (Donizetti)	Leonora (ms/s) T. Parodi Fernando (t) I. Gardoni Balthasar (bs) L. Lablache Alfonso (br) F. Coletti
26 April	*La sonnambula* (Bellini)	Amina (s) J. Lind Elvino (t) E. Calzolari Rodolfo (bs) G. Belletti Lisa (ms/s) S. Howson
28 April	*Lucia di Lammermoor* (Donizetti)	Lucia (s) J. Lind Edgardo (t) I. Gardoni Enrico (br) F. Coletti Raimondo (bs) Sig. Arnoldi Arturo (t) Sig. Bartolini
3 May	*La Figlia del Reggimento* (Donizetti)	Maria (s) J. Lind Tonio (t) I. Gardoni Sulpice (bfb) F. Lablache

10 May	*Roberto il Diavolo* (Meyerbeer)	Alice (s) J. Lind
		Isabella (s) J. van Gelder
		Roberto (t) I. Gardoni
		Rambaldo (t) Sig. Bartolini
		Bertram (bs) G. Belletti

15 May	*Il barbiere di Siviglia* (Rossini)	Rosina (s) M. Alboni
		Almaviva (t) I. Gardoni
		Figaro (br) G. Belletti
		Bartolo (bfb) L. Lablache
		Basilio (bs) F. Lablache

19 May	*Semiramide* (Rossini)	Semiramide (s) T. Parodi
		Arsace (ms) M. Alboni
		Assur (bs) F. Coletti
		Idreno (t) Sig. Bartolini
		Oroe (bs) L. Lablache

24 May	*La Gazza Ladra* (Rossini)	Ninetta (s) M. Alboni
		Giannetto (t) E. Calzolari
		Il Podesta (bs) L. Lablache
		Pippo (ms/ct) Mlle. Casaloni
		Fernando (bs) F. Coletti

31 May	*Don Giovanni* (Mozart)	Don Giovanni (br) F. Coletti
		Donna Anna (s) T. Parodi
		Zerlina (s/ms) M. Alboni
		Donna Elvira (s) C. Giuliani
		Don Ottavio (t) I. Gardoni
		Masetto (br) F. Lablache
		Leporello (bfb) L. Lablache

14 June	*Il Matrimonio Segreto* (Cimarosa)	Fidelma (ct) M. Alboni
		Carolina (s) T. Parodi
		Elisetta (ms/s) C. Giuliani
		Paolina (t) E. Calzolari
		Count Robinson (bs) F. Lablache
		Geronimo (bfb) L. Lablache

21 June	*Lucrezia Borgia* (Donizetti)	Lucrezia Borgia (s) T. Parodi
		Maffio Orsini (ms) M. Alboni
		Gennaro (t) N. Moriani
		Alfonso (bs) L. Lablache

28 June	*Don Pasquale* (Donizetti)	Norina (s) M. Alboni Ernesto (t) E. Calzolari Don Pasquale (bfb) L. Lablache Malatesta (br) G. Belletti
7 July	*Linda di Chamounix* (Donizetti)	Linda (s) H. Sontag Carlo (t) I. Gardoni Antonio (br) F. Coletti Pierotto (ms) Mlle.Casaloni
19 July	*La sonnambula* (Bellini)	Amina (s) H. Sontag Elvino (t) E. Calzolari Rodolfo (bs) G. Belletti Lisa (ms) S. Howson
28 July	*Otello* (Rossini)	Otello (t) N. Moriani Desdemona (s) H. Sontag Rodrigo (t) E. Calzolari Jago (t/br) G. Belletti Elmiro (bs) L. Lablache
7 August	*Don Giovanni* (Mozart)	Don Giovanni (br) F. Coletti Donna Anna (s) T. Parodi Zerlina (s) M. Alboni Donna Elvira (s) H. Sontag Don Ottavio (t) I. Gardoni Masetto (br) F. Lablache Leporello (bfb) L. Lablache
14 August	*Le Nozze de Figaro* (Mozart)	Figaro (br) G. Belletti Susanna (s) H. Sontag Il Conte (br) F. Coletti La Contessa (s) T. Parodi Cherubino (ms) M. Alboni Bartolo (bfb) L. Lablache

1850

12 March	*Medea in Corinto* (Mayr)	Medea (s) T. Parodi Jason (t) Sig. Micheli Egeo (t) E. Calzolari Creonte (bs) G. Belletti Creusa (s) C. Giuliani

19 March	*Nabucco/Nino* (Verdi)	Nabucco/Nino (br) L. di Montemerli Abigaille (s) T. Parodi Fenena (ms) C. Giuliani
21 March	*Ernani* (Verdi)	Ernani (t) S. Reeves Leonora (s) T. Parodi Carlo (br) L. di Montemerli Da Silva (bs) G. Belletti
2 April	*Lucia di Lammermoor* (Donizetti)	Lucia (s) C. Hayes Edgardo (t) S. Reeves Enrico (br) G. Belletti Raimondo (bs) F. Lablache
4 April	*Don Pasquale* (Donizetti)	Norina (s) H. Sontag Ernesto (t) E. Calzolari Don Pasquale (bfb) L. Lablache Malatesta (br) G. Belletti
9 April	*Il barbiere di Siviglia* (Rossini)	Rosina (s) H. Sontag Almaviva (t) E. Calzolari Figaro (br) G. Belletti Bartolo (bfb) L. Lablache Basilio (bs) F. Lablache
11 April	*Don Giovanni* (Mozart)	Don Giovanni (br) F. Coletti Donna Anna (s) T. Parodi Zerlina (s) H. Sontag Donna Elvira (s) C. Giuliani Don Ottavio (t) E. Calzolari Masetto (br) F. Lablache Leporello (bfb) L. Lablache
18 April	*Le Nozze de Figaro* (Mozart)	Figaro (br) G. Belletti Susanna (s) H. Sontag Il Conte (br) F. Coletti La Contessa (s) T. Parodi Cherubino (ms) C. Hayes Bartolo (bfb) L. Lablache
20 April	*I Lombardi* (Verdi) LP	Giselda (s) C. Giuliani Oronte (t) C. Baucade Pagano (bs) F. Coletti

27 April	*Linda di Chamounix* (Donizetti)	Linda (s) H. Sontag Carlo (t) C. Baucade Antonio (br) F. Coletti Pierotto (ms/ct) I. Bertrand
2 May	*La sonnambula* (Bellini)	Amina (s) H. Sontag Elvino (t) S. Reeves Rodolfo (bs) G. Belletti
4 May	*I due Foscari* (Verdi)	Doge (br) F. Coletti Jacopo (t) C. Baucade Lucrezia (s) T. Parodi Pisana (s) Mde Giuliani
9 May	*I Puritani* (Bellini)	Elvira (s) H. Sontag Arturo (t) C. Baucade Riccardo (br) F. Coletti Giorgio (bs) L. Lablache
21 May	*Lucrezia Borgia* (Donizetti)	Lucrezia Borgia (s) E. Frezzolini Maffio Orsini (ms) I. Bertrand Gennaro (t) C. Baucade Alfonso (bs) L. Lablache
25 May	*L'elisir d'amore* (Donizetti)	Adina (s) E. Frezzolini Nemorino (t) E. Calzolari Belcore (br) G. Belletti Dulcamara (bs) L. Lablache
4 June	*Lucia di Lammermoor* (Donizetti)	Lucia (s) E. Frezzolini Edgardo (t) S. Reeves Enrico (br) G. Belletti Raimondo (bs) F. Lablache
8 June	*La Tempesta* (Halévy) (Opera premiere)	Prospero (br) F. Coletti Miranda (s) H. Sontag Antonio (bs) F. Lablache Caliban (bs) L. Lablache Sycorax (s) T. Parodi Ferdinand (t) C. Baucade Spirit of the Air (s) C. Giuliani
29 June	*I Capuleti e i Montecchi* (Bellini)	Giulietta (s) E. Frezzolini Romeo (ms) T. Parodi

		Tebaldo (t) I. Gardoni Capellio (bs) G. Belletti
4 July	*Il Matrimonio Segreto* (Cimarosa)	Fidelma (ct) T. Parodi Carolina (s) H. Sontag Elisetta (ms/s) E. Frezzolini Paolina (t) E. Calzolari Count Robinson (bs) F. Lablache Geronimo (bfb) L. Lablache
15 July	Giuditta Pasta 'Farewell' Concert Scenes from *Tancredi, Medea* and *Orfeo ed Euridice*	Assisted by: T. Parodi, I. Gardoni, E. Calzolari, F. Coletti, F. Lablache L. Lablache Chorus & orchestra conducted by Balfe
	Giuditta Pasta gave a second concert the same week with scenes from *Anna Bolena*	
16 July	*I Puritani* (Bellini)	Elvira (s) E. Frezzolini Arturo (t) C. Baucade Riccardo (br) F. Coletti Giorgio (bs) L. Lablache
18 July	*La Figlia del Reggimento* (Donizetti)	Maria (s) H. Sontag Tonio (t) I. Gardoni Sulpice (bfb) F. Lablache
13 August	*Norma* (Bellini)	Norma (s) Mde Fiorentini Pollione (t) I. Gardoni Oroveso (bs) L. Lablache Adalgisa (ms) C. Giuliani
	La sonnambula (Bellini) (Last act only)	*Norma* was followed by the last act of *La sonnambula* with C. Hayes and S. Reeves.

1851

22 March	*Lucia di Lammermoor* (Donizetti)	Lucia (s) C. Duprez Edgardo (t) E. Calzolari Enrico (br) Sig. Lorenzo Raimondo (bs) Sig. Balanchi

29 March	*Gustave III* (Auber)	Amelia (s) Mme Fiorentini Gustavus (t) E. Calzolari Oscar (s) C. Duprez Ankerstron (br) Sig. Lorenzo Dehorn (bs) F. Lablache Arvedson (ms) Mlle Feller Ribbing (bs) M. Poultier
8 April	*La sonnambula* (Bellini)	Amina (s) C. Duprez Elvino (t) E. Calzolari Rodolfo (bs) F. Coletti Lisa (ms) Mlle Feller
10 April	*Masaniello* (Auber)	Elvira (s) Mme Fiorentini Masaniello (t) Sig. Pardini Alfonso (t) Sig. Scotti Lorenzo (t) Sig. Mecuriali Silva (bs) Sig. Balanchi Borella (br) Sig. Lorenzo Fenella (ms) Mlle Monti
22 April	*L'elisir d'amore* (Donizetti)	Adina (s) C. Duprez Nemorino (t) E. Calzolari Belcore (br) F. Coletti Dulcamara (bs) L. Lablache
26 April	*Lucrezia Borgia* (Donizetti)	Lucrezia Borgia (s) Mlle Alaimo Maffio Orsini (ms) I. Bertrand Gennaro (t) I. Gardoni Alfonso (bs) L. Lablache
3 May	*La Figlia del Reggimento* (Donizetti)	Maria (s) H. Sontag Tonio (t) I. Gardoni Sulpice (bfb) F. Lablache
10 May	*Le tre Nozze* (Alary)	Luisa (s) H. Sontag Il Barone (b) L. Lablache Vespens (s) Mde. Giuliani La Marchesa (ms) I. Bertrand Cav. Villafranca (t) I. Gardoni Cricca (bs) Sig, Ferrante
15 May	*Don Giovanni* (Mozart)	Don Giovanni (br) F. Coletti Donna Anna (s) Mme. Fiorentini Zerlina (s) H. Sontag

		Donna Elvira (s) C. Giuliani
		Don Ottavio (t) E. Calzolari
		Masetto (br) F. Lablache
		Leporello (bfb) L. Lablache

20 May	*Fidelio* (Beethoven) (Balfe wrote the recitatives for this performance)	Florestan (t) S. Reeves
		Leonore/Fidelio (s) S. Cruvelli
		Rocco (bs) Sig. Balanchi
		Marzelline (s) C. Giuliani
		Jaquino/Fritz (t) Sig. Mecuriali
		Don Pizzaro (bs/br) F. Coletti
		Don Fernando (bs) Sig. Casanova

22 May	*Il barbiere di Siviglia* (Rossini)	Rosina (s) H. Sontag
		Almaviva (t) E. Calzolari
		Figaro (br) Sig. Ferranti
		Bartolo (bfb) L. Lablache

3 June	*Norma* (Bellini)	Norma (s) S. Cruvelli
		Pollione (t) Sig. Pardini
		Oroveso (bs) L. Lablache
		Adalgisa (s/ms) C. Giuliani

7 June	*Don Pasquale* (Donizetti)	Norina (s) H. Sontag
		Ernesto (t) E. Calzolari
		Don Pasquale (bfb) L. Lablache
		Malatesta (br) Sig. Ferranti

12 June	*Il Prodigo/Enfant Prodigue* (Auber)	Nefte (s) D. Ugalde
		Reuben (br) J. A. Massol
		Azael (t) I. Gardoni
		Jeftele (s) H. Sontag
		Amenofi (t) Sig. Mercuriali
		Nemroud (bs/br) Sig. Casanova
		Bocchoris (br) F. Coletti
		Canope (t) Sig. Scotti

26 June	*La prova d'un opera seria* (Gnecco)	Composer (bs) L. Lablache
		Prima Donna (s) D. Ugalde
		? (t) E. Calzolari

3 July	*Florinda* (Thalberg)	Julian (bs) L. Lablache
		Florinda (s) S. Cruvelli
		Teodomiro (ct) M. Cruvelli

Rodrigo (t) E. Calzolari
Favila (t) S. Reeves
Munuzza (br) F. Coletti

10 July   *Le Nozze de Figaro* (Mozart)   Figaro (br) Sig. Ferranti
Susanna (s) H. Sontag
Il Conte (br) F. Coletti
La Contessa (s) Mme. Fiorentini
Cherubino (ms) S. Cruvelli
Bartolo (bfb) L. Lablache

12 July   *La Cenerentola* (Rossini)   Cenerentola (ms) M. Alboni
Thisbe (ms) Mlle Grimalde
Clorinda (s) Mlle Feller
Don Ramiro (t) E. Calzolari
Don Magnifico (bs) L. Lablache
Dandini (br/bs) Sig. Ferranti
Alindoro (bs) F. Lablache

19 July   *Ernani* (Verdi)   Ernani (t) S. Reeves
Leonora (s) S. Cruvelli
Carlo (br) F. Coletti
Da Silva (bs) Sig. Scapini

22 July   *La Corbeille d'Oranges* (Auber)   Zerlina (ms) M. Alboni
Jemma (s) M. Nau
Rodolfo (t) E. Calzolari
Roccanera (br) Sig. Scapini
Buttura (bs) Sig. Casanova

29 July   *Linda di Chamounix* (Donizetti)   Linda (s) S. Cruvelli
Carlo (t) S. Reeves
Antonio (br) F. Coletti
Pierotto (ms) M. Cruvelli

31 July   *La Gazza Ladra* (Rossini)   Ninetta (s/ms) M. Alboni
Giannetto (t) E. Calzolari
Il Podesta (bs) L. Lablache
Pippo (ms) I. Bertrand
Fernando (br/bs) F. Coletti

5 August   *Lucrezia Borgia* (Donizetti)   Lucrezia (s) Mme Barbieri Nini
Maffio Orsini (ms) I. Bertrand
Gennaro (t) I. Gardoni
Alfonso (bs) L. Lablache

7 August	*La Figlia del Reggimento* (Donizetti)	Maria (s/ms) M. Alboni Tonio (t) I. Gardoni Sulpice (bfb) F. Lablache
11 August	*I Quattro Fratelli* (Balfe)	Erminia (s) S. Cruvelli Beaumanoir (br) J. A. Massol Olivero (t) I. Gardoni Ricciardio (t) Sig. Pardini Allardo (t) Sig. Mercuriali Rinaldo (bs/br) Sig. Balanchi Clara (ms/s) C. Giuliani Iolanda (s) MmeFeller Eglantina (ct) Mme Lanza Uberto (t) Sig. Dai Fiore Ivon (bs/br) F. Coletti
	Followed by: *Il Matrimonio Segreto* (Cimarosa) (Act I only)	Carolina (s) Mme Fiorentini Fidalma (ms) M. Alboni Paolina (t) E. Calzolari Robinson (bs) F. Lablache Geronimo (bs) L. Lablache
26 August	Anna Bolena (Donizetti)	Anna Bolena (s) Mme Barbieri Nini Jane Seymour (s) C. Giuliani Smeaton (ms) I. Bertrand Percy (t) E. Calzolari Henry (bs) L. Lablache Rochfort (bs) Sig. Casanova Sir Harvey (t) Sig. Mercuriali
29 August	*La sonnambula* (Bellini)	Amina (s) H. Sontag Elvino (t) E. Calzolari Rodolfo (bs) Sig. Lorenzo Lisa (ms) Mlle Feller
0 Sept.	*La sonnambula* (Bellini)	Amina (s) S. Cruvelli Elvino (t) E. Calzolari Rodolfo (bs) Sig. Lorenzo Lisa (s) Mlle Feller

Note: There was an extension of the season that included a mixture of different acts from various operas and a repeat of some of the above operas with Sophie Cruvelli. The last performance took place on 11 October1851.

1852

1 April	*Maria di Rohan* (Donizetti)	Chevreuse (br) Sig. Ferlotti Maria (s) Mme Fiorentini Chalais (t) E. Calzolari Armando (br/ct) I. Bertrand
13 April	*L'Italiana in Algeri* (Rossini)	Mustaffa (bs) G. Belletti Elvira (s) Mlle Feller Lindoro (t) E. Calzolari Isabella (ct) Mlle. Angri Taddeo (bs) Sig. Ferranti
17 April	*Norma* (Bellini)	Norma (s) S. Cruvelli Pollione (t) I. Gardoni Oroveso (bs) L. Lablache Adalgisa (s/ms) Mlle Feller
22 April	*Il barbiere di Siviglia* (Rossini)	Rosina (s) S. Cruvelli Almaviva (t) E. Calzolari Figaro (br) G. Belletti Bartolo (bfb) L. Lablache Basilio (bs) Sig. Ferlotti
29 April	*Fidelio* (Beethoven)	Florestan (t) E. Calzolari Leonore/Fidelio (s) S. Cruvelli Rocco (bs) Sig. Sussini Marzelline (s) MlleFeller Jaquino/Fritz (t) Sig. Mecuriali Don Pizzaro (bs/br) G. Belletti Don Fernando (bs) Sig. Fortini
1 May	*La Cenerentola* (Rossini)	Cenerentola (ms) Mlle Angri Thisbe (ms) ? Clorinda (s) Mlle. Feller Don Ramiro (t) E. Calzolari Don Magnifico (bs) L. Lablache Dandini (br/bs) G. Belletti Alindoro (bs) Sig, Fortini
8 May	*Ernani* (Verdi)	Ernani (t) E. Calzolari Leonora (s) S. Cruvelli Carlo (br) Sig. Ferlotti Da Silva (bs) G. Belletti

13 May	*La sonnambula* (Bellini)	Amina (s) S. Cruvelli Elvino (t) I. Gardoni Rodolfo (bs) G. Belletti Lisa (s) Mlle Feller
22 May	*Lucia di Lammermoor* (Donizetti)	Lucia (s) Mme de la Grange Edgardo (t) I. Gardoni Enrico (br) Sig. Ferlotti Raimondo (bs) Sig. Sussini
29 May	*La prova d'un opera seria* (Gnecco)	Composer (bs) L. Lablache Prima Donna (s) Mme de la Grange ? (t) E. Calzolari
3 June	*Don Pasquale* (Donizetti)	Norina (s) Mme de la Grange Ernesto (t) E. Calzolari Don Pasquale (bfb) L. Lablache Malatesta (br) Sig. Ferranti
1 July	*Il barbiere di Siviglia* (Rossini)	Rosina (s) Mme de la Grange Almaviva (t) E. Calzolari Figaro (br) A. De Bassini Bartolo (bfb) L. Lablache Basilio (bs) Sig. Fortini

(Announcement in MW that various artists have left the theatres including Cruvelli, Gardoni, Belletti and Angri.) July 3 MW

6 July	*Maria di Rohan* (Donizetti)	Chevreuse (br) A. De Bassini Maria (s) Mme de la Grange Chalais (t) E. Calzolari Armando (br/ct) I. Bertrand
8 July	*I Puritani* (Bellini)	Elvira (s) Mme de la Grange Arturo (t) I. Gardoni Riccardo (br) A. De Bassini Giorgio (bs) L. Lablache Gualtiero (bs) Sig. Fortini Enrichetta (ms) Mme Grimaldi
15 July	Otello (Rossini)	Otello (t) Sig. Bettini Iago (br) A. De Bassini

Desdemona (s) Mme de la
Grange
Elmiro (bs) L. Lablache

29 July   *Lucrezia Borgia* (Donizetti)   Lucrezia (s) MmeFiorentini
Maffio Orsini (ms) I. Bertrand
Gennaro (t) I. Gardoni
Alfonso (bs) A. De Bassini

5 August   *Casilda* (RH Duke of Saxe Coburg)Don Alfonso (t) E. Calzolari
Casilda (s) Mme Charton
Donna Anna (s) Mme de la
Grange
Don Luigi (br) A. De Bassini
Gomez (bs) Sig. Sussini

9 August   *Don Giovanni* (Mozart)   Don Giovanni (br) A. De Bassini
(Balfe benefit)   Donna Anna (s) Mme Fiorentini
Zerlina (s) Mde. Taccani-Tasco
Donna Elvira (s) Mme E. Garcia
Don Ottavio (t) E. Calzolari
Masetto (br) F. Lablache
Leporello (bfb) L. Lablache

Summary of Balfe performances at Her Majesty's Theatre, 1846—1852

Operas by Donizetti 11, Verdi 6, Rossini 6, Bellini 4, Auber, 3, Mozart 3, Halevy 2, Meyerbeer 1, Beethoven 1, Balfe 1 and 5 operas by various other composers.

Total operas conducted 43. Each opera would have been performed several times during each season. During his seven years as musical director and conductor Balfe probably would have conducted more than 300 operatic performances.

APPENDIX IX - SELECTED OTHER (FORTY) LITTLE-KNOWN
BALFE MUSICAL COMPOSITIONS

The music pieces featured in this section are unusual, mostly relatively unknown works that Balfe composed at various times over a period of forty years. They are presented chronologically. Many of these pieces demonstrate the diversity of Balfe's talents and style as a composer.

The majority are vocal pieces with Italian words. There are some rare and unusual pieces. The list expands on the known number of cantatas composed by Balfe. Some of these are autograph scores which should interest musicians who study the Victorian period.

To endeavour to compile a complete listing of Balfe's works other than his operas would be virtually impossible. Balfe's output was enormous. He composed around 250 English-language songs alone. Additionally, so many of his individual pieces are scattered around libraries in Europe, America, Canada, and Australia and in private collections. The National Library of Ireland and the *Royal Irish Academy of Music*, Dublin, both have Balfe holdings. However, details of these are not yet fully available online. It is possible to check the card index collection at the National Library of Ireland in Dublin.

The 1829 Sinfonia is a unique piece since it is believed that this was the only symphonic work that Balfe ever composed. It comprises eighty-eight pages of manuscript. Balfe was twenty-one years old when he wrote it in Bologna for a friend of Rossini's.

A great many of Balfe's songs and arias from his operas were also published in American cities (New York, Boston, Philadelphia, St. Louis, New Orleans, etc.) over a period of about seventy-five years. As a result, many libraries in the US hold Balfe sheet music in addition to the Library of Congress. The Library of Congress holdings can be researched online. Also a number of the leading University libraries with theatre and music collections, such as Harvard, Yale, Columbia, Duke, Stanford and the University of Texas, Indiana University and others have extensive collections of his music and other Balfe documents. For example, Yale has autograph sketches for his opera *Satanella*.

Similar to other composer's music of the time many of Balfe's operatic pieces were published in reductions, for piano, piano and violin, two-pianos four-hands, occasionally piano and horn or flute, and paraphrases. Fantasias by Moscheles, Osborne, Chotek, Voss and others are available from the British Library. Publication also happened not only in Britain and Italy but also in Germany and Austria. The sheet music for many of these is available from various Italian libraries.

The British Library in London has the single largest collection of Balfe music, manuscripts and scores; over eleven hundred items. Their integrated catalogue can be researched online, and in the process copies can be ordered. The contact is: www.bl.uk – Balfe's music is located in several different collections at the British Library. For ordering copies of any item you should go to www.bl.uk/reproductions. The British Library accepts credit cards and will mail orders to virtually anywhere in the world.

Amazon.com in the UK also features over 800 Balfe musical items, many of which are also featured in the British Library catalogue.

Work, Title, where Published and Year

1. Song – *The Lover's mistake* (Dublin 1822)
This is Balfe's first published song. It is remarkable piece and of great historical significance since it was written by Balfe in Dublin when he had just turned fifteen years old. It was published by Isaac Willis of Dublin in December 1822. The sheet music is held by the British library, ref: H1661(3). A copy is also held at the Library of Congress in Washington DC, ref: M1619.S684 no. 15 1820z. There is also a copy in the National Library of Ireland in Dublin.

2. Aria & Scena – *Ildegonda nel Carcere –Sventurata Ildegonda* (Paris ?)
This scene and aria was written for interpolation into an opera by Marco Marliani of the same name. The location of the music is not known. The music has been recorded. See discography section.

3. *Sinfonia in F* (Bologna 1829)
This is Balfe's only known *Sinfonia* (88 pages). It was written on 31 March, 1829 for the birthday of for the Marchese Francesco Giovanni Sampieri of Bologna, a friend of Rossini's. Original mss. music held by the *Academia di Filarmonica*, Bologna. The author has a hard copy of the mss. score.

4. Cantata – *for four voices* (Bologna-1829)
This piece was also written for the Marchese Sampieri of Bologna. The original manuscript score (33 pages) is held by the Accademia di Filarmonica Archives, Bologna. The author has a hard copy of the manuscript.

5. *Fantasia per il pianoforte*; Guglielmo Balfe (Milan 1831)
This is a composition for piano written by Balfe in his early years and published by Ricordi of Milano, circa 1831. The piece was dedicated to Giuseppina de Marchi; it contains 19 pages. Music held by: Biblioteca del Conservatorio di musica Giuseppe Verdi, Milan IT\ICCU\DE\89020600671; IT\ICCU\DE\89020600672.

6. Cantata – *for two voices* (Bergamo 1832)
This manuscript appears to be some type of a greeting or fanfare. It is for tenor and bass. It is difficult to read. It is dedicated to 'Guglielmo Balfe's' friend, Francesco Maria Zanchi, in Bergamo and dated February 1832. The manuscript score is held by the Biblioteca Angelo Mai in Bergamo in its Mayr collection. The author has a copy on microfilm.

7. Aria – *Oh! Suoni un di soave. Recitativo, e Ahi che Alfredo in questo loco?* (London 1835)

This piece for a mezzo-soprano was composed in Italy, probably around 1830 or 1831, possibly as a scene to be interpolated into another composer's opera. The text was written by Count Carlo Pepoli, a poet and political activist who was imprisoned in 1831. After his release he went to Paris, where he had the distinction of writing the libretto for Bellini's *I Puritani* in 1835. Based on the plate number when it was published in London the publication date was circa July/August 1835. It shows the composer as 'Guglielmo Balfe'. The sheet music is held by the British Library, ref: H.2832.c (7).

8. Aria – *Ho giarto tutto il mondo* (London 1835)
When Balfe arrived in London from Italy in May 1835, he joined forces with a number of the leading Italian singers of the time (Lablache, Grisi, Rubini and others) and participated in concerts. He wrote this concert aria for his friend Luigi Lablache. The words were by Arcangelo Berettoni an important former singer and friend of Lablache. The British Library ref: H.2832.c.(7) and H.1660.d. (7). There is also a copy (15 pages) in the Biblioteca del Conservatorio di musica S. Pietro a Majell in Naples; code identifier: IT\ICCU\NAP\0332455

9. Arietta – *Io sentiti tremar* (London 1835)
Shortly after his arrival in London in 1835 Balfe composed a number of Ariettas. This is possibly one of them, or Balfe may have brought it with him from Italy since the words are by the poet and librettist Felice Romani. The sheet music is held by the British Library, ref: H193. (5). And G.807.d. (2).

10. Cantata – for soloists and five part choir 'Now the spring' (London-circa 1836)
The accompaniment is for piano. Balfe dedicated this to the Princess Victoria. The music is held in the Royal Music Collection, British Library, ref: R.M.21.e28 (16)

11. Cantata – for one voice, orchestra and horn (London 1836)
This Cantata was written by Balfe for his friend Maria Malibran, presumably while she was in London preparing for Balfe's opera *The Maid of Artois*, which premiered in 1836. The music is in a private collection, or possibly held by *OperaRara* who recorded it. The piece has been recorded. See the discography section for details.

12. Cavatina – *Una Donna più felice* (London 1837)
This is a soprano aria from Balfe's opera *Enrico IV, al passo della Marna*. Lina Balfe sang in the premiere of the opera at the Teatro Carcano in Milan in 1833. The sheet music also shows that it was sung by 'Madame Balfe'. The fact that Balfe wrote this for his wife makes it a particularly interesting piece, since Lina Balfe was an excellent singer. It also provides an indication of Lina Balfe's vocal style. British Library ref: H2832.c (6).

13. Coronation Stanzas – Celebrating Queen Victoria's Coronation (London 1838)
The words for these works were provided by J.A. Hoy. Balfe composed other music with this poet. The music is in the British Library, ref: H.1661.(4), and R.M.13.d.26.

14. Cantata – *Il Postiglione ... Col capello* **London 1840?)**
The words were by Carlo Pepoli; see item 7 mentioned above for details of Count Pepoli. This concert aria which was also described as a "cantata" in contemporary reports was written for the composer's friend, the great bass, Luigi Lablache. Several well know bases and even Balfe himself sang this piece. The music is available from the British Library, call ref: H.2832.c (8).

15. Aria –*La Speranza ... Dolce soave speme* **(London 1840?)**
The poet who wrote the words for this aria was N. di Santo Mango. Nothing is known about the piece. Perhaps Balfe brought it with him from Italy. British Library ref: H.2832.i (5)

16. Song – *Le Crépuscule ... voici la nuit ...* **(Paris 1841)**
The words for this song were provided by M. de Lamartine, the romantic poet and political activist in Paris. Balfe, who was fluent in French, spent a considerable time in Paris throughout his lifetime. British Library holding ref: G.808. (9). There is also a copy in the Biblioteca musicale governativa del Conservatorio di musica Santa Cecilia, Rome, code identifier: IT\ICCU\DE\02042300991.

17. Cantata – for seven voices (Paris 1842)
This important work was composed while Balfe was in Paris in 1842. It is unpublished. The text is in Italian. The singers were all very prominent at the time. They included, P. Viardot Garcia, G. Duprez, H. Nissen, A. Dupont and W.H. Weiss. Balfe and his wife Lina also sang in it. The original manuscript (35 pages) is at the Pierpont Morgan Library, New York, under Balfe's name in the Mary Flagler Cary Music collection. The cantata was dedicated to Mademoiselle Zimmermann, daughter of Pierre Zimmermann, a professor at the Paris Conservatoire who was a friend of Balfe's. The author has a copy of the cantata on microfilm.

18. *La Curiosita, original air with variations for Piano and Flute* **(London 1844).**
Nothing is known about the origins of this piece. British Library; ref: H.248. (2)

19. Aria – *Ognor costante t'amero* **(London 1846)**
This was music written by Balfe and introduced into the opera Don Pasquale,which he conducted at Her Majesty's Theatre in April, 1846. The soloists at the time were with Grisi, Mario and Lablache, who created the opera in Paris in 1843. All of them were close friends of Balfe. The music is available from the British Library, ref: H.194.f (2).

20. The Prayer to the Nation (London 1846)
This is a song Balfe composed in 1846 to words by J.A. Hoy. The songs opens with the words 'God Save the Queen' The music is available from the British Library, ref: H.2345.

21. Aria – *Qual fior novello* **(London 1847)**
The words for this aria were provided by Francesco Jannetti, who did translations of Donizetti and Rossini works, some of which are still used today. Whether Jannetti was in England or not during this period is not known; if not this may have been music that Balfe had originally composed in Italy. The reviewers at the time were under the impression that Balfe wrote the piece specifically for the tenor Gardoni. Balfe conducted this Italian concert aria for the tenor Italo Gardoni, who partnered Jenny Lind, Luigi Lablache and others in Birmingham in late August 1847. The tenor aria, which created quite a furore, was described by one of the critics to be one of the most beautiful pieces of the evening, despite other numbers by Meyerbeer, Donizetti and Bellini. The music is held in the British Library collection, ref: H193 (5).

22. *Duet – M'offrian cittadi e popli ... Recitative and duet ...* **(London 1847)**
This is another piece with words by Francesco Jannetti. While the sheet music states 'Composed expressly for, and sung by Jenny Lind and Italo Gardoni', it indicates character names of 'Nello' for the tenor's music and 'Elvira' for the soprano line, which would suggest that this duet may have been part of a larger manuscript that Balfe was working on for an opera that was never completed, possibly while he was in Italy or France. During this period Balfe was said to have been working on an opera based on the Victor Hugo play *Le roi s'amuse*. However, the names of the characters featured on the sheet music do not match the names in Hugo's play. In any event, the duet was performed at the Birmingham concert in August 1847 with much applause. British Library holding, ref: H193 (5).

23. Moore's Irish Melodies, with new symphonies and accompaniments for the pianoforte by M.W. Balfe (London 1850)
Balfe worked on this project under contract from Novello & Co. The selection includes eighty-four of Thomas Moore's Irish Melodies as published by Novello & Co. in 1850.

24. Italian School of Singing – *Exercises on solfeggi* **(London 1850/1851?)**
These singing exercises were composed by Balfe from the works of Rossini and Giulio Bordogni. Balfe was an excellent singer who performed in that capacity for many years. Rossini, recognizing Balfe's vocal talents early on, had specifically requested him to study with Bordogni in Paris in 1827. Balfe spent almost a year taking vocal lessons from the great teacher. British Library ref: H.1797 (1.

25. Arietta - *Un pensiero d'amore* **(London 1850)**

The words for this piece were provided by G. Torre. Torres wrote the words for the Balfe Cantata detailed at item 25, so it's possible that this piece may actually be from the Cantata. British Library ref: H.193 (11).

26. Arietta – *Il bacio* (London 1851)
This piece was dedicated to the operatic composer and diplomat, Count Poniatowski, who lived in London 1850–1853. The words were written by, Luigi Capranica. This piece should not be confused with a very popular song of the same title composed by Luigi Arditi in 1860 for the soprano M. Piccolomini. The Balfe song is at Biblioteca del Conservatorio di musica Giuseppe Verdi, Milano, reference numbers ML B.25.h.249.22 – IT\CCU\DE\89013000044.

27. Cantata – *for nine female voices; Inno Delle Nazioni; Onore Alla Gran Bretagna* (London/Milan 1851)
This is quite an extraordinary piece, which Balfe composed for a benefit concert for the well-known singer and vocal teacher, Giacinta Puzzi, wife of Balfe's friend Giovanni Puzzi, the horn player and concert impresario. The cantata was for *nine female voices* with each singer represented a country. The concert was held in May 1851 at Her Majesty's Theatre just before the start of the first Great International Exhibition in London in 1851.

The singers who performed in Balfe's work were H. Sontag (Italy), F. Lablache (Russia), C. Duprez (France), S. Cruvelli (Germany), E. Biscaccianti (America), Mme Giuliani (Ireland), I. Bertrand (Scotland), Mlle Fiorentini (England) and Mme Alaimo (Spain). The Irish soprano Catherine Hayes, who arrived back in London from a highly successful season of opera in Rome just shortly before this event, apparently was not offered the 'role' of Ireland by her fellow countryman, Mr Balfe!

The amazing coincidence is that ten years later Giuseppe Verdi wrote a piece with the exact same title for London for the 1861 Great Exhibition. However, the structure of Verdi's work was quite different.

Balfe's music for this work is not in the British Library. Possibly it is with the Giovanni Puzzi collection in Biblioteca e gli Archivi del Commune, Parma, where, among other items, a horn concerto composed (1835) by Balfe for his friend Puzzi is held.

28. Bravura Aria – *Di duchessa il nome altero ... Rondo & finale ... Dal momento avventurato* (London 1851)
This is a long and very difficult aria with fioriture and a classic Italian rondo finale including trills, scales and roulades that was written by Balfe especially for the dramatic coloratura soprano Sophie Cruvelli for his opera *I Quattro Fratelli*. It was apparently superbly executed by Cruvelli. The vocal range needed is almost three octaves. It created a furore in the opera house at the premiere in 1851. The music is held by the British Library, ref: H.193.q.

29. Aria – *Pari A Bella Fresca Rosa* (London 1851)
This is a short tenor aria from *I Quatro Fratelli* sung by the tenor Italo Gardoni at the London premiere in August 1851. The music is held by the British Library, ref: H.193.q.

30. Aria – *Dice Ognun Che il Guardo Ho Fiero* (London 1851)
This is another tenor aria from *I Quatro Fratelli*. The music is held by the British Library, ref: H.193.q.

31. Aria – *So Felice Appieno* (London 1851)
This is a more lyrical soprano aria from the opera *I Quatro Fratelli* and sung by Mme Giuliani in London, August 1851. The music is held by the British Library, ref: H.193.q.

33. Aria - *Pei sentier del bosco ombross* ... (London 1851)
This is another aria from the opera *I Quattro Fratelli*, which premiered in London in 1851. The British Library holds the music, ref: H.194.e (7).

34. *The Joy of Tears* – Song for Catherine Hayes (London 1851)
This song was specifically written for the Irish soprano Catherine Hayes during the time she was singing in opera at Her Majesty's Theatre in London, with Balfe as the conductor.

35. *Fidelio* by Beethoven – with Italian recitatives by M.W. Balfe (London 1851).
In May 1851, when Balfe was musical director and conductor at the Italian Opera at Her Majesty's Theatre, where Beethoven's *Fidelio* was being performed in Italian, he wrote recitatives in Italian for the score. British Library ref: Add 34226.

36. *Hark the Wind upon the Hill!* – Becky Sharp's Song (London 1857)
Balfe composed this song in 1857 to words by his friend, William M. Thackeray. The music is available in the British Library, ref: H.194.a. (2).

37. *Victoria and England Forever* - Patriotic Song (London 1861)
This was written around the time of the death of Prince Albert. The music is held by the British Library, ref: H.194.c (9).

38. Cantata – *Mazeppa, for four voices and chorus* (London 1862)
Jessica Rankin wrote the words for this work. The drama is based on the Ukrainian character of the same name and the Byron poem. Rankin had also worked with Balfe on a number of songs. The Cantata was first performed at Exeter Hall in London on 23 July, 1862 at the benefit concert of the famous tenor Sims Reeves. Balfe conducted. The original score has been lost. A piano vocal score (106 pages) is held by the Biblioteca Nationale Centrale Firenze, code identifier: IT\ICCU\CFI\0581351. There is also one in the British Library, ref: H.193.n.

39. Duet – *Cara nel Cielo from the opera Keolanthe* **(London 1862)**
The Italian words for this piece were written by the great tenor Giovanni Mario.
When Balfe and Mario were in St Petersburg' together in 1853, Mario included
music from this Balfe opera in his concerts. Possibly it was at that time that this
tenor/soprano duet was given its Italian words by Mario. The British Library
holds the music; ref: H.194c. (28).

40. Trio in A major for Pianoforte, Violin and Violoncello (London 1866)
This work was first performed by the pianist Marie Krebs, violinist Joseph
Joachim and the cellist Alfredo Piatti.

APPENDIX X – DISCOGRAPHY OF RECORDINGS OF BALFE'S WORKS

Recordings are listed chronology based on the year the specific piece was composed. Only professional recordings are listed.

The Siège of Rochelle (London 1835)

Excerpt

Twas in that Garden Beautiful

One CD Melba label CD 301082 Conducted by Richard Bonynge with soprano Deborah Riedel and the Australian Opera and Ballet Orchestra:

The Maid of Artois (London 1836)

Opera on two CDs issued in 2005, CD 2042/3. Conducted by Philip Mackenzie with the Victorian Opera Northwest Group.

Excerpts

The Rapture Dwelling in My heart

One CD Melba label CD 301082 Conducted by Richard Bonynge with soprano Deborah Riedel and the Australian Opera and Ballet Orchestra.

Yon Moon O're the Mountain

One CD Melba label CD 301082 Conducted by Richard Bonynge with soprano Deborah Riedel and the Australian Opera and Ballet Orchestra.

Cantata (London 1836?)

Sempre Pensoso e Torbido - written for the great mezzo-soprano Maria Malibran.

One CD Opera Rara ORR227, featuring mezzo-soprano, Manuela Custer and Richard Bissell, horn.

Ildegonda nel Cacere (Balfe/Marliani Paris 1837?)

Excerpt

Sventurata Ildegonda... Chiuso nell'armi e splendido

Decca CD 475 6812, featuring mezzo-soprano Huguette Tourangeau and l'Orchestre de la Suisse Romande, conducted by Richard Bonynge.

Falstaff (London 1838)

Excerpts

Vorrei parlar ma l'ira – trio.

One CD Opera Rara ORR221, featuring various soloists and orchestras conducted by David Parry.

Le puits d'amour (Paris 1843)

Excerpts

Rêves d'amour, rêves de gloire
One CD London CD, 440679-2 featuring Sumi Jo, soprano, and the English Chamber Orchestra conducted by Richard Bonynge.

The Bohemian Girl (London 1843)

Opera on two CDs originally issued in 1991 on Argo CD 433 324-2; reissued in 2002 on Decca label CD 473077-2. Richard Bonynge conducting the National Symphony Orchestra of Ireland with an international cast of singers.

Excerpts

Highlights from *The Bohemian Girl* with Veronica Dunne, soprano, Uel Deane tenor, and Eric Hines, baritone. Orchestra conducted by Havelock Nelson. EMI CD 3359482.

I Dreamt I Dwelt in Marble Halls

London CD 425048-2 featuring soprano Joan Sutherland with the London Symphony Orchestra conducted by Richard Bonynge.
Erato CD 1224296 featuring soprano Sumi Jo and orchestra conducted by E. Stratta.
EMI LP MBS1 featuring soprano, Margaret Burke Sheridan with a string quintet conducted by Lawrence Collingwood. Recorded in 1929.

When Other Lips and Other Hearts

RCA Victor CD, 68030-2, featuring tenor Jerry Hadley singing with the English Chamber Orchestra conducted by Richard Bonynge.
Symposium CD 1163 featuring John McCormack. Recorded in 1910.
Testament CDSBT 1165, featuring tenor Beniamino Gigli singing with orchestra conducted by Enrico Sivieri.

The Heart Bow'd Down

Preiser CD 89172, featuring bass-baritone Wilhelm Hesch singing in German withunknown accompanist. Recorded in 1907.
Symposium CD 1081 featuring baritone Clarence Whitehill. Recorded in 1914.

The Rose of Castille (London 1857)

Excerpts

The Convent Cell

One CD Melba label CD 301082. Conducted by Richard Bonynge with soprano Deborah Riedel and the Australian Opera and Ballet Orchestra.

'Twas Rank and Fame

RCA Victor CD, 68030-2, featuring tenor Jerry Hadley singing with the English Chamber Orchestra conducted by Richard Bonynge.

Satanella (London 1858)

Excerpts

Oh! Could I but His Heart Enslave

One CD Melba label CD 301082. Conducted by Richard Bonynge with soprano Deborah   Riedel and the Australian Opera and Ballet Orchestra.

The Puritan's Daughter (London 1861)

Excerpts

Bliss for ever Past

One CD Melba label CD 301082. Conducted by Richard Bonynge with soprano Deborah Riedel and the Australian Opera and Ballet Orchestra.

Il Talismano (London 1874)

Excerpts

Nella Dolce Trepidanza

One CD Melba label CD 301082. Conducted by Richard Bonynge with soprano Deborah Riedel and the Australian Opera and Ballet Orchestra.

Che Calmo Asil: Placida Notte

One CD Melba label CD 301082. Conducted by Richard Bonynge with soprano Deborah Riedel and the Australian Opera and Ballet Orchestra.

APPENDIX XI – COMPOSERS WHO WERE BALFE'S CONTEMPORARIES

The overall environment in which Balfe worked in London, Paris and Vienna was a crowded, competitive field. Balfe achieved prominence as an operatic composer during the period 1835–1870.

Composer	Dates
Auber, Daniel F.	1782 — 1871
Balfe, Michael W.	1808 — 1870
Barnett, John	1802 — 1890
Beethoven, Ludwig	1770 — 1827
Bellini, Vincenzo	1801 — 1835
Benedict, Jules	1804 — 1885
Bennett, William S.	1816 — 1875
Beriot, Charles de	1802 — 1870
Berlioz, Hector	1803 — 1869
Bishop, Henry	1786 — 1855
Cherubini, Luigi	1760 — 1842
Chopin, Frederic	1810 — 1849
David, Félicen	1810 — 1876
Donizetti, Gaetano	1797 — 1848
Gounod, Charles	1818 — 1893
Liszt, Franz	1811 — 1886
Loder, Edward	1813 — 1865

(Timeline axis: 1770, 1790, 1810, 1830, 1850, 1870, 1890, 1910)

APPENDIX XI – COMPOSERS WHO WERE BALFE'S CONTEMPORARIES

	1770	1790	1810	1830	1850	1870	1890	1910

Massenet, Jules — 1842—1912

Mercadante, Saverio — 1795—1870

Meyerbeer, Giacomo — 1791—1864

Osborne, George A. — 1806—1893

Pacini, Giovanni — 1796—1867

Pugni, Cesare — 1802—1870

Ricci, Federico — 1809—1877

Ricci, Luigi — 1805—1859

Rossini, Gioachino — 1792—1868

Schubert, Franz — 1797—1828

Thalberg, Sigismond — 1812—1871

Verdi, Giuseppe — 1813—1901

Wallace, Vincent — 1812—1865

Wagner, Richard — 1813—1883

APPENDIX XII– BALFE'S CIRCLE OF FRIENDS AND ASSOCIATES

Balfe's active career covered almost fifty years. He met many people over the course of the years. Because of his profession his relationships tended to gravitate towards people in the field of music and associated areas. This included singers, composers, performers, theatre managers, music publishers, biographers, critics, poets and others. The list shown below of fifty selected people represents some of the more prominent individuals. Members of Balfe's family are not featured in this listing as they are dealt with in the text.

Alboni, Marietta (1826–1894), Italian contralto who made her debut in 1842 after study with Rossini and others. She quickly became a leading singer at La Scala, Milan. She had a brilliant career that brought her to the principal operatic centres of Europe and to St Petersburg and New York. She first met Balfe in London in 1849 when he was conducting at Her Majesty's Theatre, London. Later in 1858 she sang in the London premiere of Balfe's *La Zingara* in the role of the Queen.

Barton, James, was a violinist and teacher. He was born in Dublin, where he taught music. In addition to teaching he also played in various theatre orchestras in the city. He taught Balfe from around 1817 for two to three years, as Balfe was emerging and performing as a child prodigy in concerts at the Rotunda and various other venues in Dublin.

Beale T. Willert (1828–189?) was the son of Frederick Beale, one of the partners in the music publishing firm of Cramer in Beale of 201 Regent Street, London, who published many of Balfe's works. Beale in his autobiography talks about Balfe with great affection. Later in life Beale became an agent manager for many of the leading singers visiting London, including Grisi and Mario, Catherine Hayes, and others who sang under Balfe's direction at Her Majesty's theatre. He also conducted opera tours of Ireland, taking his principal singers with him to Dublin, Cork, Limerick and Belfast. He wrote two books. See the bibliography for details.

Benedict, Julius (1804–1885), was a composer and conductor. Benedict was an excellent musician and teacher who studied with the composer Carl Maria von Weber in Germany. He initially started as a conductor of opera in Vienna and later went Naples. He arrived in London around the same time as Balfe in 1835. He and Balfe became good friends. He conducted a number of Balfe's operas. Balfe conducted the Mozart Requiem Mass at the funeral of Benedict's wife in London in May 1852. Benedict was the composer of the opera *The Lily of Killarney* with a libretto by Balfe's close friend Dion Boucicault.

Behrend, Maxmillian (1823–1890) was a wealthy lumber and commodities merchant from Danzig who married Balfe's eldest daughter Louisa 'Gigia' in London in 1850. They went to live in Danzig. They had eight children. The family moved to London in the late 1850s. When Balfe died in 1870, Behrend took care of Balfe's wife Lina and helped her relocate from the composer's country home to central London. He also made a generous donation to the fund that erected the large marble statue of Balfe that stands in the lobby of the Theatre Royal, Drury Lane, today.

Bordogni, Giulio (1789–1856) was a well-established tenor and singing teacher when Balfe met him in Paris in 1827. Bordogni was also a professor of singing at the Conservatory. At the direction of Rossini Balfe studied voice with Bordogni. Balfe later made his operatic debut in *Il barbiere di Siviglia* in the role of Figaro, singing opposite Bordogni, who had the role of Almaviva. They became good friends..

Boucicault, Dion Lardner (c.1829–1890), Dublin-born actor, dramatist and theatre manager. He wrote several successful plays starting in 1841 in London, where he and Balfe first met. Later in life, Balfe asked him to write an operatic libretto for him. Boucicault presented a layout to the composer who criticized him for producing something that was 'structured so badly'. Balfe proceeded to show the dramatist how an opera libretto should be written. Many years later Boucicault wrote a lengthy article about his amusing experience with his friend Balfe. Boucicault was one of those instrumental in arranging for the large marble commemorative Balfe statue to be erected in the lobby of the Drury Lane Theatre in London in 1874.

Bunn, Alfred (1797–1860), poet, librettist and theatre manager. Bunn managed the Theatre Royal at Drury Lane at the time Balfe returned to London from Italy in May 1835. Through the influence of Maria Malibran, Balfe's first opera *The Siege of Rochelle* was produced with great success at Drury Lane the same year. Bunn and Balfe collaborated on a number of operas which were produced at the same theatre, including Balfe's most famous work, *The Bohemian Girl*, in 1843. Bunn's librettos were considered mediocre at best.

Cherubini, Luigi (1760–1842), composer. Balfe was introduced to Cherubini in Paris around 1825. Cherubini was impressed with the young composer. Balfe later studied with the Italian composer for about a year. Cherubini introduced Balfe to Rossini in Paris during this period. The meeting with Rossini set Balfe on course for becoming an excellent singer and eventually becoming a composer of opera.

Chorley, Henry F. (1808–1872), playwright, novelist (none of the plays or novels was particularly successful) and long-time music critic of the London news weekly, *The Athenaeum*. He was an eccentric person and a caustic critic who had little time for Balfe or his music. Balfe never worked with Chorley on a libretto for an opera, unlike others of the period. Chorley crafted a cynical obituary on Balfe's death in *The Athenaeum*, so much so that the orchestra members at Drury Lane Theatre wrote a letter to *The Times* chastising the critic about it. Chorley's memoirs, *Thirty Years' Musical Recollections*, published in 1862 and detailing his life as a London music critic, have endured. See the bibliography for details.

Cooke, Thomas S. (1782–1848), Dublin born singer, musician and composer who had studied with Giordani in Dublin. In 1823 he became the leader of the orchestra at the Theatre Royal Drury Lane in London. It was at that time that the fifteen-year-old Balfe met Simpson, who gave him a job in the orchestra. Balfe and Simpson remained friends for life. When Simpson died in 1848, Balfe organized a benefit concert for his family.

Costa, Michael (1808-1884), was a conductor composer. He was born in Naples. He came to England in 1929. Sometime afterwards he became the director of music at the Italian Opera. In 1846 he resigned to form a new venture, the Royal Italian Opera at Covent Garden, where he became director. Balfe took over from him at the Italian Opera at Her Majesty's Theatre. While the two in effect competed they remained friends all their lives. In 1874 Costa officiated at the dedication of the large Balfe statue that stands in the lobby of the Theatre Royal in Drury Lane today.

Crampton, Sir John (1807–1886) was the British Minister to the Court of Russia. He met and married Balfe's youngest daughter, Victoire, when she and her parents were visiting Russia in 1860. Crampton and his wife lived in Paris and Madrid afterwards. The marriage was eventually annulled by the Pope in 1863 on the grounds of his impotence. Balfe was directly involved in the divorce proceedings on behalf of his daughter in the courts in London. Victoria Balfe remarried a year later.

Davison, James W. (1813–1885) was the long-time music critic of *The Times* of London from 1846 to 1878. Davidson was a trained musician. He was married to his former pupil, the much younger talented pianist Arabella Goddard. In addition, he also became the editor of the important weekly periodical, *The Musical World*, a position he held from 1843 until 1883. Davison and Balfe were close friends. They exchanged letters from abroad when one or the other was travelling. Balfe and Davison also dined together occasionally. Davison's reviews of Balfe's operas were generally quite favourable. He frequently complemented Balfe on his skills as a musician and conductor. He also applauded Balfe's ability for managing the members of the orchestra and singers during difficult periods and conflicts.

Dickens, Charles (1812–1870), the famous Victorian novelist, was a friend of Balfe and his family. Dickens visited the Balfe family on a number of occasions. He gave the composer a gift of a 'Pickwick Papers' initialed snuff-box during one visit. They had children of the same age. Balfe in many respects was the Charles Dickens of music in Victorian England. Both were highly popular and their work was enjoyed by the masses.

Fitzball, Edward (1792–1873) was a dramatist and writer of operatic librettos. He provided Balfe with the libretto for *The Siege of Rochelle* in 1835. He though very highly of Balfe and in particular of Balfe's personal style, referring to him 'Sunny Balfe' because of the composer's outgoing personality. Fitzball also wrote the libretto for Balfe's contemporary, Vincent Wallace's successful opera *Maritana*. In general, Fitzball's writing style was similar to Alfred Bunn's. Both were considered somewhat archaic, even for the Victorian period and style.

Gardoni, Italo (1821–1882), was an elegant lyric tenor whom Balfe first met in Paris when the composer went there to premiere a new opera at the

Académie de Musique (Paris Opera) in December 1845. Gardoni had one of the leading roles in the opera. He became good friends with Balfe and his wife. He was married to the daughter of the great baritone Antonio Tamburini another Balfe friend. Gardoni later performed in London in several operas under Balfe's direction at the Italian Opera. He also attended Balfe's funeral in London in 1870.

Grisi, Giulia (1811–1869) was one of the nineteenth century's greatest sopranos. Balfe and Grisi first met in Bologna in 1829 when they were in their early twenties. They became life-long friends. Grisi may have had some influence on the management of the King's Theatre in London in 1838 in arranging for Balfe to composer his opera *Falstaff*. Balfe conducted her in various operas in London in the 1840s. Grisi had a long distinguished career; she created the principal soprano roles in Bellini's *I Puritani* and Donizetti's *Don Pasquale* in Paris. She was immensely popular in London and Paris.

Harrison, William (1813–1868) was a tenor who premiered ten Balfe operas in London. The most important was *The Bohemian Girl* in 1843. He and Balfe worked together on selected arias in the opera so that the music suited Harrison's vocal range, which was somewhat limited to the top of the range. He formed an opera company with the soprano Louisa Pyne in 1856. He and his partner commissioned Balfe to compose various operas for the new season starting in 1856. They created a programme that was to become known as the *English Ring* in which they gave successive performances of *The Bohemian Girl*, *Maritana* and *The Lily of Killarney*. The group also performed in New York.

Kenny, Charles Lamb (1823–1881) was one of Balfe's biographers. He was born in London, where he became a writer on drama for *The Times*. He also wrote a number of light operas and songs. He translated several works from French into English. Most of his input for his Balfe biography came from Balfe's widow, Lina. The biography was published five years after the composer's death. Kenney's father, James Kenny, was a Dublin-born playwright and manager and or proprietor of a major social club in London's West End.

Kupelwiser, Josef (1792–1866) was a librettist and author of numerous plays. Kupelwiser was associated with the Kärntnertor-theater in Vienna. He was also a translator and located in Vienna. He translated *The Bohemian Girl* and reworked the libretto and story into German for performances as *Die Zigeunerin* in Vienna, where Balfe conducted the local premiere. Kupelwiser also translated other Balfe operas into German for performances in Vienna and elsewhere.

Lablache, Luigi (1794–1858) was the foremost bass in nineteenth-century Europe. He was born in Naples. His mother was Irish, her maiden name Bietach. He created many roles in Rossini, Bellini, Donizetti and other operas. He was renowned in Naples, Paris, London, Vienna and St Petersburg in Russia. Balfe met him in London in 1835 when Balfe sang in a concert with Lablache, Grisi and others in the Vauxhall Gardens. Lablache also created the title role in Balfe's opera *Falstaff* in 1838. Lablache appeared in several operas conducted by Balfe in London in the 1840s. He was vocal coach to Queen Victoria for almost twenty years.

Levey, (O'Shaughnessy) Richard M. (1811–1899) was a violinist, orchestra leader and teacher of music. Levey was born O'Shaughnessy in Dublin. He was a remarkable musician who was a lifelong friend of Balfe's. He and Balfe were students together at James Barton's musical establishment. He changed his name to Levey as he felt it was a more appropriate name for a musician. It was apparently his mother's maiden name. He conducted the Dublin premiere of Balfe's *The Maid of Artois* in 1840. He was a co-author of the book *Annals of the Theatre Royal, Dublin,* detailing the Italian opera season in Dublin in the nineteenth century. He was also a founder of the Royal Irish Academy of Music.

Lind, Jenny (1820–1887) was a Swedish-born soprano of great renown. Balfe first met Lind in Vienna in 1846. She came to London under contract with Benjamin Lumley in 1847. Balfe conducted her debut at Her Majesty's Theatre in May of that year. He subsequently conducted virtually all of her operatic performances in England and in Dublin. He also worked with Lind and Verdi when the Italian composer came to London to premiere his new opera. Balfe accompanied Lind on various concert tours. He wrote songs and concert arias for her. They had an excellent relationship.

Lover, Samuel (1797–1868) was a composer, prolific writer and artist. Dublin-born Lover was a close friend of Balfe's most of his life. In London in 1841 Balfe sang the leading role in Lover's operetta *Il Paddy whack in Italia,* which had considerable success. Balfe's singing of the song *Molly Bawn* had great appeal. He later gave Balfe three librettos for potential operas; however, Balfe for whatever reason, never used them.

Lucca, Francesco (1802-1872) was a music publisher located in Milan. Lucca was an employee of the Ricordi publishing establishment in Milan. He opened his own publishing business in 1825. Lucca published the basically unknown early Balfe Italian opera *Enrico IV, al passo della Marna* in cooperation with Dova in Milan in 1832. The opera was quite successful, being performed in a number of cities.

Lumley (Levy) Benjamin (1810–1875) was a lawyer and impresario of the Italian Opera in London for many years. His Canadian father, businessman Sion Levy, had moved to Birmingham. His son was born either in Canada or in Birmingham around 1810. His name change came early in life, possibly when he was entering public school. In 1832 Lumley (Levy junior) qualified as a lawyer. He became involved professionally with the bankrupt Italian Opera in London, ultimately taking it over in 1841 and changing the approach for marketing Italian opera and selling tickets. He was a talented business person. When his musical director, the esteemed Michael Costa, resigned, he hired Balfe in 1846 to be his replacement and for the next seven years he and Balfe ran the Italian Opera in London at Her Majesty's Theatre. Under his administration Jenny Lind and Giuseppe Verdi both appeared in London for the first time. Lumley was also responsible for the local premiere of several Verdi operas during the 1840s.

Malibran, Maria (1808–1836) was one of the foremost singers of the nineteenth century. She was the daughter of Manuel Garcia, the creator of a number of Rossini operas. Her brother, Manuel Patricio Garcia, was a famous singing teacher and coach. Her sister, Pauline Viardot-Garcia, was a renowned singer. Balfe first met Malibran in Paris, where they sang together in Rossini operas. Later Malibran was influential in arranging for Balfe to partner with her at La Scala, Milan, in Rossini's *Otello* and in various operas in Venice. Balfe wrote *The Maid of Artois* for her in London in 1836.

Maggione, S. Manfredo (1810–1862?) was a prominent London-based Italian librettist and translator. He was associated with the Royal Academy of Music and with various leading musicians in London. He knew Balfe from the mid-1830s in London. He created the libretto for Balfe's first London Italian-language opera, *Falstaff*, using Shakespeare's *Merry Wives of Windsor* play as the basis for his libretto. Maggione, successfully translated Donizetti's *Lucia di Lammermoor* into an English libretto for performances in London. He also did translations of Auber's operas and Halevy's operas.

Maretzek, Max (1821–1897) was a musician, chorus master and impresario. When Balfe took over the Italian opera at Her Majesty's Theatre in 1846, Maretzek was the chorus master. Balfe and he became friends. Maretzek went to New York to become director of the Astor Place Italian Opera in 1848. He later was director at the Academy of Music at 14th Street in New York and he also managed touring Italian opera groups. Maretzek and Balfe continued to communicate with each other despite the distance. In Maretzek's memoirs (see bibliography section) he has an extended reference to a New York rumour that Balfe was going to replace him at the Academy of Music. He wrote to Balfe, who was in Italy at the time, advising him about the difficulties of managing opera in America and commenting on the problems Balfe's countrywoman, Catherine Haye, had had in New York during her time there in 1852. As it turned out, Balfe never went to America so he never had to face replacing his friend Maretzek.

Mario, Giovanni Matteo (1810–1883) was the most distinguished tenor of the middle decades of the nineteenth century in London and Paris. He had made his debut in Paris in 1838. Balfe and he probably became friends in Paris in the early 1840s. He later sang in various operas in London which were conducted by Balfe. He translated some of Balfe's English opera arias into Italian and performed them. He was the life-long companion of the soprano Giulia Grisi. Both of them also visited Dublin and other cities in Ireland regularly.

Nilsson, Christine (1843–1921) was a Swedish- born soprano who met Balfe in Paris in 1869, when she appeared in Gounod's *Faust*. Balfe was in Paris working on his revisions of *La Bohémienne*, the French version of *The Bohemian Girl*. Nilsson must have learned that he was also working on a new opera. She later created the soprano role in the premiere of Balfe's *Il talismano* in London in 1874, claiming that Balfe had written it for her. She also donated a significant contribution towards the Balfe memorial statue that stands in the lobby of the Theatre Royal, Drury Lane, London.

Osborne, George Alexander (1806–1893), was a Limerick-born pianist, composer and music teacher. His best-known pupil was Charles Hallé. Osborne met Balfe in Paris in 1827. Osborne was a close friend of Chopin, Rossini, Berlioz and the composer's Irish-born wife Henriette Smithson. At Balfe's request he was helping him with his study of the role of Figaro in Rossini's *Il barbiere di Siviglia*, in preparation for the baritone's operatic debut. Osborne expressed shock at Balfe's wild antics during his Figaro rehearsals, when the baritone started to throw plates, napkins, cushions and anything he could find at Osborne, as part of his enthusiasm for the role. The two remained good friends all their lives.

Pasta, Giuditta (1797–1865) was one of the great legendary singers of the early nineteenth century. She created the title roles in the premieres of *Norma*, *La Sonnambula*, *Beatrice di Tenda*, *Anna Bolena* and other operas. Balfe sang with her at a concert in Milan in December 1828. In July 1850, when Pasta visited London and decided to come 'out of retirement' to perform at Her Majesty's Theatre, Balfe conducted these concerts. Balfe's wife Lina had also sung with her in Milan in 1830.

Piave, Francesco Maria (1810–1876) was a prominent writer who provided Verdi with many librettos for his operas including *Ernani*, *Macbeth*, *Rigoletto*, *La Traviata* and others. In 1854 Piave worked with Balfe on the libretto for a new opera, *Pittore e Duca*, which premiered in Trieste. The opera, however, was not a success and it was cancelled, possibly because of the soprano, Fanny Salvini-Donatelli. Donatelli had been associated with a comparable failure a year earlier when she had created Verdi's *La Traviata* in Venice.

Puzzi, Giovanni (1785–1876) was a prominent horn player, impresario and concert manager. His wife, Giacinta Tosi Puzzi, was also an important singer and teacher. Balfe met the Puzzis through Malibran in Milan in 1834. Some time early in 1835 in Venice or Milan, Puzzi was planning to go to London and he probably suggested to Balfe that he should return there too. Balfe remained friends with Puzzi and his wife and frequently performed with them in London. In 1851 Balfe composed a very unusual cantata for nine female voices for a benefit concert for Giacinta, and later he wrote a horn concerto for husband, Giovanni.

Ricordi, Giovanni (1785–1853) was the founder of the Ricordi music publishing house in Milan early in the nineteenth-century. Balfe met him in Milan, probably through his friend Maria Malibran. In Turin in 1835 Balfe wrote a very personal letter to Giovanni Ricordi in Italian talking about Hérold's opera *Zampa*, in which Balfe's wife Lina was performing along with the baritone Giorgio Ronconi in Turin. Later Balfe also sang in this opera in Turin.

Ronconi, Giorgio (1810–1890) was a very important baritone during the nineteenth century. Balfe met Ronconi in Pavia in 1831. Ronconi was at the very start of his long and successful international career when he sang in one of Balfe's early Italian operas, *Un avvertimento ai gelosi*, at the Teatro Re in Milan in 1831. Ronconi went on to create many roles for Donizetti and later for Verdi, including *Nabucco* at La Scala in 1842, the composer's first great success.

Rossini, Gioachino (1792–1868) was the most famous Italian composer in the first half of the nineteenth century. Balfe met him in Paris in 1827. Rossini took an interest in Balfe and encouraged him to study singing. The great Italian composer became Balfe's mentor, helping him to study singing and to make his debut at the Italian opera in Paris.

Rothschild, Lionel (1808–1879) and Charlotte (1819—1884) Lionel was the head of the London-based Rothschild banking establishment. Balfe, as a prominent London-based musical personality, knew the Rothschilds. He corresponded with them occasionally. Charlotte, Lionel's wife, was interested enough in the Balfe family to make comments in one of her letters about an invitation they had received to the wedding of Balfe's daughter to a Spanish duke.

Ryan, Michael Desmond (1816–1868) was a music critic, poet and librettist. He was born in Kilkenny, Ireland. He was the son of a doctor, and was educated at Edinburgh University. Afterwards he became music critic for leading London newspapers in the 1840s and the sub-editor to Davison for the weekly periodical *The Musical World*. He and Balfe became friends and he continually mentioned Balfe in his writings. He also provided Balfe with the text for at least one song.

Scribe, Eugène (1791–1861) was one of the most important Paris-based librettists who provided French librettos for leading operatic composers such as, Auber, Donizetti, Gounod, Halévy, Verdi and Meyerbeer. Scribe and Balfe collaborated on a new opera for the Opéra Comique in 1843. The opera, *Le puits d'amour*, was Balfe's first composition for Paris and was very successful.

Sontag, Henriette (1806–1854) from an early age was a very successful prima donna. In 1824 she sang in the premiere of Beethoven's Ninth Symphony in Vienna, with the composer conducting. In Paris in 1828 she sang the role of Rosina when Balfe made his operatic debut as Figaro in Rossini's *Il barbiere di Siviglia* at the Théâtre des Italiens. Afterwards Balfe and Sontag came to know each other well and he conducted all of her operatic performances in London at Her Majesty's Theatre in the early 1850s. Sontag died in Mexico in 1854.

Staudigl, Joseph (1807–1861) was a bass who made his Viennese debut in 1845. When Balfe went to Vienna in 1846 Staudigl worked on a German translation of the composer's *The Bohemian Girl*. He also sang in the opera. Staudigl's translation was later replaced by Kupelwiser's German libretto. Balfe conducted Staudigl and Jenny Lind in her London debut in *Roberto le Diable* in May 1847.

Stoltz, Rosine (1815–1903) was a famous mezzo-soprano at the Paris Opéra during Balfe's time. She created operas for Donizetti, Berlioz and others. When Balfe composed a new opera, *L'étoile de Séville*, for the, Académie Royale de Musique (Paris Opéra) in December 1845, Stoltz sang the leading role. The opera was quite successful and had fifteen performances.

Strauss, Johann, Sr (1804–1849) born in Vienna, was a musician and orchestra director. He became famous as a composer of waltzes, dances and marches. He met Balfe in Vienna when the Irish composer was conducting his *Die Zigeunerin*. Strauss was so impressed with Balfe's talents and melodies that he later made arrangements of music from four of Balfe's operas, some of which were played as late as 2003 in Vienna for the New Year's Eve concert.

Tamburini, Antonio (1800–1876) was one of the early important baritones in Italy who created many roles for Donizetti and Bellini. Balfe, while singing in Ital, was sometimes compared to him because of his vocal flexibility. Tamburini's daughter was married to the tenor Italo Gardoni, who was a close friend of Balfe's. In 1838 in London Tamburini sang in the premiere of Balfe's *Falstaff*.

Viardot-García, Pauline (1821–1910) wasa mezzo-soprano, and, like her sister, Maria Malibran Garcia, she became one of the outstanding performers in nineteenth-century opera. Balfe first met her in the early 1840s when she sang in a cantata which Balfe composed while in Paris. She later performed in Balfe's *La Zingara*, the Italian version of *The Bohemian Girl*, in Dublin in 1858.

Zaffira, Giuseppe (1825–1887?) was a Paris-based librettist and translator. He translated operas for Gounod and A. Thomas. In 1869 when Balfe was working in Paris on his revised version of *La Bohémienne* (*The Bohemian Girl*), Zaffira also completed an Italian translation, possibly for a performance at the Théâtre des Italiens, which apparently never took place. In 1873, Zaffira also wrote the Italian libretto for Balfe's final opera *Il talismano*, which had its premiere in London in 1874.

APPENDIX XIII – BALFE'S FAMILY TREE

Michael W. Balfe's Family Tree

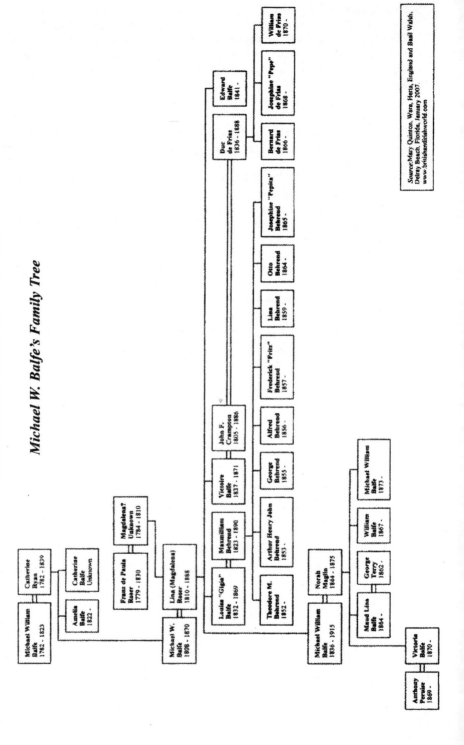

Source: Mary Quinton, Ware, Herts, England and Basil Walsh,
Delray Beach, Florida, January 2007.
www.britishandirishworld.com

Select Bibliography

BOOKS, PERIODICALS, JOURNALS, NEWSPAPERS AND LETTERS

Ahlquist, Karen. *Democracy at the Opera. Music, Theatre and Culture in New York City 1815–60.* University of Illinois Press, Chicago, IL, 1997.

Allsbrook, David I. *Liszt: My Travelling Circus Life.* Southern Illinois University Press, Carbondale, IL, 1991.

Appolonia, Giorgio. *Giuditta Pasta, Gloria del Bel Canto.* EDA Torino, Italy. 2000.

Arditti, Luigi. *My Reminiscences.* Skeffington, London, 1896.

Ashbrook, William. *Donizetti and His Operas.* Cambridge University Press, New York, 1982.

Banister, Henry C. *George Alexander Macfarren, His Life, Works and Influence.* George Bell & Sons, London, 1892.

Barbier, Patrick. *Opera in Paris 1800–1850.* Amadeus Press, Portland, OR, 1987.

Barrett, William A. *Balfe, His Life and Works.* William Reeves, London, 1882.

Beale, Willert. *The Light of other Days.* 2 vols. Bentley & Son, London, 1890.

Berlioz, Hector. Edited by Barzun, Jacques, *Evenings with the Orchestra.* University of Chicago Press, Chicago, IL, 1973.

Bernard, Bayle. *The Life of Samuel Lover.* Appleton & Co., New York, 1874.

Biddlecombe, George. *English Opera from 1834 to 1864 with Particular Reference to the Works of Michael Balfe.* Garland Publishing, New York, 1994.

Biggi, Maria I. and Mangini, Giorgio. *Teatro Malibran.* Marsilio, Venice, 2001.

Blanning, T. C. W. *The Nineteenth Century.* Oxford University Press, Oxford, UK, 2000.

Bledsoe, Robert T. *Henry Fothergill Chorley, Victorian Journalist.* Ashgate, Aldershot, UK, 1998.

Boydell, Brian. *Rotunda Music in Eighteenth-Century Dublin.* Irish Academic Press, Dublin, 1992.

Brown, James D. and Stratton, Stephen S. *British Musical Biography,* Birmingham, UK. 1897.

Bunn, Alfred. *The Stage, Both Before and Behind the Curtain.* 3 vols. Bentley, Philadelphia, PA., 1840.

Bushnell, Howard. *Maria Malibran: A Biography of the Singer.* Pennsylvania State University Press, PA., 1979.

Cambi, Luisa. *Vincenzo Bellini Epistolario.* Mondadori, Italy. 1943.

Cheke, Dudley. *Joséphine and Emilie, Stars of the Bel Canto in Europe and America 1823–1889.* John Carpenter, *Oxford, England*, 1993.

Chorley, Henry F. *Thirty Years' Musical Recollections.* Vienna House reprint, New York, 1972.

Clive, Peter. *Mozart and His Circle.* Yale University Press, New Haven, CT., 1993.

———. *Beethoven and His World.* Oxford University Press, Oxford, UK, 2001.

Cox, Rev. John E. *Musical Recollections of the Last Half-Century.* 2 Vols Tindsley, London, 1872.

Crawford, E. Margaret. *Counting the People: A Survey of the Irish Censuses, 1813–1911,* Four Courts Press, Dublin, 2003.

Crosten, William L. *French Grand Opera, an Art and a Business,* King's Crown Press, New York, 1948.

Current Musicology, No. 10, 1970. Article, 'Ricordi Plate Numbers in the Earlier 19th Century' by Thomas F. Heck. Columbia University, New York, 1970.

Curtis Jr., L. Perry. *Apes and Angels, The Irishman in Victorian Caricature,* Smithsonian Press, Washington, DC, 1998.

Davison, Henry. *From Mendelssohn to Wagner, being the Memoirs of J. W. Davison.* W. Reeves, London, 1912.

Davey, Henry. *History of English Music,* Curwen & Sons, London, 1921.

De Nie, Michael. *The Eternal Paddy, Irish Identity and the British Press, 1798–1882.* University of Wisconsin Press, Madison, WS. 2004.

Dent, Edward. *Foundation of English Opera*. Da Capo Press, New York, 1965.

Dizikes, John. *Opera in America, a Cultural History*. Yale University Press, New Haven, CT, 1993.

Ebers, John. *Seven Years of the King's Theatre*. Blom reprint, New York, 1969.

Ehrlich, Cyril. *First Philharmonic A History of the Royal Philharmonic Society*. Clarendon Press, Oxford, UK, 1995.

Ellis, Katherine. *Music Criticism in Nineteenth-Century France*. Cambridge University Press, Cambridge, UK, 1995.

Ellis, Roger. *Who's Who in Victorian Britain 1851–1901*, Stackpoole, 1997.

Fenner, Theodore. *Leigh Hunt and His Opera Criticism*. University Press of Kansas, Wichita, KS, 1972.

——. *Opera in London, Views of the Press 1785–1830*, Southern Illinois University Press, Carbondale, IL, 1994.

Ferguson, Niall. *The House of Rothschild, Money's Prophets 1798–1848*. Viking, London, 1998.

Fitzlyon, April. *Maria Malibran, Diva of the Romantic Age*, Souvenir Press, London, 1987.

Flood, W.H. Grattan. *Irish Musical History*. William Reeves, London, 1920.

Ford, Boris, Editor. *The Cambridge Cultural History of Britain vol. 6: The Romantic Age in Britain*, Cambridge: Cambridge University Press, 1992.

Forbes, Elizabeth. *Mario and Grisi*. Gollancz, London, 1985.

Foster, R.F. *Paddy & Puck, Connections in Irish and English History*. Penguin Group, London, 1993.

Friel, Mary. *Dancing as a Social Pastime in the South-East of Ireland 1800–1897*. Four Courts Press, Dublin, 2004.

Fuller Maitland, J.A. *English Music in the XIXth Century*, Longwood Press, Portland, ME, 1976.

Galatopoulos, Stelios. *Bellini, Life, Times, Music 1801–1835*. Sanctuary Publishing, London, 2002.

Garibaldi, Luigi A. *Giuseppe Verdi nelle Lettere di Emanuele Muzio ad Antonio Barezzi*. Treves, Milan,. 1931.

Gatti, Carlo. *Verdi the Man and His Music*. Putnam, New York, 1955.

Gossett, Philip, *Divas and Scholars, Performing Italian Opera*, University of Chicago Press, Chicago, IL, 2006.

Gray, Peter, ed. *Victoria's Ireland? Irishness and Britishness, 1837–1901.*Four Courts Press, Dublin, 2004.

Graziano, John. *European Music and Musicians in New York City 1840–1890*, University of Rochester Press, Rochester, NY,2006.

Grove, Sir George. *Dictionary of Music and Musicians*, 4 vols. Presser Philadelphia, PA, 1889.

Gutierrez, Beniamino. *Il Teatro Carcano (1803–1914)*. Arnaldo Forni reprint, Milan, 1916.

Gyger, Alison. *Opera for the Antipodes*, Currency Press, Sydney, 1990.

——. *Civilising the Colonies, Pioneering Opera in Australia*, Pellinor, Sydney. 1999.

Harrison, Clifford. *Stray Records*. Bentley, London, 1892.

Harrison, J.F.C. *The Early Victorians 1832–1851*. Weidenfeld and Nicolson, London. 1971.

Hepokoski, James A. *Giuseppe Verdi: Falstaff*, Cambridge University Press, Cambridge, UK, 1983.

History Ireland, Vol. 11, No. 1, Spring 2003. 'Michel W. Balfe, the Irish Italian Ireland's uniquely gifted composer.' pp. 28–32. Wordwell, Dublin.

Holland, Henry S. and Rockstro, W.S. *Memoir of Madame Jenny Lind-Goldschmidt: Her early Art-life and Dramatic Career 1820–1851.* 2 vols. John Murray, London, 1891.

Hurd, Michael. *The Romantic Age 1800–1914*. Blackwell Reference, London, 1958.

——. *The Orchestra*. Chartwell, Secaucus, NJ, 1981.

Irvin, Eric. *Dictionary of the Australian Theatre 1788–1914*. Hale & Iremonger, Sydney. 1985.

Jensen, Luke. *Giuseppe Verdi & Giovanni Ricordi with Notes on Francesco Lucca*. Garland, New York, 1989.

Kaufman, Thomas, G. *Verdi and His Major Contemporaries. A Selected Chronology of Performances with Casts*. Garland, New York,. 1990.

Kelly, Michael, *Reminiscences of Michael Kelly of the King's Theatre and the Theatre Royal Drury Lane*. 2 vols. Da Capo reprint, New York, 1968.

Kendall-Davies, Barbara. *The Life and Work of Pauline Viardot Garcia: The Years 1836–1863*. Vol.1.Cambridge Scolars Press, Cambridge, UK, 2003.

Kennedy, Michael, Ed. *The Autobiography of Charles Hallé*. Barnes & Noble, New York, 1972.

Kenney, Charles Lamb. *A Memoir of Michael William Balfe*. Da Capo Press reprint, New York. 1978.

Kilgarriff, Michael. *Sing Us One of the Old Songs*. Oxford University Press, New York, 1998.

Kimbell, David. *Vincenzo Bellini, Norma*. Cambridge University Press, Cambridge, UK, 1998.

Klein, Axel. *Irish Classical Recordings, a Discography of Irish Art Music*. Greenwood Press, Westport, CT, 2001.

Lacombe, Hervé. *The Key to French Opera in the Nineteenth Century*. University of California Press, London, 2001.

Lawrence, Vera Brodsky. *Strong on Music. Vol. 1 1836–1849*. Oxford University Press, New York 1988.

—— *Strong on Music. Vol. 2. 1850–1856*. University of Chicago Press, Chicago, 1995.

—— *Strong on Music. Vol. 3 1857–1862*. University of Chicago Press, Chicago, 1999.

Lee, Edward. *Musical London*. Omnibus Press, London, 1995.

Levey, R.M. and J. O'Rorke. *Annals of the Theatre Royal Dublin*. Dollard, Dublin, 1880.

Love, Harold. *The Golden Age of Australian Opera, 1861–1880*, Currency Press, Sydney, 1981.

Lover, Samuel and Croker, T.C. *Ireland.* Senate, London, 1995.

Lowenberg, Alfred. *Annals of Opera 1597–1940*. Rowman and Littlefield, Totowa, NJ, 1978.

Lumley, Benjamin. *Reminiscences of the Opera*, London, 1864.

Mackenzie-Grieve, Averil. *Clara Novello 1818–1908*. Geoffrey Bles, London, 1955.

Mackinlay, M. Sterling. *Garcia the Centenarian and His Times*. Da Capo Press reprint, New York, 1976.

McSpadden, J. Walker. *Opera and Musical Comedies.* Crowell & Co., New York. 1946.

Mapleson, James H. *The Mapleson Memoirs, 1848–1888*. 2 Vols. Remington, London, 1888.

Macqueen Pope, W. *Theatre Royal Drury Lane*. W.H. Allen, London, 1945.

Maretzek, Max. *Crochets and Quavers*. S. French, New York, 1855.

Mattfeld, Julius. *Variety Musical Cavalcade, Musical Historical review 1620–1961*. Prentice-Hall, New York, 1962.

——. *A Handbook of American Operatic Premieres 1731–1962*. Information Services, Detroit, MI, 1963.

Maude, Mrs. Raymond, *The Life of Jenny Lind*. Cassell, London, 1926.

Maxwell, Constantia. *Dublin Under the Georges 1714–1830*, Faber, London, 1956.

Merlin, Countess de, *Memoirs of Malibran*. 2 vols. Colburn, London, 1844.

Morash, Christopher. *A History of Irish Theatre 1601–2000*. Cambridge University Press, Cambridge, UK, 2002.

Musgrave, Michael. *The Musical Life of The Crystal Palace*. Cambridge University Press, Cambridge, UK, 1995.

Nalbach, Daniel. *The King's Theatre 1704–1867, London's First Italian Opera House*. Society for Theatre Research, London, 1972.

Neighbour, Oliver and Tyson, Alan. *English Music Publishers' Plate Numbers*. Faber, London, 1965.

Norris, Gerald. *A Musical Gazetteer of Great Britain and Ireland*. David and Charles, London, 1981.

Orrey, Leslie. *Bellini*, Dent & Sons, London, 1969.

Ottenberg, June C. *Opera Odyssey, Towards a History of Opera in Nineteenth-Century America*. Greenwood Press, Westport, CT, 1994.

Pearce, Charles E., *Sims Reeves, Fifty Years of Music in England*. Paul and Co. London, 1924.

Pearse, Mrs. Godfrey & Hird, Frank. *The Romance of a Great Singer*, A Memoir of Mario, Smith, Elder & Co. London, 1910.

Phillips-Matz, Mary Jane. *Verdi, A Biography*. Oxford University Press, New York. 1993.

Pine, Richard. *Music in Ireland 1848–1998*. Mercier Press, Dublin, 1998.

Pine, Richard & Charles Acton, eds. *To Talent Alone. The Royal Irish Academy of Music 1848–1998*. Gill & Macmillan, Dublin, 1998.

Pistone, Danièl, *Nineteenth-Century Italian Opera from Rossini to Puccini*. Amadeus Press, Portland, OR, 1985.

Preston, Katherine K. *Opera on the Road, Traveling Opera Troupes in the United States 1825–60*. University of Illinois Press, Urbana, IL, 1993.

Radomski, James, *Manuel García (1775–1832) Chronicle of the life of a bel canto Tenor*. Oxford University Press, New York, 2000.

Reeves, Sims, *My Jubilee, or Fifty Years of Singing*, London, 1889.

Reid, Charles. *The Music Monster, a Biography of James William Davison*. Quartet, London, 1984.

Robertson, Priscilla, *Revolutions of 1848*. Princeton University Press, Princeton, NJ, 1952.

Rosenthal, Harold. *Two Centuries of Opera at Covent Garden*, Putnam, London, 1958.

Rosselli, John. *The Life of Bellini*. Cambridge University Press, Cambridge, UK, 1996.

——. *Music & Musicians in Nineteenth-Century Italy*. Amadeus, Portland, OR, 1991.

Russell, Frank. *Queen of Song, the Life of Henrietta Sontag*, Exposition Press, New York, 1964.

Sadie, Stanley, ed. *The New Grove Dictionary of Opera* 4.vols. Macmillan, New York, 1992.

St, Leger, H.J. *Reminiscences of Balfe*. Nimmo, London, 1840.

Santley, Charles, *Student and Singer*. Arnold, London, 1892

Schenk, Erich. *Mozart and His Times*. Knopf, New York, 1959.

Scholes, Percy A. *The Mirror of Music 1844–1944*. 2 vols. Novello & Co. London, 1947.

Servadio, Gaia. *The Real Traviata, the Life of Giuseppina Strepponi*. Hodder & Stoughton, London, 1994.

Shaw, George Bernard. *Music in London 1890–94*. 3 vols. Constable & Co., London. 1949.

Simpson, Adrienne. *Opera's Farthest Frontier, a History of Professional Opera in New Zealand*, Birkenhead, Auckland, NZ, 1996.

Smith, Gus. *Ring up the Curtain, Wexford Festival Opera*. Celtic Publishers, Dublin, 1976.

Stendhal, M. *The Life of Rossini*. Riverrun Press, New York. 1985.

Sydow, Bronislaw E, trans. Hedley, Edward. *Selected Correspondence of Fryderyk Chopin*, Heinemann, London, 1996.

Taylor, A.J.P. *From Napoleon to the Second International, Essays on Nineteenth-Century Europe*. Penguin, London, 1993.

Temperley, Nicholas, ed. *The Romantic Age 1800–1914*. Blackwell Reference, Oxford, UK, 1998.

Thompson, David. *England in the Nineteenth-Century, 1815–1914*. Penguin London, 1978.

Tintori, Giampiero. *Duecento Anni di Teatro alla Scala, Cronologia 1778–1977*. Rome, 1979.

Todd, R. Larry. *Mendelssohn, A Life of Music*, Oxford University Press, New York, 2003.

Tyldesley, William, *Michael William Balfe, His Life and His English Operas*. Ashgate Publishing, Aldershot, UK, 2003.

Upton, William T. *William Henry Fry, American Journalist and Composer-Critic*, Crowell & Co. New York, 1954.

Voynich, E.L. *Chopin's Letters*. Dover, New York, 1988.

Walker, Alan. Franz Liszt, *The Virtuoso Years 1811–1847*. Cornell University Press, Ithaca, NY, 1988.

Walker, Frank. *The Man Verdi*. University of Chicago Press, Chicago, IL, 1982.

Walsh, Basil. *Catherine Hayes, the Hibernian Prima Donna*. Irish Academic Press, Dublin & Portland, OR, 2000.

—— *Opera Quarterly*, Vol. 18, No. 4, Autumn 2002, 'Balfe in Italy' article, pp. 484–502. Oxford University Press, Cary, NC.

——. *History Ireland*, Vol. 11, No. 1, Spring 2003. 'Michel W. Balfe, the Irish Italian Ireland's uniquely gifted composer'. pp. 28–32. Wordwell, Dublin.

—— *Donizetti Society Newsletter No. 85*, February 2002, London. Article, Balfe's Italian Operas.

—— *Donizetti Society Newsletter* No. 92, June 2004, London. Article, 'A visit to Donizetti (by Balfe & his wife)'.

—— *Donizetti Society Newsletter* No. 98, June 2006, London. Article, 'Balfe and Malibran'.

Walsh, T. J. *Opera in Dublin 1798–1820*. Oxford University Press, New York, 1993.

—— *Monte Carlo Opera 1910–1951*. Boethius Press, Kilkenny, Ireland, 1986.

——. *Second Empire, Théâtre Lyrique, Paris 1851-1870*. John Calder, Riverrun Press, London, 1981.

Weaver, William. *The Golden Century of Italian Opera*. Thames and Hudson, New York, 1980.

—— and Chusid, Martin. *The Verdi Companion*, Norton & Co, New York, 1968.

Weinstock, Herbert. *Donizetti and the World of Opera*. Pantheon Books, New York, 1963.

—— *Rossini, a Biography*. Knopf, New York, 1968.

—— *Vincenzo Bellini, His Life and His Operas*. Knopf, New York, 1971.

Weintraub, Stanley. *Uncrowned King, the Life of Prince Albert*. The Free Press, New York, 1997.

——. *Charlotte and Lionel, a Rothschild Love Story*. The Free Press, New York.
White, Eric W. *The Rise of English Opera*, Lehmann, London, 1951.
——. *A History of English Opera*, Faber, New York, 1983.
White, Harry, *The Keeper's Recital, Music and Cultural History in Ireland 1770–1970*. University of Notre Dame Press, Indiana, IN, 1998.
Williams, William H. A. *Twas Only an Irishman's Dream*. University of Illinois Press, Chicago, IL, 1996.
Wilson, A.N. *The Victorians*, Arrow, London, 2002.
Wollenberg, Susan. *Music at Oxford in Eighteenth and Nineteenth Centuries*, Oxford University Press, Oxford, UK, 1997.
Wyndham, Henry Saxe. *The Annals of Covent Garden Theatre from 1732 to 1897*. 2 Vols. Chatto & Windus, London, 1906.
Young, Percy M. *George Grove 1820–1900.*; Macmillan, London, 1980.

PERIODICALS/JOURNALS/NEWSPAPERS AND LETTERS

Allegemeiner Wiener Musik-Zeitung
Athenaeum, London
Donitzetti Society Journals
Dublins Historical Record
Dublin University Magazine
Dwight's Journal of Music
Freeman's Journal, Dublin
Gazetta Musicale di, Milano
Harmonicon, London
Hibernia Magazine
History Ireland
Il Barbiere di Siviglia, Giornale di Musica, Teatri e Varieta, Milano
Illustrated London News
Irish Times, Dublin
Journal des Débats, Paris
La France Musicale, Paris
Le Ménestrel, Paris
Le Siècle, Paris

Musical Gazette, London
Musicxl Magazine, Boston
Musical World, London
Neus Preussische Zeitung, Berlin
New York Times
Quarterly Musical Magazine & Review, London
The Record Collector
Répertoire Internatinale de la Presse Musicale
Revue e Gazette Musicale, Paris
Rothschild Charlotte, letters, Rothschild Arcives, London
Saunders News-Letter, Dublin

Letters of Queen Victoria, 3 vols,
  London

The Opera Quarterly
The Times, London
Wexford Herald
Weford Independent

Index

(Opera references are shown under the respective composer's name. See cities for specific opera houses, Balfe's arrival/debut and his other activity in that city)